REPORT ON
THE ASIANS

ALSO BY W. L. WHITE:

WILLIAM L. WHITE

REPORT ON THE ASIANS

Reynal & Company
in association with
WILLIAM MORROW AND COMPANY, INC.
NEW YORK
1969

TO EUGENE REYNAL

College classmate and life-long friend who wanted to publish this book, and who died as it was going to press.

CONTENTS

Prelude: Paris   1
India   23
Bangkok   101
Vietnam   125
The Delta   149
Saigon   195
Hong Kong   209
Taiwan   229
South Korea   245
Japan   253
Communist China   265
Index   285

PRELUDE: PARIS

M Y wife, Kathrine, and I are in Paris on our way to Asia, and most particularly to Vietnam, to get a different perspective on Vietnam and to get some idea of where the United States now stands in the world. As World War II was closing the late Henry R. Luce proudly trumpeted the beginning of The American Century. Twenty years later the country was tied down in the most unpopular war of our time, seemingly on the verge of bankruptcy, its price level on a dangerously steepening upward curve, its gold draining away.

During the stop-over in Paris, still for us the hub of Europe, we were told right away that in Europe, at least, an era is ending, and that Americans should understand why. At the end of World War II when Europe feared Stalin's land armies, America's monopoly of The Bomb was freedom's only shield, so Free Europe huddled with the United States in NATO for protection. When Russia got The Bomb, a shift began. Both sides had a weapon so terrible that maybe neither would use it except as the last means of self-defense. Should the Russians advance in Europe, would Washington use it against Moscow, with the certainty of instant Russian retaliation from the skies? Safety for France, as de Gaulle saw it, lay in neutrality, and presently NATO began to come unbuttoned. So with the Warsaw Pact, for the Marxist world is afflicted with like woes. The Balkan and Central European tributaries are restless. And most unsettling of all is that widening gap between Moscow and Peking.

World-wide, youth is in ferment, seemingly against all forms of government: you name it, they don't want it. In Spain, they riot against Franco. In China, against the old-line Communist bureaucracy. In America, against Lyndon Johnson and His War. In Warsaw and Prague, against the Stalinist Establishment—craving freedom. In Berlin, even in that Free University we built there, where once they demonstrated against The Wall, now under the banners of Mao and Castro German youths denounce parliamentary government and demand that the Yankees go home. Even Moscow's writers seem no longer content to dedicate their talents unquestioningly to Mother State.

It was well that, in the lovely Paris of that fall, we could not foresee the immediate future; could not know that riots and strikes presently would shake the Gaullist government to its foundations, putting its solidly gold-based franc in peril; could not foresee that Soviet tanks presently would roll in to crush budding freedoms in Czechoslovakia. Instead we are glad to find Paris an island of calm in an ocean of change, with the French enjoying the good life of a free-market economy. True, Louis XV's great Place de la Concorde has been degraded to a parking lot, but above the tops of Renaults and Citroëns, the seated, plump, toga-draped granite ladies representing the provinces of France still rise. When first I saw them in 1909 the stone lady representing Strasbourg was swathed in black crepe of mourning for the Lost Provinces. When I next saw her shortly after the 1918 Armistice, her granite lap was heaped high with flowers of rejoicing. Now both crepe and blossoms are gone. It is another day.

Years later I learned that I shared that Paris of the 1918–19 winter and spring, while statesmen were busy writing the Treaty of Versailles, with a man who has since done well. He now rules the village where he was born, in northern Annam province of old Indo-China, for his name (I use the last of many pseudonyms) is Ho Chi Minh. In that land of his birth he was the son of a middle-class (mandarin) official, and so attended a French *lycée*. But his father was a passionate Vietnamese nationalist, and the boy was expelled from his *lycée* for similar activities at the age of twelve.

France was then ruling Indo-China with an iron hand; the climate was not hospitable to Vietnamese nationalists; and so the boy signed on as a kitchen hand aboard a French liner. He was not to see his native land for forty years, when he would return as a conqueror. During those years he visited not only France but America; and in England he got a job in the world's most celebrated kitchen, that of the old Carlton in London presided over by the great Escoffier, whose cross-channel version of French cooking was so renowned that Parisian gourmets often came to London to sample it. The smart Vietnamese youngster caught the eye of Escoffier, who presently moved Ho up to pastry cook —the highest-paid post in any French-cuisine kitchen.

Yet Ho could not forget his father's lost cause: freedom for Indo-China. In late 1918, at the close of World War I, the world's statesmen—Wilson, Clemenceau, Lloyd George, and others—were gathering in Paris to reshape the world. Ho, then, forsook Escoffier's cream tubes and *mille feuilles* and went to Paris to plead the cause of his country, making his living as a retoucher of photographs; under wartime rationing, pastry was unobtainable in France. That winter and spring the city was thronged with hopeful, half-starved nationalists from all countries—from Armenia, from Poland and Bohemia, from India, from the Balkans, from the wreckage of the Hapsburg Empire, from the Baltic States, from China, from the Dodecanese Islands, from the Ukraine and Czarist Russia, from the Arab world—each seeking his own kind of freedom for his own land.

In the Paris of 1918–19, the only ears Ho found even casually attentive to the wrongs of French imperialism were a few in the French Socialist Party, then in the throes of a schism which stemmed from the newly born Russian revolution. The old Bolshevik-Menshevik split had its counterpart in France, with the result that Ho presently peeled off of the main body of the French Socialist Party to go with its left wing, thus becoming a founding member of the French Communist Party and one of its authorities on colonial problems.

His duties entailed several extensive trips to the Soviet Union, during which he could complete his education (interrupted at that French *lycée*) with a degree from Moscow's University for the Toilers of the East, with the usual basic courses in dialectics, espionage, subversion and guerrilla tactics. He also became a Soviet citizen.

In 1924 he was sent to China as part of a military mission under Michael Borodin to help guide the Chinese revolution. From China, Ho sent about two hundred trained agents into Indo-China to make trouble for the French. Chiang Kai-shek became increasingly aware that the Soviet purpose was not so much to aid his Kuomintang as to get control of it, and in 1927 he turned on the Communists, in a sizable massacre, sending the Russian mission home. Ho escaped by hopping over to Hong Kong, from where, protected by the British flag and the civil liberties of

England, he could direct his agents in Hanoi and Saigon. He had occasional problems of discipline that he solved by having the dissenters denounced as Communist terrorists, which of course they were: the French then took care of the punishment.

At long last, however, the French, finally tracing their troubles back to Ho in Hong Kong, had him condemned to death in absentia as a traitor, and demanded his extradition. British justice went ponderously into action, with Stafford Cripps (a power in the Labour Party) defending Ho before the Privy Council in London. Might not Ho be a political refugee, seeking freedom under the British flag? Their Lordships were inclined to go along and Ho, freed in Hong Kong, promptly skipped out to the mainland, where his Communist colleagues were fighting Chiang Kai-shek and (when they could spare the time) the Japanese.

But Mao Tse-tung had other plans for Ho, who, in 1940, surfaced in Vietnam, the homeland he had not seen since, almost forty years before, he had signed aboard that French liner. He resumed contact with that web of agents he had woven from Hong Kong, and presently got support from the American OSS. For was not Ho a patriotic nationalist, fighting the Vichy French? Were we not against imperialism everywhere? As for his old record as a founding member of the French Communist Party, either we did not know or did not care. Back in the jungles, Ho and his agents organized the government of the Vietnamese Democratic Republic, with the Viet Minh as its open political party, this containing a light top dressing of non-Communist nationalists, following the United Front formula.

During World War II the Japanese demanded and got from the Vichy French governor of Indo-China various coastal bases. After the liberation of France in 1944, Gaullist agents entered Indo-China and the Vichy governor faded from the scene. The French garrison under Gaullist command would have then turned on the Japanese bases had the Japanese not first turned on the French, capturing most but not all of their garrison. Those who survived continued to struggle against the Japanese from a base at Langson. Allied intelligence was good, and British air force planes dropped desperately needed supplies.

U.S. policy differed. General Claire Chennault, commander of the 14th Air Force whose planes were then pounding the Japanese in Saigon, remembers that he got orders "stating that no arms or ammunition be provided to French troops under any circumstances" because Washington "was interested in seeing the French forcibly ejected from Indo-China, so the problem of postwar separation from their colony would be easier," and perhaps because the OSS was still in helpful contact with our gallant ally, Ho Chi Minh. So the Japanese overran and butchered the Gaullist garrison at Langson, and why should President de Gaulle forget this?

At the war's end in 1945, de Gaulle forces were not able to move into Indo-China immediately, and so it was agreed that, to accept the Japanese surrender there, a British force would land in Saigon while Chiang Kai-shek's Nationalist Chinese would move into Hanoi. Chiang's generals then turned over civil affairs in Tonkin province to Ho and his Viet Minh, and why not? Was not Ho the protégé of the American OSS? Were we not against imperialism?

In 1946 there was a change of the guard in Indo-China— the British left Saigon and Chiang's troops were moved out of Hanoi, both to be replaced by the Gaullist French. There followed an uneasy period of negotiations between them and Ho Chi Minh on details of independence for the country within the French Union. But how much freedom? Would Bao Dai retain his throne? Would the union include Cochin China (the Delta) then claimed by the French as a colony? Even the shrewd French in this period were not sure that

Ho was a Communist. But in November, when his Viet Minh staged an uprising against the French in the north, most doubts were removed, particularly those of Emperor Bao Dai, who now sought safety in France. And many nationalist groups who, heretofore, had played with Ho (or had failed to unite against him) now felt that a truly free Vietnam could be achieved only with French help in getting rid of Ho and his armed guerrillas, and so turned to Emperor Bao Dai in France to negotiate in Paris for this freedom and this help.

Bao Dai returned to Vietnam with his agreement, signed early in 1949, which was almost everything a non-Communist nationalist could hope for. Cochin China, Annam, and Tonkin were to merge into a Vietnam as completely free in domestic affairs as are Canada or New Zealand, and with a voice in the French Union, of which they would remain a part. Elections would be held when the country was pacified.

But of course Ho Chi Minh hoped for more; Emperor Bao Dai and his government were French puppets; imperialism must be rolled back into the sea, and so the war went on. It could continue now with open support from the Chinese Communists, for Chiang had left for Taiwan, and Mao's troops occupied the frontier of Tonkin Province. Washington began to wonder if Ho was truly just a nationalist; might he not, after all, be a disciplined Communist?

So in 1951 the United States decided to make common cause with the embattled French: Korea and Vietnam were two fronts in one struggle against Communism, and we now promised the French supplies which we had withheld from them at Langson. These proved to be too little and too late.

Then another character appeared on the stage—a man who for a decade was to be our ally—a brilliant, tragic figure, a Vietnamese patriot without flaw; unswerving, incorruptible, but with character defects (later to emerge) almost as

great as his virtues. Jean Baptiste Ngo Diem was, like Ho
Chi Minh, born of a mandarin family. His father, like Ho's,
bitterly opposed the French. Then differences begin. Diem's
family were devout Catholics. The elder Diem broke with
the French when he was a minister to the Emperor Thanh
Thai. When the Quai d'Orsay in Paris decided in 1907 to
depose Thanh Thai, Diem's father, furious, refused to serve
the French further, and from then on fought to get them
out of Indo-China.

Presently young Diem graduated from a French *lycée* at
Hué, the seat of the imperial court. Diem went on to study
law at the great university the French had established for
bright young colonials at Hanoi, where he topped his gradu-
ating class. Then came World War II, which brought the
able young Diem a wealth of choices. The Japanese moved
in, ruling the land through the new Emperor Bao Dai, who
offered Diem a high post. He refused; in his eyes the last
free emperor of Annam had been deposed in the days of
his father. The times were troubled. Diem's brother was
buried alive, by the Viet Minh—maybe because the family
was too ardently Catholic: an uncle was a bishop. Then
Diem himself was captured by the Viet Minh but not killed;
might so able a man be equally ambitious? He was taken
instead to a camp back in the hills, and, in an interview
with Ho himself, was offered a post in the government of
the Democratic Republic of Vietnam.

"Why did you kill my brother?"

"A mistake," insisted Ho. "The country was in confusion."
A mistake, however, which could not be wiped out by offer
of a government job, for young Diem was too proud to
serve puppets, whether of the French, of the Japanese, of
Moscow, or of any other foreign invader of his homeland.
Freedom, it seemed, now could only be had abroad, and
since his patrician family had money Diem could go. He
visited neighboring Asian countries, America, and Europe,

during which period he spent some time in a Belgian monastery brooding on the plight of his country. He encountered a young American senator named Kennedy—also a Catholic and also opposed to French colonialism. The senator had spoken out loudly against it when Algiers was torn by civil war, to the intense annoyance of de Gaulle. Diem and Kennedy did not forget each other.

Meanwhile in spite of American aid (arms, not men) the Indo-Chinese war was going from bad to worse, following a pattern now familiar to us: patrols in strength were sent out to hit an enemy who would vanish into the jungles, the Viet Minh controlling half the villages by day and still more by night. In France, government after government fell; this Vietnam war was not popular. More young French officers were getting killed each year than graduated from Saint-Cyr (the French West Point), and to what end? In 1953, America got out of her Korean tangle, but in Vietnam war still dragged on.

Could not a Korean-type settlement end it? An international conference was called at Geneva, just as reports were coming out that a large French force under a General de Lattre was in danger of being encircled in the valley of Dienbienphu. Assembled in Geneva were representatives of the French, the Americans, the British, the Russians, the Viet Minh, and of course the government of Emperor Bao Dai. During the conference His Majesty made the supreme gesture of calling in, as his premier and negotiator, his enormously able but not too loyal subject Jean Baptiste Ngo Diem, who was conveniently in Paris. At this conference Diem and the Viet Minh representatives at first agreed on only one point: that their country should not be divided. But divided it was on the Korean model, at the 17th Parallel. There was to be: (1) an international supervisory commission (Poland, Canada, India); (2) an immediate and permanent departure of the French; (3) an exchange between

North and South of all people who did or did not want to live under freedom or Communism; and (4) ultimately, an election on the country's unification. To these points Diem understandably could not agree, since the North was more populous than the South and, under Ho, would of course be voted as a monolith for his Communist regime.

In the exchange of peoples, the Vietnamese voted with their feet. One hundred thousand Viet Minh guerrillas and Communists moved up from the South to join Ho's regime. From the North moved, by official count, 860,000—but observers think the true total of those who sought freedom was more than a million. And then came the first official breech of the Geneva Agreement, for observers insist that an additional two million anti-Communists tried to leave North Vietnam but could not. It was not just priests and intellectuals who wanted to flee Communism; it was also scientists, doctors, engineers, and skilled laborers. Without them, North Vietnam's industries and transport would come to a halt. When Ho saw the extent of the exodus, he had no choice but to throw up his own type of Berlin Wall.

Of the million who got out, many were both middle-class and Catholic, for in Indo-China the cross had preceded the flag. Catholic schools had opened the door to Western thought and technology: in the process of getting educated, many people had also been converted. But Holy Church in Indo-China was most wise: all Vietnamese bishops are native Vietnamese, and it is routine for a Vietnamese of any education to be both a devout Catholic (often more fervent than in France) and an even more passionately anti-French nationalist. Many rice farmers also left; single villages moved as a unit, each following its priest, his baggage being the carefully packed sacramental vessels of the village altar, and this vastly simplified matters for Ho, who, following Mao's text, had to have land reform. Ninety-eight per cent of North Vietnam's farmers owned the rice paddies they tilled, although most fields were tiny and living standards low. Now land left by the departing anti-Communist million could be divided among those who stayed. As for landlords, Ho created them by fiat; he proclaimed any peasant who owned as much as two acres to be an exploiter and further (following the Chinese example) ordained that each village and hamlet should select at least one such landlord, and then gather to witness his execution.

A combination of this land reform and bad crops led, in November 1956, to a greatly underpublicized North Vietnamese peasant uprising. At least two divisions were required to quell it, and the Canadian member of the International Control Commission reported crowds of peasants thronging around his jeep, imploring him to help them get to the South. Ho's answer was to admit that, in land reform, "mistakes had been made," perhaps almost an apology for the murder of those "landlords," in numbers estimated at 50,000.

Down south across the 17th Parallel, Diem's problems were even greater; land must be found for that anti-Communist million which had managed to flee the North. In the South much of the best land was owned by landlords, many of them French, and farmed by sharecroppers on a 50–50 basis. Diem vigorously moved in on this situation. No landlords were butchered, but under Diem's decrees no man could own more than 100 hectares (about 250 acres), the surplus being bought by the government—10 per cent cash, the rest in bonds. Thus he acquired half a million hectares (1.25 million acres) which were sold to 122,000 peasant families, who got full title by agreeing to pay only 20 per cent of the crop for 20 years. Rice farming needs capital for seed and fertilizer and, squeezed by both landlords and Chinese moneylenders, a peasant sometimes was left with only an eighth of his crop. Diem took care of the moneylenders by government loans to peasants—enough for seed and fertilizer, and enough to support their families until the crop could be threshed and sold.

On the whole it was a good plan and, considering wartime conditions, well administered. Its critics argued only that it should be extended and the ceiling on land ownership dropped to maybe 10 hectares (25 acres) with more money lent to buy fertilizer. But it was money Diem did not have, for a war was beginning and America had come in.

Just how did we get involved (or entrapped)? When the French pulled out in 1956, an American Military Assistance Advisory group replaced them in training the Vietnamese army. This group grew until at the time of John F. Kennedy's inauguration we had 900 of them in the country; we could be said to have wet our toes in Vietnam. Then came our humiliation at the Bay of Pigs and, following that, Kennedy's meeting with Khrushchev in Vienna at which, according to Kennedy, Khrushchev "bullied" him. A firm gesture was needed to show the Communist world that we were not irresolute. Therefore, on the President's return to Washington, and after threshing the proposal out with his top advisers (there were serious pros and cons), 12,000 combat troops were sent to join the advisers in Vietnam, which put us in that war up to our knees.

Some Vietnamese had objected that our advisers were training the Vietnamese army for a war they would never fight, for in those early days the Pentagon was haunted by the example of Korea. True, there were many similarities. Both countries were divided in the middle by a parallel across a narrow neck of land. So South Vietnamese divisions were trained to defend this tapering waist, just as South Korean divisions manned the strong points behind Panmunjom.

But now came the enormous difference: Korea is a peninsula around which the American navy controls the seas, while Vietnam is a coastal strip backed up against the trackless jungles of Laos and Cambodia—trackless until the Communists began building trails through them, along which supplies could be packed to guerrilla units (the Viet Minh was now renamed the Viet Cong) deep within the country. So the war in 1960 came not with guns thundering along that heavily defended 17th Parallel, but with assassination of headmen and schoolteachers in villages deep in the country. At first both Diem and his advisers brushed these off as a flare-up of banditry, to be dealt with by local militia. They soon found that they were forced to repair and re-man the old block houses defending each hamlet, which were originally built by the French against the Viet Minh.

It was in this period that some serious flaws emerged in the character of Jean Baptiste Ngo Diem. He fell out with Emperor Bao Dai who, from his home on the French Riviera, made the mistake of ordering Diem to relinquish command of the army. Diem's answer was a plebiscite under which His Majesty was deposed, and power handed to Diem by the preposterous majority of 98 per cent—a landslide not even equaled in Ho's Communist elections. True, the monarch's popularity had waned, and, even in an honest count, he probably would have lost. But, unfortunately, the throne was the only unifying force the country had, and in its place, Diem attempted to substitute a hazy doctrine he called "democratic personalism." In practice it came to mean rule by the Diem family. In the old imperial city of Hué, a Diem uncle reigned as Roman Catholic archbishop. A Diem brother governed the province and at Diem's elbow in Saigon was his brother-in-law, Ngo Dinh Nhu, who was head of the all-powerful secret police. While political killings were few (we Americans had no taste for them) many were jailed on suspicion, for the police were apt to view any opposition to "democratic personalism" as evidence of Communist sympathies.

Perhaps an even more serious mistake was Diem's abolition—by decree in June 1956—of elections for village councilmen and mayors. For centuries these had been chosen by the people; now they were to be appointed from Saigon. Diem's purpose was to bring the hamlets closer to the government. The effect was the opposite. The ancient system of local government was an extension of the family. Four or five families would make up a hamlet, each led by its senior grandfather. These in turn would pick one of their number as headman or mayor. This form of democracy should not seem strange to us as, under the ancient Teutonic system, a village also was ruled by its council of elders, whence our word "alderman" came. Diem wanted mayors loyal to his government in Saigon. Often they were those the village would have chosen, but occasionally they were corrupt. And since all were now government appointees, the Viet Cong felt free to declare open season on them. By 1961 they, and their government-appointed successors, were being killed at the rate of eleven a day, and in areas controlled by the VC after dark, Saigon could find no one brave enough to take these jobs.

Diem's answer was the idea of "strategic hamlets," which had worked for the British in Malaya. Elaborate fortifications would be built around an area, and then people from surrounding hamlets moved into these, protected by adequate soldiers. By day, the peasants could move out to cultivate their paddies; by night, they would be secure. Further, the headman was secure from VC assassins, the peasants from any need to pay VC taxes.

Of course it took time, but it seemed to work. By 1963 a third of the peasant population was safely housed in villages where the VC could no longer requisition their teen-agers for its army. Assassinations of village officials had dropped to almost zero, for Ngo Dinh Nhu's secret police were all-pervasive. But sometimes it took force—villagers often were loath to leave their old homes.

Diem's family was intensely Catholic and some of the reforms, reportedly instigated by Madame Nhu, Diem's sister-in-law, imposed on the land what most Vietnamese felt was an alien Puritanism. Multiple marriage is an ancient tradition and Diem decrees forbade it. True, a man might choose to legalize either his No. 1 or No. 2 wife, but the children of the others became bastards.

Prostitution was also abolished, a move which might evoke cheers in the West but not in Vietnam. Had not concubines risen to sit on the throne of Imperial China?

Lastly, Madame Nhu meddled with the native costume—bell-bottomed black trousers, over which women wear an enchanting long gown, with a high Chinese collar, and slit to the waist at the sides. These, she ordained, must be replaced by European-type smocks. Dancing and love songs likewise were forbidden.

All of which Vietnam might have endured had not the Catholic Diems collided violently with the Buddhists, some 70 per cent of the population. Catholics, while they may include a majority of Vietnam's educated class, make up hardly 15 per cent—some say only 11 per cent—of the population.

Could it be that the Venerable Tri Quang, leader of the militant Buddhists, was a crypto-Communist? The point has been heavily debated and it is possible. More probably, however, he could on occasion work with the Communists because they had so much in common. For Tri Quang was bitterly against the Catholic Diems and as bitterly anti-American—in fact, against all foreign influence. It later became clear, however, that Tri Quang and his politically active militants were a small and uninfluential portion of Vietnam's Buddhists. Yet in 1963, Tri Quang could be the focal point for all opposition to Diem, for in the spring of that year Diem jailed a number of Buddhist leaders agitating against his government, on the grounds that they were Communists.

In May in the city of Hué, which is both a revered center of Buddhism and also a Diem stronghold, the Buddhists were refused permission to fly Buddhist flags on Buddha's birthday. Their answer was the inevitable student protest parade. Since Diem's brother was governor of this province he could inevitably view this only as a Communist uprising upon which his troops opened fire, killing a dozen and wounding a hundred. Again inevitably, the surviving Buddhists could view this only as a religious massacre.

Then in a Saigon public square in early June 1963, in full view of press television cameras summoned for the occasion, an elderly monk, Quang Doc, after his followers had drenched him with gasoline, struck a match, and went up in flames of protest which moved not only Vietnam but the whole world. The little country was now deep in civil turmoil. Marchers in protest parades included all who had grievances of any kind against the Diems—every shade of political or religious opinion—since marching was now the only permitted form of protest.

In Saigon, American advisers, profoundly upset, were putting pressure on Diem to make peace with the Buddhists. Already the war had cost us the lives of about a hundred advisers and almost $400,000,000. While the situation in the countryside was, we felt, improving, it was falling to pieces in the towns. Back in the State Department, Averell Harriman and Roger Hilsman were already anti-Diem. Our able ambassador in Saigon, Frederick Nolting, had established a close relationship with Diem, and was sure the situation could be controlled.

Also in Saigon a segment of the American press corps had become violently anti-Diem, and almost equally critical of Nolting. Noting this, the left-wing Buddhists would tip them off to prospective immolations. By May, President Kennedy had been persuaded to quietly dump Nolting and send Henry Cabot Lodge to Saigon. Lodge was instructed to take a firmer line. We were not then ready to dump Diem, for no replacement was in sight, and without Diem the war might fall to pieces, as presently it did. Those who saw this clearly included John McCone, head of the CIA, Robert McNamara and Maxwell Taylor in the Defense Department, and Vice-President Lyndon Johnson, who said, "I think we should try to live with what we've got."

Meanwhile in the State Department, the anti-Diem faction was leaking to the press predictions that Diem might be overthrown, which in Saigon produced understandably strained relations between Diem and the Americans. In one of their final interviews, Diem asked Ambassador Nolting if this change of diplomats indicated a change in the attitude of the U.S. government. Nolting assured him it did not, and presently produced a cable from Washington, reinforcing this assurance.

Diem stared at him sadly. "Mr. Nolting," he finally said, "I believe you. And I believe you believe your government. But Mr. Nolting, I do not believe your government."

Nolting, on his way home, stopped in Honolulu to brief Henry Cabot Lodge on the Vietnam situation. Word came to them that on August 21 Diem had raided Xa Loi pagoda in Saigon, loaded the struggling monks and nuns into American trucks, and driven them off to prison. The raid had been conducted by Nhu's police, backed up by special Catholic-led units of the army, brought down from Hué, the Nhu stronghold. From Honolulu Nolting cabled Diem: "This is the first time you have ever broken a promise to me."

The raid was an act of madness but with some foundation in logic: in this interregnum between ambassadors, Diem and the Nhus hoped to dispose of the militant Buddhists.

Lodge, on his arrival, would then be confronted with a *fait accompli* which would bring political peace to Vietnam.

Instead Lodge, in Saigon, was confronted with a clutch of Vietnamese generals who had approached the U.S. Embassy, insisted they had had no part in the raid on Xa Loi pagoda, and asked how Washington would react if they combined to remove Diem from power. Lodge drafted a cable which ended by asking for instructions. It arrived in Washington when most high officials were out of town to escape the sweltering summer heat. The answer was drafted by the State Department's anti-Diem faction (Harriman and Hilsman) and it read, "Do not abort"—meaning, do not stop the proposed *coup d'état*. Dean Rusk, John McCone, and Robert McNamara had not been consulted. John Kennedy had been called by telephone, and had raised no objection. The cable went off, and State's anti-Diem faction gave to the press a "backgrounder" to the effect that Washington was encouraging an anti-Diem coup by Vietnamese generals.

This caused an explosion among the Kennedy top advisers, the pro-Diem faction not having been consulted. And Lodge reported from Saigon that the generals were dragging their feet, fearing that any sudden change in government would be an advantage to the Viet Cong, and adding that "It's not too late—we can still back out." President Kennedy, however, was swinging toward the anti-Diem faction, and in Saigon, Cabot Lodge was laying down the law to Diem: his regime could be saved only if he got rid of the intensely unpopular Nhus. It was true, but Diem hesitated; they were his flesh and blood.

In late September 1963, Kennedy sent McNamara to Vietnam to review the situation. Returning in early October, McNamara completely reversed his position. He was now sure Diem had to go. In mid-October the United States cut off all aid to Nhu's special forces; they had been CIA-trained and were paid by us. On October 30, Lodge could report to

Washington that his foot-dragging Vietnamese generals at long last were ready to move. Word of this might have got to Diem, for the next day, in a meeting with Lodge, the old dictator abjectly surrendered.

"Tell me what to do," he said. "If you don't know, cable Washington for instructions, and I will do it." But Washington deemed it too late. It is said that Henry Cabot Lodge offered Diem sanctuary in the embassy, but the humbled old dictator still had the pride to refuse. If he had to die, it would be as he had lived, as no one's puppet—not of the French, not of the Japanese, not of the emperor, and, finally, not of the Americans.

Diem had to go, and the next day he did. When the generals finally moved in, they butchered Diem and his brother far from any television camera, and with a quiet discretion, which, some three weeks later, was to be so lacking in Dallas.

Diem had to go, and with him went most of Vietnam's war effort; in the villages, the VC now moved in as a tide. For however hated Nhu's secret police and special forces had been by freedom-loving Vietnamese in the towns, they had been most effective in organizing the hamlets. In the chaos which followed, the VC were free to penetrate or overrun Diem's fortified hamlets until they controlled, both by day and night, not a third of the country but more than two thirds of it, rolling back the Vietnamese army and its 15,000 uniformed American allies. The ground was not recovered until four years (and thousands of American casualties) later, and then only with the aid of half a million American troops and billions of dollars. (During the 1968 Tet offensive, much of it again was lost.)

For if Diem had to go, we still had no one to replace him. His dictatorship had allowed no civilian of stature to emerge in the country. And the junta of generals now squabbled and plotted among themselves for power—coup following coup until, eighteen months later, some semblance of stability emerged under Air Marshal Ky.

Inevitably Diem had to go, but why did we not foresee what would happen when we dexterously replaced him with a vacuum? What symbol of national unity was now left to the South Vietnamese? The throne was gone, and the squabbling top generals were little known and even less respected by Vietnamese intellectuals. A few years back, had they not been (like Ky) mere sergeants under the French? It was hardly the fault of the Vietnamese that the Diem dictatorship had allowed no civilian leaders or political parties to develop. Had we not backed him with our men and guns, accepting smug assurances that the country was not ready for democracy? (If it was not, why were we fighting there?) Whose fault was it that, in the political vacuum and chaos that followed Diem, the name of Ho Chi Minh as a national leader (had he not forced out the French at Dienbienphu?) should be better known in South Vietnam than any leader of their own?

And so I learned as much as I could learn of Ho Chi Minh and his native land, before we took off from Paris to see for ourselves.

INDIA

W E are off to Asia, Kathrine and I, destination Saigon, but with a stopover in India for two reasons. First, because India from which the British have departed may give some insight into the sometimes heated emotions which separate Asia from our Western civilization. Second, because in New Delhi, where the International Press Institute is about to hold its annual meeting, editors from all over the world are gathering to learn, among other things, what the top reporters have been able to garner from Red China, which is so powerful an influence on what eventually will happen in Vietnam.

Outside our big jet all is still inky black when the wing flaps grind down; now those squares of light below us are the streets of New Delhi—that spacious, well-laid-out, utterly un-Indian capital city of India. Our Paris watches say midnight but here it is just before the quick-coming tropical dawn. Inside the airport, guards of the Indian army are on duty; by their uniforms you would think this was any provincial airport in England. The voices speak British English. All signs are in English. Slowly we get used to how brown everyone is.

At customs we are told that we need not open our bags; they are glanced at and stamped. But returning Indians get a rigid search—hands fumble into every corner, looking for, we later learn, gold in particular. In this land of economic controls there is a craving for it, and a profitable black market. New-mined South African gold goes first by plane to Beirut, then to one of several oil-rich sheikdoms on the western tip of Arabia and thence by Arab dhow across the Arabian sea toward India's west coast, where by night the ingots are transferred to Indian "fishing boats" out of Bombay. Indians are eager to pay more than the "official" gold price of $35.00 an ounce. To end this traffic would take a far greater coast-guard flotilla than India can afford.

By the time we are in our taxi a pink flush is rising in the East, lighting a road crowded with people going into the city to work: two-wheeled wooden bullock carts on their way to market, turbaned young men on bicycles, but mostly clumps of people in flowing cotton robes.

Delhi, we are to discover, is two towns: the old walled city which was a capital of the Mogul emperors, and this new town through which we pass, laid out by the British to be the capital of their India, with public buildings of appropriate stateliness, and miles of tree-planted boulevards lined with villas of rich Indians and of ambassadors from many countries.

India's separation from Britain was in the end friendly, almost tearful. Delhi was retained as the capital of the new India and is being further developed. When Indians drive in Delhi they still keep left, and in her British-built Parliament House the English language is used in debate. Not far from it still stands a statue of H.M. George V in coronation robes. And New Delhi remains a beautiful if tiny island of Western-style luxury in that ocean of more-or-less contented poverty which is India.

The ghost of the departed British Empire is everywhere. In the smart salute of the turbaned doorman at the Ashoka Hotel who might have been a sirdar in a crack British-officered Sikh regiment, defending Khyber Pass in Kipling's time. In the uniforms of India's army, which marches by with left arms swinging, and parades to the squeal of bagpipes. In the English language, which contributes so much to India's unity that this unity might well dissolve if the language is abandoned. For India has, of her own, not one language but fourteen major ones, representing, roughly, the states into which Nehru divided India. The most widespread of them is Hindi, which India's Hindus hope will someday become the national tongue.

But Hindi, native to the north, is spoken by less than half of India's half billion people; the other Indians resent Hindu efforts to force Hindi on them. English was the language of India's struggle for independence. Even Nehru learned it from his English governesses; the tongue of his ancestors was to him a second language.

That struggle for independence was led by Oxford- and Cambridge-trained young Indians. The language used in fiery debate by their Congress Party, which led that struggle, was English. When the struggle was won it was clear that the only language understood by all educated Indians, from Madras to the Himalayas, was English. Without it, they could not function as a nation, their Parliament could not debate, its ministers could not give orders that clerks could understand.

So it was agreed that, while Hindi at some future date would become India's official language, English would for a while continue in equal status as a matter of convenience. English has continued to be the language of instruction in all of India's high schools and universities. The coming generation wants it that way. An all-India student convention, recently meeting in Calcutta, demanded that English be the sole language of the Central Government. This was more than a slap at the ruling Hindus; these young people want to get on in the world. Of what use is a dialect which, a hundred miles away, may not be understood?

India's government has made some progress in literacy; about 120 million of her half billion people can read. The registrar of newspapers reports that 3.9 million read Hindi newspapers of all types. But these are slightly outnumbered by the combination of 2.5 million who read such newspapers in Tamil, and the 1.5 million who read them in Malayalam. Far outnumbering any are the 5.6 million who read Indian papers published in English—confined to no state but scattered across the nation. These are India's top-educated one per cent who must use English to communicate with each other.

When we first arrived, Indian friends invited us to a supper club in Delhi, that we might taste real Indian curries. Since we were foreigners, of course they spoke English with us. Our table was between two others, both filled with parties of handsome, well-to-do young Indians, probably sons and daughters of politicians or businessmen from all over India, since this is a capital city. They were gaily chattering away in what we assumed to be one of India's fourteen languages. But when, between curries, fragments of talk drifted over to us, we realized that the language was English—with another intonation, sometimes queerly accented, but fluent.

Down in Connaught Circle, Delhi's luxury shopping district, signs were in English, but this could be for the tourist trade. Entering one shop, we found we were the only foreigners; Indian women were picking over saris, and customers and salespeople were talking to each other in English.

Along with this language all of England's liberties—of the press, of the ballot box, and of free speech—have been left

by the departing English on these Asian shores. How long
will they last? Who can predict this for any country? But in
India, surely they will last no longer than English, that
speech which divides them least and still holds them together,
in spite of disturbing cracks now appearing in the national
structure.

Yet India's communication problems are further complicated by her poverty, as we learn from an Indian editor at
the opening session of this International Press Institute. This
editor said that of India's half billion people, more or less,
only 6,300,000 take a daily newspaper, which is less than 13
out of a thousand. In Japan the rate is 440 per thousand.

Clearly the papers in India are not reaching the people,
70 per cent of whom are in India's 500,000 villages, which
are reached by only 2 per cent of the pathetically small circulation of India's daily papers. The press is an urban affair,
with 93 per cent of its circulation in cities of more than 100,-
000. All of India uses, each day, one tenth the newsprint con-
sumed by the city of New York.

But, for the few who can read English, India produces a
truly great press, as we can judge for ourselves; throughout
our stay we feasted on it. In make-up this Anglo-Indian press
is a faithful copy of London's dailies before World War II.
But in content this press is lively, it is often brilliantly
written, it is free, it is brave, and it has a conscience.

At the editors' meeting an editor from Taiwan follows the
Indian to boast that in 1950, when Chiang Kai-shek moved
there from the mainland (with some assist from the Communists), its capital city of Taipei had only one newspaper. Today the island of Taiwan, although it has only 1,400 square
miles, has 50 newspapers.

Before 1961, Taiwan's papers carried little advertising, but
this is now increasing between 15 and 20 per cent a year, with

the result that the average paper on the island has eight
pages.

More important, those papers enjoy freedom of the press.
Although it has in the past been charged that the newspapers
were government-controlled, there was, the speaker insisted,
no news censorship; editorially the papers are free to criticize
the government. Of course, he went on to say, "we in Taiwan
are unanimously anti-Communist since we are under constant threat from mainland China, and no one on the island
would speak for Communism."

Perhaps the high point of the week was the program
on China, and its star was Charles Taylor, who until recently
covered Peking for the Toronto *Globe and Mail*. The official
briefings the Chinese offer to the press, he says, are ludicrous;
you get a spoken version of editorials which already have
appeared in their morning Chinese Communist press. "And
when we protest, they say we are 'not friendly.' But we can
use our eyes and ears in this matter of their Red Guards and
Cultural Revolution. We can report wall posters, attacking
people still high in power—but for how long?"

Reporters, he says, are restricted to a 25-mile radius of
Peking. You can request permission for other trips, but half
are refused. In Peking, you can get around on your own to
go into markets and stores. But it is impossible for a foreigner to have an "authorized" conversation with any Chinese. Nevertheless, Taylor made a few contacts the government would not like, and got out a few stories they did not
want.

We then heard from an old China hand, Hans Bernischke,
of the German Press Agency in Hamburg. He says that
agencies such as his must put together the puzzle of China
from a very few pieces. There is in China no such thing as
inside information, so primary sources are the same: reading
the Chinese press, listening to its radio, trying to keep wish-
ful thinking out of your conclusions. But still, Bernischke

says, it helps an agency to have a man on the spot in Peking. For while such a reporter can provide no hard news not given in the Chinese press and radio, he can add detail and color to his stories. There is, he says, no restriction on critical reporting, and the embassies and reporters in Peking pool their information and theories.

Journalists are free to report the Red Guards smashing art objects if they catch them doing it. As for getting news out, the telephone connections between Peking and Tokyo work well. In the past, many reporters telephoned their stories out via Moscow, but service on this line seems to deteriorate along with Chinese diplomatic relations with Russia.

It is, says Bernischke, most important to analyze the news systematically, for a sensation may lie buried in one phrase of an otherwise dreary 15,000-word Chinese press release.

L. La Dany, a China watcher based in Hong Kong, who covers the mainland through his organization, China News Analysis, points out that Hong Kong is too close to the reality of China to be fooled, and the Hong Kong Chinese are sensitive to any change on the mainland. They get their information from letters of friends or relatives, and sometimes such letters contain hints that contact must be broken off; it is too dangerous.

Hong Kong has many daily papers, and their reporters interview people arriving from China on every train. From such sources they got the first picture of the Red Guard riots—so factual that the Chinese Communist press in Hong Kong did not deny it.

Foreigners, returning from mainland China through Hong Kong, are another source, but a poor one. They come out, says La Dany, either enthusiastic about mainland China or disgusted, but they seldom bring any hard facts not already known. So the main news source is Red China's three daily papers.

The American consulate has an excellent translating serv-

ice. While all mainland China's papers are ruled by the
Propaganda Department of the party, discipline is not perfect. Editors are often purged as a prelude to getting at the
man higher up.

Formerly the *People's Daily* had been the voice of the
Communist Party, and the *Liberation Army Daily* a less-
important paper published by the army. But once there was
a 24-hour delay on the *People's Daily,* in reprinting an article
from *Liberation,* a hint that all was not serene between the
two.

But the *People's Daily* now is completely in line, and de-
votes a daily page to the greatness of Chairman Mao and the
power of his "Thoughts." The Chinese people, La Dany
tells us, seldom believe what they read in the party press. In
general, he says, "Hard news out of China is so meager that,
to many questions, the answer must be that we don't know.
But we are finding that, in many outlying provinces, farms
and factories are being run, not by peasants and workers'
co-operatives, but by the Security Department—the police.
We find that, for a Chinese, there are few restrictions on
travel, but on his journey he can get no rations, so how can
he go?

"In private we learn that there are party members in China
who have not lost their common sense, as you would think
they had by reading their press. Before all this, there was in
China a long tradition of good reporting, and we feel that
the present status of the press in China is only a passing
episode.

"There is an agreement," he says, "between China and
Japan to exchange nine newspapermen, but they must change
every year. The Chinese now have only two in Japan; the
other seven have gone home and disappeared."

A Japanese who speaks excellent English picks up the story.
He is Teruo Fujikura, who represents the *Nihon Keizai*

Shinbun, which could be called the *Wall Street Journal* of Japan.

"China," he warns, "is growing stronger, and a reporter's role there is important." Japanese correspondents were the first to report the rise of the Red Guards, and during this period the foreign agencies, trying to report China, filed heavily from Tokyo, basing their stories on the reports of Japanese correspondents from China.

Japan and China, he says, while they have no diplomatic relations, do have official "cultural" ties. In the exchange of newspaper correspondents, it has been the Chinese who had insisted on that one-year time limit, to avoid a Japanese law which stipulates that foreigners residing in Japan more than a year must be fingerprinted, to which the Chinese violently objected.

As Japan and China have no diplomatic relations, their exchange of correspondents had to be arranged through the Japan-China Friendship Society. The exchange enabled the Japanese public to get eyewitness reports from China.

When the Chinese Great Proletarian Cultural Revolution began, the Japanese correspondents in Peking could read the wall newspapers, while other correspondents could not. Chinese and Japanese writing systems are the same however greatly their spoken languages differ.

But a reporter's life in Peking, Fujikura tells us, is hard. Interviews are never granted with people more important than the deputy head of a department in a province. For a while there was a monthly breakfast with the Peking branch of the Japan-China Friendship Society, but when things got hot it was discontinued.

And Chinese economic figures are deliberately confusing. In their press, government officials will boast that the monthly production of something has increased by 12 per cent over last year, but you never can find out just how much of this something was actually grown or raised, either last year or this. It is also hard to dig out solid facts on their trade with the West.

In Japan, four out of the nine Chinese correspondents who once were there did not compete with each other; they pooled their copy and gave it to the New China News Agency for transmission back home.

China, Fujikura concludes, is a world problem. And by giving objective reports on what is going on, the Japanese correspondents feel that they ultimately are benefiting the Chinese people.

Another Hong Kong newspaperman rose, saying he would like to tell us his main sources in reporting China from Hong Kong. First come the official Communist newspapers with their long documents which Chinese can translate more accurately than foreigners, digging out that single phrase which may have high news value.

From returning travelers—2,000 come out each day—he tries to sort out the hard facts. He also monitors the radio and reads the provincial Chinese papers, and finally, gets letters out of China to friends in Hong Kong.

His newspaper, he says, has a staff of about a hundred, including many who formerly were students on the mainland. And he thinks that "our foreign friends," in interpreting the facts, usually misunderstand the psychology of the mainland regime. He believes that attacks on those holding power are frequently fake attacks.

"The Peking regime thinks it is the center of the world. Foreigners believe the regime's foreign policy is important, but we think its domestic policy is still more important. Some mainland changes are improvements—the industrial development, and the fact that they have cleaned out beggars and whores. But the Cultural Revolution saddens us.

"And foreign correspondents who know nothing of relations between people on the mainland do not realize that even a man and his wife dare not discuss politics."

But the Chinese, he tells us, are not fools. Many, in high places, also think the Peking regime is ridiculous. There was, for instance, a high-placed Communist, the propaganda head for five provinces, and in one of the provinces a newspaper mentioned the fact that, when Chairman Mao speaks Mandarin, his accent is not perfect. This propaganda chief savagely attacked the newspaper for daring to criticize Mao, but then himself defected to Taiwan a few days later.

We question our experts: to what stories do the Peking censors object? A Peking magazine went to press with, on its back cover, an intricate painting in which were hidden the characters "Long Live Chiang Kai-shek!" Quickly all copies were pulled back from newsstands, and the *Globe and Mail*'s Taylor was severely reprimanded for cabling the story abroad.

This is passing strange. Most foreigners are sure that pro-Chiang sentiment is long dead on the mainland. If only the mainland's rulers could share this certainty, they would not need to maintain so many divisions on the beaches of Fukien, a province no foreigner may visit. For Chiang's name is the only alternative to Communism that any Chinese remembers.

Mr. Taylor also mildly takes issue with Fujikura San on the importance of knowing Chinese, arguing that a knowledge of the language adds only 10 per cent to a writer's ability to cover that country. "We employ interpreters," he explained, "furnished by the Chinese government, who may vary in age, sex, and political outlook. We know they are in a delicate position, for some of them have a bourgeois background," he explained.

Why are there not more foreign correspondents in Peking? he was asked. "Because the Chinese are reluctant to have too many. Generally it is a trade, for it is important to them to have their correspondents in foreign capitals."

A Calcutta editor now complained that the panelists had reported only on Peking. What about the rest of China—

Tibet, for instance? How much of the country is closed, and how much open? Taylor answered that vast areas are ruled out. When you ask to visit them, the polite Chinese answer is that it would not be convenient at this time. But no one could ever get permission to visit the coastal areas, or Tibet.

"But when you get out of Peking," added Taylor, "the atmosphere is different. Often the people in charge of large factories are not aware of Peking's propaganda line." China, he says, is not the monolith it appears to be.

What about incidents on the Sino-Soviet border? What do the Chinese think of the atom bomb?

The experts on China answered that even very anti-Communist Chinese were proud that the Chinese had been able to devise a bomb. As for border disputes, all foreign correspondents are barred from Sinkiang; news of such conflicts comes only from outside China.

The Chinese have become adept in reading between the lines. The Chinese who come out say they know only what was in their newspapers, but have no real opinions of their own. As an example, the Chinese Communist press for ten days completely ignored the anti-Communist explosion within Indonesia which stripped Sukarno of power. Then they printed a letter from a Chinese saying he was delighted to learn that Sukarno was in good health: nothing else.

Often the Chinese officials cracked down on correspondents—on a Reuters man, for example, who reported on demonstrations outside the British Embassy during the Lebanon crisis. And some newsmen get warnings, usually calls late at night, as a reporter did when he had gone to Peking University during the "Flower Blooming" period, and cabled abroad the attacks on the government printed in the wall newspapers.

During the sessions of the International Press Institute meeting we were entertained each night by some Indian group, but never more spectacularly than by the government of India's Information Service, in the palace of the deposed Nizam of Hyderabad, whose quarters were taken over by the Indian government.

The palace is now a century old, and its architecture reflects what the British were then building in India. In that phase of their history the British clearly thought of themselves as the heirs of Rome, so it was fitting that Rome's columns should be the symbol of their rule. Such columns stand today as a sheltering colonnade around Connaught Circle, the business center of New Delhi, named for a viceroy-brother of Edward VII.

The new city adjoins Old Delhi, site of the Mogul emperors' palace and the Red Fort. Beyond this, Old Delhi is a vast bazaar. Dirty, yes; crowded, yes; and fascinating. Merchants sitting cross-legged on low platforms in the midst of their wares. Goats, sacred cows, and ownerless dogs wandering about. Food-shop vendors frying over a single kerosene flame delicious little cubes of mysterious things that give off a wonderful smell.

Rows and rows of such open-air stalls, swarming with people. Shops selling copper pots and water jars, shops selling curious herbs, shops selling grains and spices from bins, and types of dried peas and beans we had never seen. Tiny (maybe filthy) restaurants of four or five tables, where you could be served such things if you only knew the language. Shops where they were cutting curiously spiced and frosted cakes into little cubes.

Shops where, if you so much as glance inside, salesmen will start unfolding many-hued saris for your inspection. Saris from Madras, silver painted on cotton as fine as gossamer. Silk saris loaded with the daintiest 18-karat gold embroidery from Benares, which the shopkeepers continue to unfold and shake at you so long as there is the faintest chance that you may be coaxed inside.

Beggar women carrying diseased babies. What affliction most deeply touches your heart—a three-year-old hunchback? A two-year-old whose scalp is covered with sores?

A brass shop where they hammer out graceful pitchers of a design 2,000 years old.

A shop selling ring scarves from Kashmir worked with lovely Persian floral designs, in area enough to cover a woman's head and shoulders (say, two square yards), but of a wool so fine that you can pull a scarf completely through a wedding ring—hence the name.

Nearby a shop sells dried yellow disks of sacred cow dung, which women take home under the arm like loaves of bread to use as fuel for the family cooking fire. You laugh? Remember that on our plains, when the covered wagons halted to make camp for the night, it was the children's chore to fan out and gather dried buffalo chips before the light failed.

So it must have been with the covered wagons of the invading Aryans, 5,000 years ago.

For this India has not changed. It was the India which Alexander saw, and then the Moslem Moguls who, in about the year 1500, moved from Persia across the Indus, carrying with them Persia's high civilization and some of their nomadic own. It was the India which the British East India Company saw in the late seventeenth century, when they moved in to take over the country from the collapsing Mogul Empire. It was the India of which Kipling sang and of which Mark Twain briefly but so vividly wrote on his short visit here—all of it still in Old Delhi.

India's conquerors always have built with majesty, of which much is reflected in Hyderabad Palace, where the new British-Socialist-trained Congress Party rulers entertain us tonight, in a square surrounded by mighty Doric columns enclosing flower beds, and in their center a roaring log fire over which, in happier days, His Highness the Nizam surely roasted his goats. But what will remain a thousand years from now is not, I think, these columns, but the market we saw in Old Delhi.

At a safe distance from this roaring fire we glanced around the quadrangle formed by the Nizam's palace and noted one wing that, we were told, had once been occupied by His Highness' extensive and variegated harem, in its day the pride of the countryside and the wonder of all India. We were busting for a tour of those quarters, which once echoed to the clicks of jeweled bangles and ankle bracelets. We were told that they were occupied by the secretariat of the Ministry of Information of the new government, and now echo only to the click of typewriters, powered by the prim daughters, nieces, or granddaughters of the ruling Congress Party, all of them without doubt highly educated, speaking the purest clipped British English, relentlessly efficient and unswervingly progressive in outlook, qualities which may have been lacking in that wing in the old days.

We asked about the Nizam and were told not to worry about him; His Highness was living elsewhere in somewhat reduced circumstances, with his harem commensurately shrunk to a streamlined task force.

But when reading, shortly after we left India, of the old gentleman's death, we wondered if the socialist state which had fallen heir to his palace had made any provision for senior-citizen's benefits to his sadly shrunken harem.

India's original inhabitants were what anthropologists call an Australoid people, today found in a band stretching from southern India down into Australia, where they were and are the aborigines.

In skin color these people are a dark brown, but are unrelated to the Congoid races which developed in Central Africa. Australoids are short in stature with low foreheads, heavy brows, and short, flat noses with wide nostrils. Although you find this type throughout India, it is most common in the extreme south, which has languages derived from Dravidian, presumably the original language of India.

The first conquerors of this subcontinent, some 5,000 years ago, were a people who called themselves Aryans (the Proud People) and who descended on India through the passes in the Himalaya Mountains. They were by race Caucasoid, but anthropologists further divide this race into three types: Nordics (tall, blond, and blue-eyed) are found in northern Europe, Alpines (shorter, brown-haired, round headed) are mostly in central Europe, and, farthest south, the Mediterranean strain of this Caucasoid race—originally inhabiting both shores of the Mediterranean Sea—comprising Spaniards, southern French, Italians, Greeks, Egyptians, Arabs, Jews, Armenians, Syrians, and Persians. The "Aryan" conquerors of India came from this Mediterranean branch of the Caucasoid race—a dark strain of what we call the white race.

They crowded the still-darker Dravidian-speaking Australoids into the south, but in 5,000 years there has been much mixture, producing a handsome race. Yet it is still true that today the peoples of south India are darker than those of the North, who live closer to the mountain passes through which the Caucasoid invaders marched.

The Aryans brought with them a social structure of four classes which scholars think is the basis of India's caste system today. At the top were the Brahmans (priests). Under these the Kshatriyas (warriors), beneath these, the Vaisyas (merchants), and still below, the Sudras (farmers and artisans).

India's Brahmans claim descent from this old Aryan priestly class, and today the Brahmans are India's priests, and also supply a large part of the country's teachers, scholars, scientists, and top administrators. Brahmans are light in color, although to this rule there are countless exceptions; you may find, in southern India, Brahmans as black as any Congo Negro, but this dark skin is stretched over European-type facial bones.

Below these four main castes in India are the outcastes or untouchables. Once they were limited in occupation to street sweepers, latrine cleaners, and tanners of hides. Even their touch was contaminating to one of higher caste, so they lived apart, and a Brahman could not eat food if the shadow of an outcaste man had fallen on it.

You will hear, abroad, that the new government has abolished caste. This is not true. It has abolished only the legal barriers between castes, admitting the children of the outcastes to its schools and colleges on an equality with others.

But beyond this legal equality, not much has changed. With caste goes division of labor, still cherished in this crowded land. An American woman, breaking a dish, was told by her houseboy and cook that the pieces would be swept up only when the sweeper returned from an errand. To shame them, she swept up the pieces herself. Next morning she found all three servants had gone, rather than lose face by working in a house where the mistress would do the sweeper's work. How does this differ from the jurisdictional disputes of labor unions?

To make conversation with a diplomat's young wife at an embassy reception, I remarked that I understood servants' wages were low in India.

"They seem to be," she said. "Then you find that you need servants of different castes for various kinds of work which one alone might do, and you must feed their families; if you don't, they will steal it, which is understandable. And next you find they have made you into a kind of feudal lord; if one of the family gets sick, it is up to you to get a doctor and help out. In the end you will find you are running a welfare state, which is not easy to do on our salaries."

To get a look at India's social structure, disregard the editorials in the papers and read the matrimonial ads that come out every Sunday. Caste (social class) in India is as alive as it always was, for the caste of the person seeking to marry is always stressed in these advertisements.

India's four main castes are divided into innumerable sub-castes. Color is also important. By and large (with exceptions) the Brahmans are lighter than the others, and the lower castes progressively darker. Frequently a boy, advertising for a wife, insists that she be "fair" or proclaims himself to be "fair." For instance:

"Wanted: Beautiful, educated Brahman match for an M.A. [this is his college degree] Kanyakubja Brahman [this is his subcaste and caste] boy, 30 years old, government service drawing 300 rupees per month [about $40.00, a salary for a young man to brag about in India]."

And another:

"Wanted: A tall, slim, fair, graduate [he means high school] accomplished girl below 25 for a Srisvatava Dusre [subcaste and caste] Captain in the Army. Father retired senior gazetted office, brothers well placed." (This young officer will settle for a girl of any subcaste within his Dusre caste, but those of lower caste are out. He announces that his father and brothers are well placed because there will be no need to spend any of his military salary supporting them or their families.)

And now comes a real catch, a boy who advertises himself as "U.S.A.- and Europe-trained, young, handsome, tall, outstanding personality, age 28, has his own flourishing industry, Vaishnav [this is his caste] highly respectable family, invites matrimonial proposals with full particulars from beautiful, tall, home-loving girls or their parents."

Now, the parents of a girl who want a "suitable Brahman groom, preferably of West Bengal origin, for a fair-complexioned high school graduate girl of 23."

Now, a man who describes himself as a "highly qualified chartered accountant, aged 28, Lingayet Banagiga [subcaste and caste] earning four figures in the Central Government service, subcaste no bar [but of course it must be a subcaste within his caste]. Well-placed parents of a fair, domesticated, graduate girl may please write in strict confidence, giving full particulars."

Then, the catch of all time. A young man who advertises: "Wanted: a beautiful, homely [they mean home-loving] preferably convent-educated, high school graduate bride for a tall, Rajvanshi Vaish [subcaste and caste] foreign-qualified Civil Engineer of 29, having permanent residenceship in U.S.A., drawing about Dollars 10,000 per annum [a salary fabulous beyond belief in India]. Marriage proposed March or April 1967."

From the parents of a girl: "Wanted: suitable match for a fair-complected Aggarwal [no subcaste given] girl, college graduate, aged 20½, belongs to respectable family. Well-qualified persons only, such as scientists and industrialists. Non-Aggarwal may also write." This girl, a college graduate, probably insisted that this last sentence go in. She may want a smart husband, and if he is also tall and fair with good prospects, she might settle for a lower caste in spite of the protests of her parents.

From such ads and countless others, one gathers that the prime factor in seeking a mate in India is suitable caste. Other factors, in descending order of importance, are that the mate should be fair, tall, rich, or with good prospects.

Our friend is by caste a Brahman. By education he has a doctor's degree and by profession holds a high administrative post in a scholarly field. He is tall, slender, gentle, with graceful manners, and resembles Julius Caesar. He is light-skinned for India, but on the streets of Rome his complexion would pass without notice. As for caste, he explained:

"You cannot see it from the outside: only from within. There are two Indias. Educated and literate people are free of caste feeling. But the illiterates in the village [about 70 per cent of India] still have the same feeling.

"In India, every name is a caste name. When I am introduced to a man, instantly I know his caste and he knows mine. With educated people, this means increasingly less.

"In the old days, noncaste people had to draw their water from separate wells, their children could not mix with others in schools [which meant that they got no schooling] and could not enter temples. They were Hindus, of course, so they would kneel outside, palms raised and pressed together.

"Overnight the law changed all this. In the beginning there was resistance, particularly in the villages. Priests, trying to oppose noncaste people entering the temples, were jailed. This has long since changed. Today even the villages accept these three things, but the feeling is still there.

"Today, at the university level, boys and girls are picking their own mates as they do in the West, and this continues after they graduate and are working together in jobs. Noncaste people get positions and earn promotions on the basis of competitive examinations and merit, like the others.

"Of course this is good. But even I would tell my son, 'Unless you are very much in love with a noncaste girl, it is better not. For how would we explain such a marriage to relatives back in our village?' "

We also hear that if India's almost unsolvable problems of food and birth rate should bring about a collapse of government, it could never be a revolution in the European meaning. Caste-thinking is too ingrained. Such a convulsion might produce a military dictatorship, but never an overturn of society. Every little subcaste of every caste, jealous of its privileges, would be horrified.

In America, we knew what his real name was—had written it down—but never used it because, in that free way we Americans have, the sponsor who brought him to us already was calling him Dom, a version of his name. So we called him "Dom" too.

A few years ago Dom was on tour in our country. He was in his middle forties and the editor of one of India's biggest newspapers. It fell to us to show him around for about a week.

All Indians, arriving in America, are obsessed with our problems in relation to Negroes, just as, to them, we seem obsessed with their cow riots or frictions over caste. Each, viewed from across the water, bewilders the other. We felt that, if we failed to get for Dom a reserved seat at a lynching, he would feel that we were covering up.

After we met him it was not this bad. But there were so many things he simply had not learned. His visit took place at the time of Little Rock. When we casually told him that such troubles were largely confined to a dozen states, and that in most of the others, Negro and white children had always peacefully gone to grade school, high school, and college together, we could see amazement in his stare. Since he had come to trust us, he did not doubt it. But he pulled out his notebook and asked us to spell out the names of these other states. Back in India, such a list would be important news.

As the days went by, we came to like him very much. He was smart, and there also was about him a deep sweetness not too common in our land. His diet was such a problem that it was each day's fascinating challenge for us to solve it. We already had been told he was a vegetarian, but this was just the beginning. Not that Dom ever made trouble. But when any dish came on the table, he would gently bring up the topic of what had gone into it. When told, he would then either eat it all with many compliments, or not touch it. Coaxing the rules out of him took several days. Beef, pork, poultry, and lamb we had known were out. We

found that so was fish. It got down to the matter of taking
a life, no matter how humble.

A mushroom omelet was quietly passed by. When we
pressed him, it was the eggs; they contained the seeds of
future life. With pastry, it got down to the individual recipe.
Had it been made with vegetable shortening? If lard, it was
sweetly passed up.

This gentle man, we could see, was deeply pained for the
trouble he was causing. His prayer was that we would not
notice what he did not eat. Finally he was almost forced to
tell us that he was not just a Hindu, but also a Jain, and
of this sect we were to learn much more after we arrived
in India on our way to Vietnam.

This sect first emerges in about 600 B.C. with a revolt
by a great teacher against the many gods and caste system
of Hinduism. In our American pantheon today, I would
compare Jains with Quakers. The four virtues which these
Asiatic puritans preach are (1) tolerance, (2) piety, (3) re-
morse for one's own shortcomings, and (4) gentleness to all
things, living or not, from whence comes this strict diet
which, Jains insist, is only the unimportant outward sign
of a deeper creed. They never flaunt it. Dom was anything
but a long-faced bluenose. He had a keen sense of humor,
and under his kindly smile was a ready laugh.

All this is a prelude to that party around the blazing
fire in the former courtyard of His Highness the Nizam of
Hyderabad. We had been told that the cream of New Delhi's
press would be there, Dom was of it, and even in that flicker-
ing firelight we instantly recognized each other after those
eight years.

He was overjoyed to see us. We must come to see his
paper. We must let him take us around the old part of
Delhi in his car, as we had driven him around our town;
and come to his house, as he had been to ours. His wife was
not well, but in a few days she would be. Meanwhile there

was his son, of whom he had told us so much, and also his three daughters.

There were no surprises in our visit to Dom's editorial office; it was very businesslike and what you would expect in any land for a paper of better than 100,000 circulation. Of course tea was brought in (apparently served each afternoon as it would be on a British newspaper) and drunk with a number of his subordinates, all bright, courteous young men.

His home should not have been a surprise but was, for we were not prepared for the cohesiveness of an Indian family. They had all come, Dom had already told us, from the same village, not far from Delhi. To this village they return, several times a year, for important festivals at its Jain temple.

To reach his house we drove into a suburb on Delhi's outskirts, where the houses were not more than ten years old. Dom had explained that they were moving to a new one, but we could not see why, for these seemed comfortable enough. They would sell in my old home town of Emporia, Kansas, for about $20,000.

In front was a tiny garden, planted, Dom said, at government urging because of the famine, in corn, beans, and tomatoes. The house was about 25 feet wide and maybe 50 feet long downstairs: a living room, a kitchen, a bathroom, and three bedrooms. We did not go upstairs, but Dom said 18 people lived in that house, of whom 14 were on hand to greet us. Dom's wife happened to be back in their village, looking after a sick relative.

We met Dom's mother, who was in her upper 70's, his older sister, his brother, his brother's wife, Dom's son, a bright and handsome man of about 28, his wife and their new baby, Dom's three daughters, and his nephew and two nieces. There was also another boy of about 12 whom we assumed to be another nephew. They laughed and said no, he was a servant.

We now understand why Dom felt they needed a larger house. From great-grandmother to baby, four generations lived there, and all the collateral branches. We would call it living in a pile; they would regard any family breakup as a shock, if not a tragedy.

With Americans, young people always move out, and grandparents are often elbowed into some nursing home or senior-citizens' city. With Indians, a bride moves in with her husband's family, and the couple may not move out until after their first son is born—daughters do not count. Often even then they do not move out.

Group living takes order and the Indian family has it. Clearly in the absence of Dom's wife, his widowed mother, who in that living room sat in the chair of honor wearing a spotless white sari, ruled the female end of that roost. Just as clearly Dom, her oldest living son, sweetly ran the male end.

In a later meeting with Dom's son, who was about to leave for a year in England to study electronics, we talked of Western family customs of which he knew something through reading but which puzzled him.

"My father and I are one person," he said, and explained he meant that they talked together on all subjects, until they agreed. "My wife and I often go to the cinema. But I would never think of going without asking his permission, which of course he always gives." What I am failing to portray is the great sweetness of these people—sweetness to us, and clearly to each other. Was it because they are Jains? Or are all Indian families like this? We do not know.

Later Dom brought the teen-age daughters to tea with us at the Ashoka. The tea included a plate of little frosted cakes, but the very polite little girls, sitting stiffly, made no move. So finally I said that each really must take one. All three gave a quick glance at Dom; then three little hands reached out in unison, three mouths opened, and down went three cakes in less than fifteen seconds, as would happen with teen-age girls in any country. Why had they been so bashful?

Later, when they had left on an errand, I remarked to Dom how much the girls had enjoyed the cakes. He smiled.

"They would not have eaten them if their mother had been here."

"Why not?"

Dom smiled again. "The eggs in them." We had forgotten about Jains.

The eldest told us she wanted to be an economist (by this time their English had thawed out). The middle one was musical, and played beautifully on the sitar. The youngest said she didn't know yet, but thought she wanted to be a doctor. All were doing well in school, but all said they had to do lots of homework, which was not easy, with so many to talk to in the same room.

Later Dom's son and his pretty young wife came to dinner with us. The girl took a little warming up. She knew English but away from home seemed shy about speaking it, maybe because her husband spoke it so well. We talked of her husband's coming year of study in England. He said he was going to work hard because the cost of it was a sacrifice to the family, which also had other financial obligations. The two eldest of his sisters would soon be out of school and thus marriageable. This meant raising, for each, a marriage portion of 25,000 rupees, a considerable sum for India. Dom's son mentioned it with pride, and we got the feeling that no less a sum would do for girls as fine as his sisters. We guessed that, for such well-raised girls, only Jain husbands would do—from this caste which opposes caste. An outsider would not fit, would be a betrayal of that close-knit family and creed.

We knew that in India marriage is a matter of serious planning—matching caste, education, and background, and then providing capital for the young couple to start in life. Indians would be deeply shocked at our system under which, with the sense of family fast weakening, marriage is sometimes a matter of teen-age whim, often to dissolve a few months later. Indian marriages last.

If you wish to know a country—to feel, rub, taste, and see its culture and history—go to a market.

For example, one shop is staffed by what we mistake for Chinese—the same straight black hair, yellow skin, and slant eyes that characterize the great Mongoloid race that stretches from Japan through China and down to Singapore. We find that these are refugees from the Communist invasion of Tibet, here selling off their belongings, vessels of hand-hammered copper inlaid with brass dragons, or sometimes set with agates or turquoises—all of it Chinese in style.

Tibetans may look Chinese to us but they want no part of Mao's China. They are devout Buddhists, and differ from the Chinese in speech and in written language. The Communist Chinese reckon differently and this brings up their border dispute with India, whose frontiers were drawn by the British in colonial days, setting it off from lands ruled by the Czar.

The Russians, in their nineteenth-century Czarist expansion, crossed the Urals and marched to the Pacific, bringing millions of Siberian Mongoloid tribesmen (Kazakhstan, Uzbekistan, Outer Mongolia) under Slavic rule, many of them severed from the Old Chinese Empire.

Now hear Mao's side of this argument which, as the Russians know, could touch off World War III. He claims, for his Marxist state, all peoples of Mongoloid blood who ever paid tribute to the Imperial Throne in Peking, and this includes not only both Vietnams and those conquered by the Russian Romanovs, but many brought within India's frontiers by the British. For Mao does not recognize these British-drawn frontiers and recently, to the exquisite anguish of India's neutralist government, broke through them to claim not only Tibet, but still other yellow-skinned, slant-eyed Himalayans ruled from New Delhi since British times. With the result that these refugees from Mao's blood-and-soil doctrines now squat in this market selling off their wares. And with the further result that Ho, in Hanoi, would fear to admit Mao's armies to help him recover South Vietnam. Recover it for whom?

The market gives other insights. An open-front grocer's shop has bins of various grains to be sold by the scoop. Birds fly in, perch on the rims, and peck their fill, the owner making no move to shoo them off. In this land where all life is held of equal value, animals have no fear of people. On our first day two birds flew in through the open French doors of our hotel room, perched on lamp shades to inspect us, and then flew quietly out. In the garden, birds fearlessly light on our shoes to peck up crumbs of fallen tea cakes.

Next this grocer is a jeweler, whose window holds a necklace of big silver rupees bearing the head of young Queen Victoria, struck in 1840 by the British East India Company and once part of some village girl's dowry. Even today much of a bride's dowry comes in jewelry of precious metal—gold if the family can afford it, never less than 18 karat, and on this hangs a tale. The present government, trying to save gold, decreed that jewelers could use only 14-karat gold: it almost caused a revolution. Such diluted gold was not suitable for wedding gifts; the marriage hardly seemed legal.

The government had to bow: 18-karat gold can be used, but only if obtained by melting down old jewelry heirlooms bought from the estates by specially licensed jewelers. This has checked but not stopped the flow of smuggled gold bars into India.

The gavel having come down on the final session in New Delhi, we editors depart, as guests of the government of India, on a week's tour of the country aboard an air-conditioned special train so solidly British that it is hard to believe that Lord Mountbatten is not still on his viceregal throne. The staterooms are paneled in teak and each car gleams with solid brass, requiring more hand polishing than is possible today in servant-short England. The train swarms with turbaned, white-gloved servants who wake us each morning with a tray of early tea and end the day by serving, in the dining car, an Indian replica of the seven-course dinner standard in Victoria's reign.

During the night the train moved north into the Punjab, arriving at dawn in the little town of Ludhiana, where we are to see an agricultural college founded as a result of India's partition back in 1947.

Prior to India's independence, and during the great debate which had preceded it—not only in the British Parliament but throughout the world—those who opposed independence warned that it surely would bring civil war between Hindus and Moslems, who in India had been fighting and rioting for centuries, kept from each other's throats only by Pax Britannica.

The other school of thought, held by those busy dismantling the British Empire, scorned this argument. The empire, they said, was founded on the strategy of "divide and rule." There were no real quarrels between Hindu and Moslem in India, or between Jew and Arab in Palestine, except those cunningly fomented by the British to serve their own ends. Once their flag was hauled down and true democracy installed, such disputes would cease; the lion and the lamb would lie down together.

What happened instead gave proof that the British Empire, whatever its faults, had been a force for peace and tolerance in the world, for when the British withdrew, the victorious lion presently lay down alone to sleep off a feast of mutton chops.

The British yoke surely rested lightly on India, for it took no more than 12,000 English (and this counts their families) to rule the hundreds of millions on this subcontinent. This small group furnished administrators of provinces or advisers to rajahs (the title was "British Resident") at the local court. They included most (but not all) of the commissioned officers in the Indian army. In the days of the struggle for independence a joking boast went from mouth to ear in the Congress Party: if Indians would only spit together, they could drown all the British in India. It was almost true because the British were so few that in thousands of villages, the people had never seen an Englishman.

True, the British practiced social discrimination which was maddening to educated Indians. It was not legal segregation, but an aloofness. The British kept rigidly to themselves. Their social life centered around their many clubs, which had no Indian members. Indians might be equal under British law, and British courts in India were scrupulously fair. They granted to Indian newspapers most of those press freedoms to attack them savagely which British newspapers enjoyed in England, but the British judge would never dream of sitting next to a "native" at dinner. And that did it.

The drive for Indian freedom was led by Oxford- and Cambridge-educated Indians, and supported in England by the British Labour Party's intellectuals. In India it was confined almost entirely to intellectuals and students in the big cities. There were mass meetings, parades, and speeches

in both Parliament and the Congress but little real violence
(Gandhi was against this), and the "struggle" for Indian
independence cost hardly a hundred lives.

But after independence, in the ensuing Hindu-Moslem
riots as India and Pakistan were split apart and peoples
exchanged, blood flowed in oceans: maybe two million were
killed. This exploded the myth of British "divide and rule."
But the myth had served its purpose.

In the Punjab traces of this old Hindu-Moslem struggle
are everywhere. The British had built two agricultural
colleges, but when, in the partition, the Punjab itself was
split, both went to Pakistan, and the government of East
Punjab was forced to build a new school in Ludhiana.

Was independence worth it—those perhaps two million
lost lives in the Moslem-Hindu civil war, and the great
displacement of peoples—India's Moslem minority being
driven into Pakistan, while Pakistan's Hindu minority likewise had to run for their lives over the border?

The ruling Hindus certainly feel that it was. The Punjab
once had a substantial Moslem minority. In every town
you see the minarets of their mosques, but from none of
these have I heard a call to prayer.

You ask about the Moslems, and they say, Oh yes, there
are still 10 or 15 per cent. Or if our party approaches a
group of women who lift veils to their faces, the Hindus
explain that they are Moslems. But today the Moslems are
quiet, perhaps frightened, in this land which their Mogul
emperors once so proudly ruled.

We begin to see rural India—its small towns and half
million villages. I have no idea how big Ludhiana is—maybe
the size of Emporia, maybe three times as big. But as we
drove through it to the Punjab Agricultural University, we
saw no other automobile or truck. We saw ox carts. We
drove around sacred cows lying in the road. We saw the
rich in rickety carriages pulled by skinny horses. We saw
fifty such carriages lined up at our railway station, each

hoping a man would get off the train rich enough to pay for a ride. I would guess they get such a customer about once every other day. But patiently these drivers and their skinny horses wait. Not much of a job, but better than no job.

We saw the upper-middle classes riding in pedicabs. This is a bicycle which, in place of its rear wheel, pulls a light, two-wheeled carriage behind the pedaling driver.

We also saw a few rickshas, pulled by men running between shafts. These are slower but also cheaper than the pedicab, because the bicycle part represents an important capital investment. We saw one oversized ricksha seating four people, pulled by one man trotting between shafts like a horse, with another turbaned man trotting behind so that he could push when they came to a grade.

We saw Ludhiana's prosperous middle classes proudly pedaling their privately owned bicycles. But you will want to know how the common man in Ludhiana gets around. Well, I can answer that. What he does is walk.

India, which discourages the importation of foreign cars, makes one of her own, called the Ambassador, about the size of an American compact, which sells for just under $2,700, a considerable sum in a land where the national income is 24 cents a day. Production of these cars has risen from 14,000 in 1950 to 70,000 today. This is one new car for every 7,000 Indians. It also follows that, in India's half million villages, there are probably many people who have not seen a car, and some who will die without seeing one.

The bicycle situation is somewhat better, and it is the dream of every village boy to own one. Last year India turned out 1,582,000 bicycles—one for every 316 Indians. In the United States there is an automobile for every three and one half persons.

We were now so far north that it was chilly—or seemed so after the sweltering November heat of New Delhi. We passed countless kinds of trees we never before had seen; in fact the only ones we recognized were the banana trees and the mimosa. We passed head-high green bushes with purple-flowering tips—not bougainvillaea, something else. We saw mud houses, like the vanishing adobe of New Mexico, with golden cow-plop plastered in patterns on the walls to dry, the center of each bearing the imprint of the hand that molded it.

Then, on the flat horizon, we finally saw a group of the agricultural college's spaciously laid-out modern buildings, some of which were faculty housing, some student dormitories. Most interesting of all, there was one building for farmers, picked by the college from widely scattered areas and brought here to learn what wonderful crops can be grown with proper seed, fertilizer, and modern methods.

When the farmers return to their own fields they serve as informal teachers, spreading modern methods among their neighbors who have watched the splendid results. The college hopes in this way to increase farm production all over the Punjab.

Rainfall in the Punjab, they told us, is thirty inches a year—about what we get in Kansas. But since the Punjab has no winter, farmers could well grow two crops a year, a summer crop watered by the monsoon rains of early spring, and a "rabi" (winter) crop from irrigation if they can get water.

At this agricultural college generous credit is given experts from Ohio State University who helped set up the school, a part of which is experimental fields. We saw rows of hybrid tomato plants, and also grapes, which are new out here. Scientists hope that the Punjab may grow wine grapes as good as California's, that should yield an income of from 10 to 15 thousand rupees per acre per year.

We also saw twisted tomato vines and warped fruit, as though crippled with a dread disease. The disease, guides told us, was radiation. By bombarding the genes within the tomato seeds it was hoped, part by skill and part by chance, to produce some useful mutant—a tomato that would grow bigger or ripen faster.

With pride they showed us a beehive, explaining that it was brought from America, since our bees produce six times more honey than native Indian bees. The Indians are also experimenting with wheats. Their native wheat responded well to fertilizer, but then produced a head so heavy that its long stalk bent over, allowing much of the ripe grain to spill. Testing all wheats, scientists had hit on a Mexican dwarf variety which is producing a 40 per cent increase in yield over the old varieties.

We paused in front of a galvanized tank about four feet high and six feet in diameter, with pipes running out of it. Of course we had been told that cow manure is the life of an Indian farm, used both for fertilizer and as cooking fuel. But with this new device the farmer, instead of drying manure for fuel, puts it in an airtight tank. Then, as it ferments, all of its heat values come out as a gas which, piped into the house, can be used for cooking. When the gas is exhausted, the remaining manure in the tank still retains all its high nitrate value as fertilizer.

On the average Indian farm, how much of the manure is used for cooking and how much put back on the land? Stupid farmers, our guides replied, often burn 60 per cent of their manure and put back only 40 per cent in the land. With the tank contrivance, they can cook and yet put 100 per cent back into the soil. On the great majority of Indian farms the only fertilizer is cow manure, and this brilliantly simple device could more than double its present supply. But how many farmers, with the government artificially holding down the price of grain to "protect" the consumer, could afford to buy even this tank?

We then saw a display of farm tools designed for the needs

of this land, each to be operated by a man or pulled by an ox, and therefore made of wood with the minimum of light steel. One tool measured out and deposited the exact amount of needed fertilizer above and at the side of each planted seed. While each tool did the job more skillfully than it had been done before, and took some of the backbreak and stooping out of farm work, none of them can be called truly labor-saving in our American sense.

Having been to Turkey, I knew why. In the early days of our aid program there, some enormously well-intentioned idiot imported several hundred of our diesel-powered mechanical monsters into one rural province. They did the job all right, and almost caused a social revolution, for they threw thousands of agricultural laborers out of work.

These mechanical marvels of ours seldom increase production per acre. They only enormously reduce the labor needed to get slightly less production per acre. The highest per acre production comes when the farmer and his family swarm into each little field, squatting over each sprouting seed, straightening its stalk, pulverizing with their fingers the earth above its roots, weeding and sometimes even watering by hand. Such labor India has—and vastly more. For example, on our way to the Punjab we had seen herds of cattle, sheep, and goats at pasture, with no fences to keep them out of growing crops. Instead each flock was watched and guided by one or two children. Young shepherds are cheaply come by, whereas iron for barbed wire is fabulous in cost, in terms of a village income.

Much nonsense gets into print about India's wastefulness of its cows, sacred or otherwise, much of it written by people who have never set foot in an Indian village. It may be that there are, in this country, half as many cows as people, but how are cows wasted? Bullocks are the tractors of India, tilling her soil. Cows give milk which is, to village children, often their only source of animal protein.

True, when a cow gets too old either to pull a plow or

to milk, the farmer disclaims ownership and the hungry old cow, wandering into a neighbor's growing field, may cause neighborhood disputes in which villagers sometimes are injured, but never the sacred cow. True, they eat grass that could go to more useful animals. But even so, much of the cow's value comes from its precious manure, carefully gathered by the villagers.

An Indian professor, H. J. Bhabha, has estimated that the nation's total energy requirements from all sources—including atomic energy, hydroelectric power, oil, coal, etc.—come to 1.3 billion kilowatts a year, of which at least a billion come from burning cow dung. Each night in India rice is boiling in millions of pots over fires made from the dung of these allegedly parasitic sacred cows.

What, in our mad world, are the true values? The West criticizes the Indians for keeping useless sacred cows alive while people starve. The Indians, holding all life to be of equal value, feel we are too narrowly humanitarian, and should be *bucolitarian* as well. If these half-starved masses wish to share their little with their starving cows, should not that choice be theirs?

We were impressed by the practical value of the training given by this university to its students—a type of learning vitally needed by India. This foreign visitor predicts that you will never read of a riot at Ludhiana Agricultural College.

India's birth rate is four per hundred people per year. In the old days one child out of five survived to age 5. With scientific advances, about half now survive and the old are living longer; thus the population increase is 2.5 per cent a year. At this rate, by 1986 India's population will reach a billion, if vast famines do not again intervene.

When their country was part of the British Empire, many Indians escaped famine by migration to British colonies in the West Indies, South America, or Africa. These doors are now closed; all countries have population problems. Until recently, new land in India could be cleared; this is no longer true.

Under the British (and for thousands of years before) there were famines. Between 1857 and 1947 there were 30, often caused by lack of transportation within India: surplus grain from areas of abundance could not reach the starving people in time. But in general India was a food-exporting nation—8 million tons a year before World War II. Now food ships move in the other direction.

Since independence, food production has gone up from 50 million tons a year to 88 million in 1964–65. But because food supplies lagged behind population growth, India still needed to import 8 million tons. But in the following crop year drought rolled production back to 72 million tons, and India had to import 11 million. Then drought struck again, producing, in the fall of 1966, severe famine in the northeastern state of Bihar. An American who inspected the area said that he saw many people crawling into their huts, waiting for the inevitable. The land was so dry that they could not plant the spring crop and were eating the seed, having no other reserves. The water table was so low that water was lacking for bullocks, the tractors of India; and if the bullocks died, how could any crop be planted?

In Bihar he saw "misery you don't see in this century; a girl of 25, trying to sell her baby for 5 rupees." The American was newly arrived in India; the sale would be less shocking to natives, for in some regions such sales are a custom. A girl who has a child she cannot feed seeks out a family who wants one (Indians love children), and as part of the sale an agreement is made that the child shall be fed and clothed, that the mother has visiting rights, and, if the child is a girl, that she be provided with a dot when she reaches marriageable age. Tradition and customs protect the child.

While famine was widespread in both Bihar and nearby Uttar Pradesh—and while India was appealing to the world for food—grain surpluses were stored (against future need) in a number of Indian states whose ministries refused the appeals of the Central Government to release food. Hence a cartoon in the Indian press with the caption "Now that we have tried U.S.A., U.S.S.R., Canada and Australia, it looks as though we shall have to try Madras and Andhra Pradesh."

Similar contrasting conditions in food supplies often existed in India during the famines of British times, but now the British are gone; the Indians have only themselves to blame, which they are doing.

Late rains brought relief to Northeast India. But as India tries to bring her population under control, she will teeter on the brink of starvation for the next 10 years, and if she cannot solve the problem then, one American expert predicts that "in this generation we will see a tragedy which would make all the wars of history seem like nothing."

In its manifesto, the Congress Party said it was winning the food-population race, claiming that per capita food consumption, as a result of three 5-year plans, had increased from a daily 12.8 ounces to 15.4. This their opponents in the opposition Swatantra Party deny, pointing out that in 1938 under the British it was 14.2 daily ounces, and has now dropped to 13.9 despite the imports.

As for clothing, the Congress Party claimed that per capita consumption in 15 years had gone up from 11 meters a year to 15. Swatantra quotes bank figures to show that before the war it was almost 14 meters, then dropped, and now is back to about 14. If their figures are right, the average Indian is not quite as well fed or clothed by the socialist Congress Party as he was under the British.

Save for a few experimental projects and what little knowledge has seeped out from them, India's acres are farmed as they were in the Late Stone Age, except that the bullock-drawn wooden plows now have iron tips. While there are still wide regions where no farmer will kill a rat gnawing into his grain bin, in others farmers are asking, "Why, just to please a few sadhus [holy men], should I let cows eat my growing crops?"

At the time of our visit India's Minister of Agriculture was C. Subramanian, whom Americans here consider one of the great men of Asia. Under him India was finally tackling the job of raising her own food as she did before the British left—even hoping for self-sufficiency at the end of the current 5-year plan, by replanting 32 million acres with new, high-yield seed which would respond to fertilizer.

But the problem then was, would Mr. Subramanian's doctrinaire socialist colleagues let him have the needed fertilizer to keep the country from starvation? In the past they had been dragging their feet. Fertilizer plants have figured in all India's 5-year plans but, lagging far behind their goals, had achieved only 3 million tons for the whole country. The Swatantra Party was pointing out that, in nitrogen alone, the target was 800,000 tons for 1965, whereas the government plants failed to turn out even 250,000. Instead, money was squandered on status symbols like atomic-energy plants, all of which contributed to the setback which India's voters gave the Congress Party shortly after we left, with the Swatantra Party, its right-wing opposition, greatly increasing in strength.

When one compares India's various 5-year plans with their fulfillment, these "targets" turn out to be stuff that dreams are made of. The "target" for 1965–66 was 100 million tons of food grains, but what with lack of fertilizer and bad weather, India raised only about 72 million tons. The "target" for 1970–71 is 120 million tons. How far off in dreamland will this be from reality?

So many things are not foreseeable. More fertilizer means more food produced, and India's planners estimated how much more of the estimated surplus would go to the cities. But they found that India's farmers were feeding much of this surplus to their own half-starved (and fast increasing) families. No one can blame the farmers, but no one had planned for it.

Farming is a gamble with the weather, as every farmer knows, but in the long term he can win out. If the weather is good, yields are high and the price drops; but the farmer still has plenty of bushels to sell at this lower price. If it is a bad year, then yields per acre are low; but the price per bushel rises, so the farmer gets a higher return for the fewer bushels he has been able to raise—except in India. For here in famine years the government steps in, forces the farmer to sell a portion of his crop at prices fixed by the government, and in turn sells this at low prices to the holders of ration cards in the cities.

Such controls reduce both the farmer's incentive to raise more, and his ability to buy needed fertilizer. However good controls may be in theory, you can't eat them, and India needs food.

Just how miserable is India's food production compared to that of the more progressive "free enterprise" nations of Asia—Japan, Taiwan, and South Korea? The diet in all four is founded on rice. Its yield (in kilograms per hectare) is:

Japan	52.8
Taiwan	33.1
South Korea	27.4
India	13.7

Why? Well, when we look at the use of chemical fertilizers we find the same pecking order:

Japan	297.6
Taiwan	210.8
South Korea	176.8
India	3.6

Again why? Are India's leaders this much more stupid than those of (for instance) Japan? We found India's leaders to be brilliant, dedicated men. But their heads were buried in the sands of Fabian Socialism, leaving the farmers at the mercy of the droppings of Mother Cow, as these figures show. Until recently it was doubted that India's illiterate farmers would accept chemical fertilizer. Now that some have tried it, their neighbors are screaming for more, and India which produced only 3 million tons in 1966 could have used 10 million, for it now spreads only an average of 2.5 pounds per acre, whereas the Japanese use 20.9 pounds.

Foreign fertilizer companies realized that this big demand was there, and clamored for permission to build plants, but the government insisted on the right to impose price controls, arguing that foreign capitalists might exploit the great need of India's farmers for fertilizer. Was this the real reason? The Swatantra Party pointed out that the government was charging their captive market the world's highest prices for fertilizer: capitalist competition would show up socialist inefficiency.

Only after its election setback did the Congress Party reverse its policy, and now a number of desperately needed fertilizer plants are being built in India by foreign companies. It was about time, for, as Mr. Subramanian had been pointing out, the country must produce 2 million more tons of food each year, just to keep India's diet at its current semi-starvation levels. In the previous year India had eaten 83 million tons; decent health for all would have required at least 100 million.

For the moment India has a respite. Good monsoon rains have helped, and the new foreign-owned fertilizer plants, when they get into production, will help still more.

One of India's best friends, Douglas Enslinger at the Ford Foundation, pleads for more time, which the world (particularly America) does not understand. But India needs and must have the time because of the size of her problems, some of which stem from our mistakes, as we shall see. Unfortunately, each shortage is presented as a unique crisis, with the result that the world says, "What—India again?"

The task of checking her birth rate to mesh with her food production will take ten years. Is not the world's largest democracy worth this much patience?

We detrain here at Chandigarh, to see an example of modern town planning. The need for such planning came with the stampedes of panicked peoples across new national boundaries, set up when India and Pakistan were torn apart as both attained their independence from the British Crown.

Before independence the capital of this state was Lahore, a lovely little town at the foot of the Himalayas. But in the carving up, Lahore was assigned to Moslem Pakistan. Its Hindu minority was resettled in the Indian portion, which needed and got a new capital—Chandigarh, built to house the state government and the refugees. It is modern beyond belief—beautiful if somewhat coldly over-logical, a fault it shares with Brasilia and all planned cities.

It is a maze of traffic circles which seem to us to be largely traffic obstacles, with cars so scarce in India. But consider Indian traffic, compounded of automobiles, rickshas, pedicabs, bicycles, and the two-wheeled, ox-drawn carts of the peasants which have neither changed in design nor gained in speed since their Aryan ancestors drove them through Khyber Pass. Such a cart would not have time to cross an intersection before the green light winked out. Consider also the sacred cows, each moving in an erratic orbit of its choice. How would these react to the challenge of a stop-go sign? And consider the traffic snarls each might create, since it is not just a traffic offense but a sin for Hindus to collide with them. Perhaps these planners know best, and in any case their city is lovely if a little rigid.

The planners have planted their main boulevards with four lines of trees, as did Baron Haussmann in Paris, choosing them so that at almost every season of the year, some are in bloom. They selected pink cassia, jacaranda, silver oak, amaltas, and Pride of India, none of which (so far as I know) is grown in our Midwest.

Studying the traffic a little more closely, we discovered it to be a highly practical application of the Hindu caste system, for certain Brahman boulevards of traffic lanes are reserved for fast traffic, while below these are three other clearly defined castes for bikes and pedicabs, rickshas, and farmers' wagons or pedestrians. To just what spot in this traffic hierarchy the sacred cow has been assigned was not clear to us. But one thing we particularly admired about this planning was that the fastest traffic lanes were enclosed by walls so high that no child, living in a nearby house, could dart out into the street.

This planned town, after several starts, was finally carried through by a team of architects under the chairmanship of the French architect Le Corbusier, a pioneer in the modern manner, and we were taken to the center of town to see the vast public buildings designed by this master.

To be fair, I should say that I have never liked the work of Le Corbusier—not in Paris and still less in India. He comes of that primitive period in modern architecture when its devotees were screaming the word "functional" at each other, and his offering at this shrine is to leave all his cumbersome, soaring concrete masses naked, so that one can still see the knot imprints of the wooden forms into which it was poured. My yearnings for nude concrete are quickly satisfied.

But still worse is his desire to shock and astound. Up from his assembly building in Chandigarh juts what seems to me to be the giant concrete replica of a plastic thermos bottle, but which appears to others to be a ship's funnel. Up from still another of his buildings pokes a huge wedge of concrete, its function seemingly to puzzle or annoy the passer-by. His Gandhi memorial, a part of Punjab University, has a beautiful setting on a lake—and looks like a gigantic replica of a lidless shoe box sat on by a child and slightly crushed.

But the work of Le Corbusier's town planners is excellent and smoothly adapted to the needs of Indian life. And it was, they say, the master himself who, while he lived and worked here, chose the varieties of flowering trees which may make this city one of the world's loveliest.

Our hosts took us to lunch at the Yacht Club on a lawn overlooking a lake, where in tents they served a superb buffet. We got, for the first time, Indian food as we had sniffed it in the bazaars, and found it delicious but hard to describe. Basically, it was bite-size tidbits of soft cheese, spinach, eggplant, and cubes of new potatoes, dipped in a light batter and then fried in deep fat (probably ghee, which is clarified butter). Candied melon rind, wrapped in gold or silver foil, was served as a sweet.

At such functions there are always two buffet tables, one providing meat dishes, and the other labeled "Vegetarian" for pious Hindus. Among Hindus there are many castes and customs. While some castes permit the eating of fish, eggs, or even goat, beef is never permitted. To the Hindu beef is sacred; he would as soon eat a slice of a cousin.

One of our British editors tells us that often in London he entertains a Hindu friend who delights in going to Simpson's-in-the-Strand where he beckons up the roast-beef trolley and eats dripping pink slices of it almost as fast as they can be carved. When discreetly questioned on this theological point, the Hindu explained that this was British cow and hence not sacred.

Our busses presently took us back through blocks of modern housing to the center of Chandigarh, where we were escorted through the Legislative Assembly, an imposing

masterpiece of Le Corbusian confusion which they told us
had cost 11 million pre-devaluation rupees. From its entrance
steps, we watched a lean, ragged man carrying on his head a
bale of hay so heavy that his thin legs were tottering as he
moved toward a nearby cluster of those mud huts which make
up India's typical villages. The government apparently had
not got around to housing their people in modern apartments.

That evening before our train pulled out I had, on the
station platform, a long talk with tall, handsome Sydney
Jacobson of the London *Sun*, who thirty years ago worked
here on *The Express* and who says things now are far better
because "the tension is much less. In those days your best and
most intelligent Indian friends—whose writing you respected
most—were in the Congress Party and constantly going to
jail, each time coming out more bitter. In those days there
was no mingling except on the highest level. But now things
are relaxed."

Jacobson thinks the Indians could conquer their economic
problems, but their political ones are most serious—separa-
tism, what Nehru called "Balkanization." The Punjab already has been partitioned twice—once at the cost of almost
two million lives. Now the Sikhs want Chandigarh included
in a Greater Sikhistan. The whole thing could crumble if
they don't stop thinking of autonomy for every little language
area or religious sect, and start thinking of themselves as a
nation.

There is a move, among violent Indian nationalists, to get
rid of statues of British viceroys which they hold to be traffic
obstacles. Yet perhaps the greatest hazards to India's future—
also relics of imperialism and foreign rule—are the doctrines
of British nineteenth-century Fabian Socialism which still
rule the thinking of India's Congress Party, however out-
moded those doctrines may now be in the rest of the world.

How could it be otherwise? For it was an English civil servant in India who, in 1885, founded this Congress Party. It was these gentle British Fabians who, in Oxford and Cambridge, first explained to Moslem and Hindu students that India was more than a geographical expression, that there could be a united India, which then should throw off the yoke of capitalist exploitation.

It was the British Labour Party that first took up India's cause in Parliament. Harold Laski, the party's principal theoretician in the twenties and thirties, was Nehru's close friend. It was England's Conservatives who opposed complete independence: "I did not become His Majesty's First Minister," rumbled Winston Churchill following World War II, "to preside over the liquidation of her empire." So it was the Labour Party that hauled down the British Jack in Delhi in 1947.

Small wonder that the Congress Party should proclaim itself socialist, that Nehru should see the socialism of Sidney and Beatrice Webb, Ramsay MacDonald and Clement Atlee as the answer to India's problems, and that Nehru should share, with most of those British Fabians of the 1930s, a blind faith in Stalin, whose grandiose 5-year plans, abandoned today in Moscow, still cast a pink sunset-glow in India. While India should remain a parliamentary democracy on the British model, Stalin (Nehru felt) had the answer to India's economic problems.

All of this combined to produce Nehru's policy of non-alignment—a neutrality so strict that he would not even permit hospital planes, bearing wounded from the Korean war, to fly over India.

This "splendid isolation" from reality, an illusion which seemed to combine sanctimony with safety, was forever shattered by the Communist Chinese attack in 1963. India in the beginning suffered humiliating defeats in part because, through some comic miracle in inept timing, Krishna Menon, the Congress Party's shrillest pro-Communist, then happened to be India's minister of defense. Before Nehru could think out a new posture he died, and his daughter now stands bewildered amid the jagged ruins of this foreign policy.

For Nehru, India was to be equated only with Russia, both of them vast, backward, peasant lands almost continental in size, recently delivered from oppressors. First things must come first (to be achieved through Stalin-type 5-year plans), and these were government-owned dams, electric power plants, coal mines, and steel mills. As with Stalin, the peasant masses in Nehru's thinking came last. Yet Nehru at least did not butcher the peasants as Stalin did in the early 1930s. He achieved his progress while maintaining all the British freedoms and without concentration camps.

In 1967 the *Times* of India carried a story that rats, during the year, would eat up more grain than India was receiving from abroad. Why are there few steel storage bins in India? Because, in this planned economy, they planned it that way. With low grain prices, farmers cannot afford bins; and anyway they have little surplus to store.

Also copying Stalin's 5-year plans, emphasis had been put on industry. Steel went into railroad cars, hydroelectric projects, showcase model-housing projects for workers, bicycles, automobiles, and even an atomic-energy plant—but little steel for bins.

So with Air India, whose great, comfortable jets, running at a handsome deficit, whoosh away rupees around the globe. Yet India shares her hankering for such baubles with all the world's "underdeveloped" nations. Showing the new flag on the world's landing strips is needed for its "image," and (in our inflationary age) far outranks a balanced budget as a status symbol.

In some instances India's planners are beginning to see the light. Cement was left in the "private sector" but under heavy controls, so that capitalists could not exploit the workers' need for housing. Result: it was worth no one's while to make cement. Finally, cement controls were lifted. Now cement production booms.

Fertilizer was another case in point. Our people argued with Indian officials, trying to make them see that if they took off ceilings, many foreign companies would bring in their own money to build fertilizer plants and this competition would force prices down.

To such arguments India's socialist rulers listened. They seemed to agree. Then they backed away. They had heard too many fiery speeches denouncing "neo-colonialism" and "capitalist exploitation." Or they may have made such speeches themselves. India's sacred cows may turn out to be a far less serious obstacle than Fabian Socialism, still the sacred cow of the Congress Party, which would protect the masses from exploitation even at the risk of starving them.

Our American contribution to India's chaos has been substantial. For some years after World War II there was a world food shortage, diminishing as war-ravaged nations struggled to their feet, with considerable food aid from America. By 1953 there was a grain surplus. In America, supply and demand could have cured this by shifting wheat lands back to the production of meat, as before the war.

But politics intervened. Our government continued to subsidize American wheat production by a guaranteed price to farmers, and then dumped the surplus abroad, under the program "Food for Peace," of which India became a heavy beneficiary.

The Communists were quick to attack it: nations receiving this grain need not feel grateful; they were doing American monopoly-capitalism a service by helping it dispose of a surplus, thus allowing big American land owners to exploit the toiling American masses through artificially high prices for food.

What was wrong with this Communist analysis? Nothing

really, except that some softening of Marxist vocabulary would give it more appeal to the American market.

Guarding our own economic interests, in this period we even refused Burma's request for technical help to increase her rice production (our South grows rice) with the result that, in foreign affairs, Burma now goes her own neutralist way.

But now look at the over-all: if, through dumping abroad, American growers get higher prices (and American consumers pay higher food costs), the result for him who gets dumped on can only be the opposite. The Indian masses got cheaper food, thus helping swell the population bulge. The Indian farmer got less for his grain, reducing both his incentive to raise more and his ability to buy fertilizer.

So, weighing our considerable responsibility for the mess India is in, we are hardly in a position to cut off all aid and complacently watch the world's biggest democracy go down the drain.

Since independence India has been ruled by the Congress Party founded by Gandhi and Nehru. Many millions of illiterate Indians have heard of no other party. Since this party won freedom from the British, these Founding Fathers have been lavished with gratitude by India's voters. With age the party has become afflicted with nepotism, and its newer recruits are motivated more by opportunism than by enthusiasm for Fabian doctrine. But until recent elections it could be complacent about its opposition, seemingly an unimportant bagful of splinter parties, dedicated to various economic, linguistic, and regional interests, from which a few emerge as important.

On the left the Communists are split into a larger Soviet right and a smaller Maoist left, but both were badly set back by the recent Chinese attack on India.

To the right of the Congress Party is the Jan Sangh Party,

abused by its opponents as Hindu-Fascist because it blames the government for not establishing Hindi as the sole official language and also is passionately anti-Moslem.

Jan Sangh also demands a federal ban on cow slaughter, which now is a matter up to each state, and organizes the naked, trident-bearing sadhus who lead parades in defense of Mother Cow. Jan Sangh opposes all foreign influence including both foreign aid and chemical fertilizers, favoring instead the dung of Mother Cow plus compost piles. If the party gained control, it would transform India into a Hindu theocracy. This will never happen because Jan Sangh is opposed, particularly in South India, by other language groups such as those who speak Tamil and who bitterly resent the attempts of this Hindu plurality to force their language on the minority language groups, who together form a majority.

India's most rapidly growing political party is a right-wing group called Swatantra, bitterly attacked as "The American Party" in spite of the fact that Swatantra criticizes American aid as a "misplaced generosity," a subsidy which has kept the Congress Party in power by allowing it to postpone needed drastic decisions.

Swatantra passionately favors free enterprise, and this has attracted many young Indian intellectuals, disillusioned by the Congress Party's fumbling. Swatantra denounces the Congress Party as India's "Permit-Quota-License Raj," charges that its succession of 5-year plans has led the new nation into bankruptcy, and favors freeing India of all economic controls and allowing foreign capital to come in "at its own risk."

It denounces India's foreign policy of nonalignment as "meaningless," favors recognition of a Tibetan government-in-exile, and supported the American position in Vietnam.

Swatantra favors the peasant (charging that the Congress Party pampers state-owned industry at his expense) and demands that he be freed from controls and thereby obtain his "right to the highest price he can get for his produce on the market."

Because this program has got for Swatantra the support of many land owners, the Congress Party scorns it as "the Party of the Rajahs," ignoring the fact that a number of captive, pro-socialist rajahs have been elected on the Congress ticket. Rajahs may be down in India but they are not out. Although shorn of hereditary power, many retain the deep respect of their former subjects who in the villages still celebrate their birthdays and weddings as holidays, and often elect them to Parliament, holding them to be smart men with the interest of the region at heart.

In the 1967 elections the Congress Party took its worst beating in its brief history, with Swatantra emerging as India's second-largest party. True, the Congress Party maintained control of India's 521-member Lok Sabh (Lower House of Parliament), but with a skinny majority; Congress Party candidates received only 44 per cent of all votes cast. State elections were even worse. The Congress Party lost power in more than half of India's state legislatures.

Meanwhile, there was a rising rash of riots—often bloody— set off by parades, or sadhus on hunger strike against cow slaughter, or against automation, or because a steel plant is being built in the wrong town, or because students complain that university regulations are unfair, or because Chandigarh is not attached to another state, or because too many rugby tickets were sold for the size of the stadium.

If riots get worse, some fear a military dictatorship may emerge. But India's army, schooled in the British tradition of divorcement from politics, is utterly unprepared for this. No brown-skinned Napoleon looms even on the far horizon: chaos would have to create one.

Our hosts have brought us to this little town of Nangal at the foot of the Himalayas to see one of the world's biggest dams, to which we are taken by bus. The town reflects modernity. Its crows, circling above in hope of garbage, are plump, and its pariah dogs sleek and well fed. Our bus bores into the Himalayan foothills and presently we see the first dam; below it boils clear, silt-free, snow water.

Our road now begins to wind up mountainsides in hairpin turns, but there are no mountain pines. We have left behind the mimosa of the plains, and now see a willowlike tree in the valley. It is Estes Park in the tropics—yet too hot for pines.

And around a turn, Bhakra Dam bursts upon us, all of its 740 feet (14 feet higher than Hoover Dam), plunging to the river bed beneath. Our guides drench us with statistics: the dam is made of enough cement to build a highway eight feet wide around the equator; inside it there is room for a 60-story skyscraper with a million rooms; and so on.

As for the storage lake behind it, this covers 66 square miles and holds eight million acre-feet of water. It inundated 366 villages from which 30,000 people had to be moved. Its power plant will produce over a million kilowatts to light more than 7,000 Punjab towns and villages, and its water, used in irrigation, will produce more than 800,000 tons of food a year, enough to feed 20 million additional Hindus. The dam has a silt life of 120 years, which they hope to extend by planting trees on its watershed.

But here is the final, frightening statistic. At the rate that the population is increasing (12 million a year) this huge, costly (1,250 million pre-devaluation rupees), and highly useful dam buys India only a year and eight months' time in the race against famine. We can hope that this time will be wisely used.

Our hosts tell us that Americans provided the technical know-how for the dam's construction. Engineers of the U.S. Bureau of Reclamation seem to have planned it, and the man every Indian on the job remembers with loving gratitude is Harvey Slocum, who was out here, living and working with them, along with fifty-five other Americans. The unlettered millions of Indians living nearest to Bhakra Dam may know only two words of English, but these are "Harvey Slocum," a name I never heard until I came to the Punjab. They say he died only recently. I wonder if his widow or children know how deeply they love him at the foot of the Himalayas.

But other nations also helped on Bhakra: Russia, England, Japan, Yugoslavia, Denmark, and Italy each gave a huge turbine.

We departed for lunch at Satlij Sadan, another government guesthouse nearby, with spacious, high-ceilinged rooms and big ceiling fans for hot weather. Just for fun I asked its prices and they are: for a room, 15 rupees a day; for three meals, another 15: total, $4.20 in our money. Can you afford to stay at home?

From our train that evening, I looked out of the window . . .

A village of mud-walled houses with thatched roofs, for which a few aristocrats have substituted tile.

A camel, not grazing, just contemplating the far horizon.

Cows, but none of them looking particularly sacred or parasitic; bullocks pulling plows, milk cows grazing.

A sugar-cane field, with the Himalayan foothills always as a backdrop.

A high-tension line, galloping across country, surely bearing power from Bhakra to light these villages.

A dozen children, half naked (only sensible in this climate), scattered out weeding a field, busy as ants. There is, in this backward country, no need for PTA committees to devise leisure-time activities for teen-agers.

Thick, golden cakes of cow dung, drying on the roof of a mud house.

Except for that high-tension line, there is nothing that I have seen out this window that could not have been there the year Christ was born, and for a millennium before that.

At one stop I discovered my supply of cigarettes had given out, and decided to venture out into the bazaar of the small village near the station. It was like all the other bazaars, throbbing with the life of India: small cooking shops, shops selling all the little things of daily life. And then I realized what life is like for a Negro in an all-white community. I was conspicuous. My toad-belly white face and hands stood out from the rich brown of all the others. It would have been impossible for me to melt into this crowd, to become just one of the other strollers.

Little children in their mother's arms looked wide-eyed at that face, pointed a little finger at it and turned to ask mother what made it. The whole street could not help being aware of me.

In Delhi every shopkeeper knew a few words of English. Here they did not, but when I held up my empty cigarette package, they nodded and beckoned me on down the street. In the middle of the block I found it, a tiny tobacco store, untended except for a little girl, sitting cross-legged upon a pile of the stock. I would say she was eight years old, but, remembering that this is India, she may have been twelve.

Instantly this little businesswoman got the signal of my empty cigarette package, and one brown hand quickly dived into the pile of stock until she came out with a paper packet of ten cigarettes which she carefully opened. She pulled out a single cigarette and offered it to me. But when I asked the price, and tried to explain that I wanted not just one cigarette but the other nine as well, she understood not a word, where-upon there appeared at my elbow (as almost always happens in India) the helpful Educated Young Man.

"What can I do for you, sar?"

He was perhaps 25, handsome, and wearing European trousers and a shirt as white as Indian laundries ever get shirts, which is not very white. With his help I was able to negotiate not for just one cigarette but for 20. But then a block. The smallest change I had was a 10-rupee note, worth $1.30. The little girl may have seen one before but could not change it; neither could the Educated Young Man nor the stalls on either side. But quickly this was solved, for the Educated Young Man handed the 10-rupee note to a small boy who had come up and who, quick as a flash, raced away with it around the corner.

To the village moneylender's? To a larger shop? In any case, he as quickly came back with the change in nickel and copper coins, the proper amount of which was carefully counted out to me, as we were watched by the small crowd which had gathered to marvel at the twin wonders of my white skin and the 10-rupee note.

It was a friendly, a self-respecting little village. Nobody begged. I may have thought they were poor, but clearly this idea had not occurred to them. I thought of tipping the Educated Young Man and then decided this would spoil it, for he had been glad to be helpful to a stranger. So instead I thanked him.

"Don't make mentions, sar," said the Educated Young Man. So not tipping had been the right thing. He had had a chance to show off his English to the whole bazaar, proving that he actually could talk to these people with white faces. This book learning had practical value.

He was not only better educated than the rest but much taller, indicating that his family, in that village, were people of substance who had been able to give him enough food as a child. Such Educated Young Men are the country's hope. But they are so few.

They are also, for the moment, India's despair. Leaving the villages they adopt Western garb. At first the height of their ambition is ownership of a ballpoint pen, a wrist watch, and a bicycle. They hope that their smattering of education will get them these things. Even if it does, they often join the hopeless ranks of India's semi-employed.

On a slightly higher level, they crowd into the universities. Professor Max Beloff (Oxford), who recently visited a number of Indian universities, reports that because of hugely inflated enrollment, students have little contact with professors. Also many are "unequipped to profit by higher education," having been admitted only because of political pull or because standards have dropped since British times.

However they got into universities, once there they pick up a concept of Western life. But ahead of them is, at best, a job paying only two or three hundred rupees a month ($26 to $39), which ends all hope for that Western living standard.

The city of Benares is as holy to Hindus as Rome is to Roman Catholics. It is not so much the city that is holy; more exactly, it is the River Ganges. Hindus from all over the world make pilgrimages to bathe in its water.

In Benares we pass through narrow streets teeming with life and poverty, moving slowly to avoid people, ducks, and sacred cows, more than we so far have seen in any town. The shops are as fascinating as always. Back of the merchandise piled in front of each we can usually see the owner's family in a room behind—squatting to eat, sometimes cooking over a charcoal or cow-dung stove.

At the river a crowd of the curious gathers about us. Begging children come because this is a tourist spot and tourists dribble pennies. We found this to be true throughout India; outside of tourist areas there are few beggars, except near shrines where pious Hindus earn merit through giving.

One little girl is selling bits of wood, to which a little flower is attached. These are tiny rafts which, when launched in Holy Ganges, will become an offering. Some of the rafts bear candles which, launched at dusk, give off pinpoints of light as they drift down the river into the dark. There are also garlands of fresh flowers, which you may float in the river.

We now stand on the river's bank from which long, wide flights of stone steps lead to the water line—a distance of perhaps fifty yards. There are the ghats of Benares, to which pious Hindus come to pray or to burn their dead. For thousands of years it was the custom for a man's widow to throw herself on his pyre, so that the ashes of both would go into Holy Ganges together, a custom called *suttee*. Failure to follow it was interpreted as a lack of wifely devotion. The British put a stop to *suttee* under pressure of public opinion (in Britain, not in India).

We are told that, at dawn, all the people of Benares throng to these ghats to wash themselves in the water of Holy Ganges; but we arrived so late that the steps were almost deserted, and the water lapping its stones, empty of people.

We are helped aboard small barges and into folding chairs on their poop decks, each barge being rowed by two men. In several places we see smoke curling up from funeral pyres into the pale, humid sky.

Suttee has gone, but there remains yet another custom deeply shocking to foreigners. After the flames have died down, and as the mourners watch, the eldest son is given a ceremonial hatchet. He then steps forward to split open the skull, so that the brains of the deceased will pour out onto the hot coals.

One of the most intelligent people we met in India, a highly educated woman and a devout Hindu, told us she hopes this terrible custom will go. At her father's funeral, when it fell to her brother to wield the hatchet, he was so shaken by love and grief that he could not strike hard enough, whereupon priests, clasping his hands with theirs, had to strike the blows needed to break open the skull. The priests assured her that unless this was done the body on its bed of coals would rise to a sitting position. Still doubting, she checked with scientists, who told her it was nonsense.

But we, in our folding chairs, saw nothing like this as the

two straining oarsmen rowed us by the half-deserted ghats. At one point a saffron-robed monk was washing himself in the thick, brown water. Then we saw a goat, sniffing between crevices near a boy who squatted to mend a great fishing net, spread out on slanting stones. A garland of saffron flowers floated by our starboard oar, and above, ravens wheeled high in the sky. On the river banks' huge cobblestones, each about eighteen inches square, long cotton saris were spread to dry.

We then approach what seems to be a group of picnickers sitting around a big campfire. We are told that this is a funeral pyre. They are mourners, waiting for the bones to char. Still farther, a very young woman and some boys come down to bathe. They step into the water and then, with a low ceremonial bow, lay a garland of flowers and one of those little rafts on the surface.

When asked if the Ganges was always such a dirty color, our guide insisted that if you dipped up a glassful of it, you would see it was crystal-clear, and furthermore it would stay fresh and pure for days. There is no doubt that, in India, Ganges water has a thundering reputation. Delhi newspaper stories, for instance, tell us of the Saint, fasting to force the government to put an end to cow slaughter. He will drink only water from Holy Ganges, sent him by followers in Benares.

Intellectual writers in the highly civilized Indian press are deeply mortified over the cow-slaughter business, pointing out that it is making India the laughing stock of the civilized world. But when the votes of those opposed are counted, what per cent of the total will they be?

Madame Gandhi, the prime minister, seemed to be handling the situation smoothly, pointing out that cow-slaughter agitation always occurs before an election, and adding that if there are so many people in India who love these unwanted cows, they can stop the slaughter overnight by buying

such a cow and feeding it. But this argument has the drawback of being logical, and logic attracts few votes in India.
We also note that hides (from unwanted cows) are one of
India's chief exports, ranking with jute as a source of foreign
exchange.

From our landing place we climb the steep steps and plunge
into the crowd. Cakes are frying in the little food stalls. We
pass an old man wearing a saffron scarf, reading to an attentive throng from a holy manuscript. We thread our way past
this audience, around a sacred cow and little girls selling
lotus flowers, and past a shop in front of which are piled
brass jugs to be used for dipping up Holy Ganges water.
Passing another shop that sells neatly piled cow dung, we
note that, on the balcony above it, a tethered monkey crawls
about. He stops to stare at us and then defiantly throws a
peanut shell, almost causing us to stumble over three geese
at our feet, so alertly pecking for garbage among the flapping
sandals of passers-by that they do not notice us. Momentarily,
we stop in front of a shop which sells saris, joining a goat
that also is contemplating their patterns, somewhat different
from those we saw up in the Punjab.

A young beggar woman holds up a diseased baby, but
when we make no move to our pockets, she goes contentedly
on her way. Clearly we are not pious Hindus, seeking merit
through charity: the mistake was hers.

There is, in this throng, no feeling of hostility in any
glance, only wonder at so many white faces. If they also consider us to be rich, this puts us beyond envy, as remote from
them as visitors from another planet. For what we consider
poverty is to this busy, happy throng only the common lot of
man.

We awaken this morning with our special train standing in
the station of Durgapur where we are to visit one of the three
steel mills the Indian government has built since independ-

ence—this one with British help, the other two with the aid of the Russians and the West Germans.

Two sentries of the Indian army are on duty at the station platform, turbaned, long-legged khaki-clad boys as clean and as smartly turned out as the British who trained them.

At the plant we are taken into a lecture hall for a briefing by R. K. Chatterjee, the manager, who explains that "There is very much delight to have you here this morning." This, he tells us, is a million-ton plant, begun in 1956 and producing by 1959. India's annual steel production is now 6 million tons, and the country hopes for 14.9 by 1970 (America's annual steel production is about 132 million tons).

Checking later, we find that many of the government estimates for such 5-year plans are far out in Dreamland. The "target" for the end of 1965 was 9.2 million tons of ingots, but actual output was half that, the right-wing Swatantra Party points out. But how much will their 1970 production fall short of the predicted 14.9?

The plant manager gives us more statistics, and presently is asked how their costs compare with those of European plants. The answer, given at some length, seemed to indicate that production costs might be a little on the high side. If the answer was vague it had to be. With a government-owned steel plant buying its coal and its ore from other government-owned industries, it is hard to keep track of actual costs.

Certainly a country with the natural resources of India needs a steel industry and before independence it had one, a private concern very well run for a profit by the TATA firm. We gather that TATA, though privately owned, is still in the picture. But how do they make out with all this government competition? And could not private industry have handled any needed expansion? These questions we were either too stupid or too polite to ask.

The plant itself was impressive, and I have seen mills from Margam in Wales to Magnitogorsk in Siberia. Over the gigantic rolling mill was the same overhead crane, and in its air-conditioned control house was the operator, a handsome, alert Indian boy who was handling those intricate controls with such ease that you would think it was a child's tricycle.

Along its production line, white-hot bars of steel thundered by on rollers as they had in Wales and Siberia.

A hot steel mill is awe-inspiring, and there is also an awareness of possible danger. If a man should slip and fall on one of those white hot bars, there would be a sudden puff of steam, and then the lime which was his bones—black, powdered ashes now—would slowly jiggle off the sides like dancing sand as the white-hot bar rumbled along those rollers. Safeguards make such a fall improbable.

At one point a boy stops us, white teeth flashing a broad smile in his dark face. "Are you from U.S.A.?"

He has just come from Youngstown, Ohio, where he served an eight-month apprenticeship with the Johnson Steel and Tube Company. "The people were very hospitable to me." But to such an eager, smiling boy, who wouldn't be?

Farther along they are making railway wheels, and we stand fascinated as another dark, handsome boy runs a tractor, the business end of which is a giant fork. The tractor races across the floor. With its pincers-fork, it picks up a glowing wheel blank and fits it into a turning lathe from which showers of sparks fly. Plucking the wheel from this, the boy and his tractor next lay it on a giant press, where 6,000 tons of weight crash down, further shaping it. The boy and his tractor next put the wheel into an open-hearth furnace, stacking it on others.

A European who knows this plant says that although these Indians lack the physique of European and American steelworkers, they are quick to pick up the needed skills.

There is no limit to the capacity of these talented people

when they have been given enough food—which is another way of saying, "If only there were not so many of them . . ."

On the way back, a talk with our Institute's brilliant new President, C. E. L. Wichremesinghe of Ceylon. His country has narrowly escaped a Communist take-over, and the winning election issue was freedom of the press, which the Communists threatened to bring under government control. He also knows India well—in fact, he knows all this part of Asia.

The cow-slaughter issue, he says, of which we read so much in the press, however ridiculous it may seem in the West, is dangerously explosive. He cites one member of a Parliament who, in his first election, won 55 per cent of the vote but, during a later campaign made the mistake of attending a barbecue. His Hindu opponent spread the story that he had butchered the cow himself, with the result that he got only 8 per cent of the votes.

Cow slaughter in India, Mr. Wichremesinghe explains, is a matter for each state to decide, but if cow slaughter is banned in Madras, countless leatherworkers will be thrown out of work. Strange issues like this boil just under the surface all over Asia. Nehru, he said, was able to keep India's thin Western-educated crust in power. But now the people are becoming aware of their poverty. Combine this with weird issues like cow slaughter and anything can happen.

An international convention of nutritionists is coming to New Delhi, and there could be no more stimulating place for such a congress than here, where the average diet is less than a pound of food per day, almost all of it grain, and low in precious proteins.

A medical team recently looked into the causes of infant mortality here to find out why, in spite of the spread of health clinics since independence, half the children still die before

the age of six: what is killing them? The team found the
virus of no dreadful children's plague, only familiar child-
hood diseases which rarely kill Westerners: mumps, chicken
pox, whooping cough, scarlet fever, measles. But India's children, weakened by bad diet, cannot survive even these.

The doctors also found that, of those who do not die, two
thirds suffer from lack of protein which so stunts growth that
the average twelve-year-old Indian boy is no taller than an
American child of eight. This in turn brings up the deeply
important discovery made only in 1965 by a Mexican nu-
tritionist, that there is a direct link between protein de-
ficiency and mental retardation.

For years doctors have known that lack of protein in early
years stunts growth. Juaquin Cravioto in 1965 proved, with
experiments on animals, that this lack stunts brains as well
and that the crucial years are between weaning and age five,
after which neither free-school lunches nor any amount of
education can correct it. The child has a permanently stunted
brain and is a predictable drop out from high school before
he enters kindergarten.

This discovery at least has silenced the left-wing sociologists
who have been shrilly blaming the drop out problem on lack
of early intellectual stimulus. Lincoln's log cabin had little
of that, but he got plenty to eat. The cause of retardation is
still in the home, but it is not a lack of a Book-of-the-Month
Club membership, but of proper protein, that permanently
cripples the child's mind. Cravioto's find has set social workers out on a sound, new tack. Still using the schools, they try
to reach mothers of newborn babies, to whom they want to
give precious proteins in the early years.

Meat and milk—any animal protein—is far too costly for
India's peasant millions. Indeed the story is told that the
Hindu taboo against eating meat stems from the edict of an
early emperor who, fighting famine, forbade meat eating as
wasteful. In terms of food-pounds it is, since it is an old rule

of thumb among farmers that it takes five pounds of grain to produce a pound of meat.

But Hindus have *dal,* a tiny bean and a staple in India's diet. It is rich in protein, but has never been ground up for baby food. Other high-protein foods are available at one fifth the cost of milk, and thereby in the reach of India's 24-cents-a-day per capita income. Yet low-income, low-intelligence groups the world over violently resist any change in food, particularly in India where Hindus abhor beef, Moslems pork, and Jains even eggs.

Not all protein foods have equal value, because protein is made up of amino acids. If a given protein is deficient in even one amino by, say, 50 per cent, then its total effectiveness as a food drops by just this much.

Here we have a second break-through, again coming only in 1965 when Charles Mertz at Purdue University, by patient crossbreeding, developed a kernel of field corn which, because its protein is complete in all amino acids, is as nourishing as milk or steak. Corn can be grown in tropical countries, those most lacking in protein foods. The majority of their peasants are familiar with and already eat corn meal; so, linking the Cravioto discovery with that of Mertz, we may have a tool which could wipe out half the world's mental retardation in a generation.

A French approach, sponsored by the Committee Against Famine, recommends the use of yeast. Experiments with it two years ago produced "astonishing results in restoring health to undernourished persons." Yeast contains much of the food value of beef, but while it takes three years to raise a steer, yeast can be grown in only a few hours and its cost is pennies per pound. Its drawback is that it is a new food with a strange taste.

Still another approach is "spiking" known foods with the missing aminos, one of which is lycine. When this is added to wheat, it triples the protein value. Wheat kernels can be sprayed with lycine or, if this is not practical, then lycine in pellet form may be mixed with the wheat kernels before they are ground into flour, in the ratio of one lycine pellet to a hundred kernels of wheat.

Seeking to sneak missing aminos into India's normal diet, nutritionists discuss the possibility of adding lycine, which has no color or taste, into salt or tea (Lipton's is sold in every village bazaar) and converting them into carriers of health to the villages.

Cravioto's discovery may account for the vast differences we see between Indians—the tall, handsome, brilliant ones we meet at dinner parties, and the shriveled figures we see in India's fields, tottering behind a wooden plow, looking almost as dull as the starved bullocks that pull it. Both peasant and aristocrat come from the same racial blends. Might not some of the difference, both in brains and brawn, lie in the food each got as a child?

From whence comes the vast gap between the torpid, listless Indian and the smart, hard-working Japanese? Nutritionists have a quick answer. Japan is surrounded by waters teeming with fish—almost pure protein, and a staple in their diet. A second staple is soya, the nearest perfect-in-protein bean known to man. India's flat, tropical plain gives a diet glutted in starches and sugars, foods that build neither muscle nor (as we now find) brains, but are useful only as fuel.

We wake from afternoon naps to find our train pulling into Howrah, the suburban railway station that serves Calcutta, located opposite on the Hooghly River. The platforms are covered with people: the men, gray-white robed; the women, sari-wrapped; the children, comfortably half naked. A few stand. Most squat; others doze, stretched out. Amongst them, down one concrete platform, lumbers a tan cow, alert for a meal. How did she get to this platform? Will anyone help her back? Is this her regular beat or perhaps, for her, an adventure?

The shops we creep by in our busses are what we have seen all over India. But in the hardware stalls we see a miracle of progress: here is the familiar set of three water jars, tapering in size to form a pyramid on the head of the women who carry water from the well, except that these are not brass but light aluminum. This is not automation. For if you buy your wife a set, you will remove ten pounds of weight from her neck muscles, but it will throw no one out of a job. In India this is the kind of progress of which all can approve.

It is now 5:30 P.M. and, since we are so near the equator, almost dark. Calcutta, we see, is an Imperial City—huge parks and wide boulevards, often lined with those noble arcades Imperial Britain borrowed from Imperial Rome. As Asian cities go, it is new, for it is a British town. Here the Ganges spreads out its delta to the sea and, losing all its holiness, is renamed the Hooghly. In 1690, Job Charnock, an enterprising employee of the British East India Company, thought his firm might do well to pick up some land here, as a possible site for industries. For remember that this B.E.I. for which he worked was a corporation like the Hudson's Bay Company, British Overseas Airways Corporation, or General Motors, eager to expand in the interests of its shareholders.

So Job Charnock bought three villages along the Hooghly's banks at a point where the ships of that day could drop anchor. In less than 300 years the villages have grown into Calcutta, and in this way the B.E.I., whose shares were bought and sold on the 'change in London, took over India piece by piece, making treaties with rajahs, appointing governors, building railroads, paying armies, and coining money, until in 1857, after the Great Mutiny, when India was taken over by the British Crown. Calcutta, which had become a great industrial city (British housewives had discovered calico), was the administrative center, and became the first capital of British India, ornamented with vast, now dilapidated public buildings and once beautiful houses.

But Calcutta (then as now) was turbulent, its almost daily street parades and demonstrations often breaking out into riots. In 1911 the British moved their capital to Delhi, where the government of Free India maintains it today.

How the British in their time maintained their former capital I do not know. I see its great buildings and boulevards as British-scrubbed and clean under this tropical sun—a London with palms. But Indians, whatever their other virtues, are not a tidy race, and the rubbish-littered great arcade down which we now pass has crumbling plaster and peeling paint—untouched, I would guess, since the British flag came down.

We pull up in a particularly run-down section—it is the entrance to the Grand Hotel. We are disheartened, for we had been told that the Grand was the finest in all Asia. Yet on this continent a couple of beat-up old doors may open into a palace. We find that the hotel is no crowded fleabag, but a complex of enormous, high-ceilinged rooms built around a vast court framed by splendid royal palms.

We know Calcutta is a city of mobs and demonstrations, which is why the British moved to New Delhi. Our somewhat air-conditioned room overlooks a city street, and even through the closed window we hear below the roar of such a mob. Maybe one of the Communist-organized demonstrations against automation? We open the window to lean out over a parade—white-clad, brown-faced men marching resolutely, carrying giant portraits of two shaggy-bearded holy men, whose pictures we now know. This is a demonstration in favor of Mother Cow, demanding a federal ban on cow slaughter. We are not yet dressed next day when another roar brings us to the window, where we see a smartly uniformed polo team of the Indian army receiving the applause of the crowd.

Our tour ends in Calcutta. No longer guests of India's hospitable socialist government, we are on our free-enterprise own and decide to tarry a day for a closer look at this swarming, turbulent town. The day starts with a visit, not far from our Grand Hotel, to the New Market, named by the British perhaps half a century ago. The market is a covered enclosure almost as vast as the Grand Bazaar in Constantinople, similarly divided into sections and with hundreds of tiny shops.

But what it *really* contained we never learned, for at its entrance we were surrounded by a swarm of little boys, each bearing an empty basket, offering to direct us to whatever we wanted to buy, and clamoring to let him carry our purchases. Each wore a badge with a number.

We explained that we had come only to look: this made no difference. They followed us from stall to stall, getting between us and the things on display, plucking our sleeves, buzzing around us like a cloud of hungry mosquitoes in a swamp at high noon. It was as pathetic as it was infuriating, for clearly in this market there were a lot more licensed basket boys than there were customers who needed them, and each was using every trick he knew to charm or threaten us. We were reminded of those scores of rickshas at every railway station waiting almost without hope for a fare—the now familiar Indian story of too many people frantically chasing too few jobs.

We began to feel uneasy, perhaps about nothing, but still we were so very conspicuous. One stall keeper to whom we appealed assured us that if any boy bothered us, we needed only to write his number down and take it to a nearby complaint office, where the matter would be promptly dealt with. But we wanted none of these children punished for the crime of wanting to work for us; we wanted only to be left alone, which we finally achieved by leaving the New Market.

What, we then wondered, would an Indian have done in our place? Maybe he would have hired one basket boy for a few pennies, whereupon the others would have left. Probably it was we, not they, who had been in the wrong. We, so clearly able to afford the customary basket boy, yet stubbornly refusing! We had not thought of this; we knew only that we did not need a basket boy.

Our feeling of uneasiness there? Surely groundless. The day before Per Momsen, the imperturbable Norwegian who heads our Press Institute, had told us that in this turbulent city of six million, with all its protest parades, slow-down strikes, and demonstrations, there were only nine murders during the previous year.

Yet blood is shed daily in Calcutta, for Per Momsen also told us that in the afternoon he had gone to see a famous Jain temple, and he happened to arrive when its priests were sacrificing a goat. Hardly had the blood from its throat followed the knife when, attracted by its smell, there arrived (seemingly from nowhere) a small pack of those thin, scab-covered pariah dogs that limp and dodge about every street in India. In the temple they snarled at each other, each wanting to lick the goat's blood from the stone floor below the Holy Statue.

All these people—half a billion of them! They are India's only problem. Without it, all others could be solved. Instead their number increases each year by twelve million—the population of New York or California.

Luckily no political party or major religious group opposes birth control, so family planning, as it is gracefully called here, can go forward. But the effort has been mostly in the cities. The Department of Family Planning and Health has established some 17,000 family planning centers, but only 5,000 are in India's 500,000 villages, where 70 per cent of this half billion live. And only one per cent of the government's budget has been devoted to family planning; of that one per cent only a third was spent.

It is a race against time, and a job only Indians can do for themselves. Can they increase their miserably low per-acre food production, while slowing down population growth, before all they have achieved or hope for is overwhelmed in a floodtide of undernourished humanity? Unless they can, there are not enough ships in the world to carry the grain to keep them from starving by the millions. This is assuming the world could spare the grain, which it cannot. For at the present rate of increase, India would need two million more tons of food each year just to keep the diet up to its present piteously low level.

The situation is not hopeless. The hardest-boiled Americans here think that India has a good 50 per cent chance of pulling through, although it will be a cliff-hang. And she has this chance because of the large number of able and dedicated Indians, in and out of government, who see this problem more clearly than any foreigner. Nothing has ever been said or written abroad in criticism of India's mistakes, that has not been said as bitterly and more effectively by brilliant Indians, speaking in her Parliament or writing in her press.

First, bring the birth-control problem into focus: of India's half billion, 100 million are women in the 14–42 age group, of which 15 million are pregnant, another 15 million are lactating, 9 million are infertile, and 11 million have not yet had a child. This leaves 50 million "targets" for family planning. Of these, only 3 million are "covered" by some form of contraception.

India first began to grapple with her population bulge in 1952. Until then, not much could be done because of the influence of Gandhi, who felt he had solved the problem of sex (it disturbed his meditations) by periodically sitting in tubs of ice water.

The new government's first efforts were concentrated on the rhythm method, which had the enormous advantage of being inexpensive, but it made no sense with an illiterate population unable to keep track of the days. For a long time, condoms have been distributed—30 million per year—but to most their cost is prohibitive, as is that of The Pill.

Under the present program, 1.6 million sterilization operations have been performed—three quarters on males, one quarter on females—but these hardly scratch that 50 million target.

In behalf of India it should be made clear that only in 1965 was a practical family planning tool perfected in "the loop"—a small, flattened spiral of plastic, to be inserted in the cervix. Any doctor can quickly insert or remove it.

The idea goes back to the mid-twenties, when a German doctor devised a prototype which worked. But it was only recently revived and perfected by Jacques Lippe, a medical school professor in Buffalo, New York. Since 1965 over a million have been inserted. About 15 per cent have been removed because they cause irregular bleeding. Others have been removed for "psychic" reasons.

A newly planned condom factory will meet all demands of those relative few who can afford the cost, and some states offer men seventeen rupees per vasectomy and also pay two or three rupees to anyone who persuades a woman to visit a family planning clinic. If the measures are desperate, so is the situation.

India supports all known birth-control methods short of abortion. The great hope is now the loop, which costs a fraction of a penny and lasts indefinitely. At Kahnpur a factory turns out 30,000 a day, far more than India can now use. In order to reach the villages, birth-control workers need to train 100,000 auxiliary nurses. The goal is 13 million loop insertions in the next 10 years.

The obstacle is the massive ignorance and superstition in

the villages. Moslems regard the whole thing as a Hindu plot to decrease the percentage of Moslems. A rumor raced all over North India that a husband, becoming entangled in a loop, was released only by amputation. And of course there are reports of cancer scares, none of them proved.

There is also tradition. Not too many decades ago, great fertility was needed in order to insure the family's survival: dare they change now? Village men also feel that, particularly in these modern times, three sons are needed to insure security in old age. For one may die, another drift off to the city and out of contact, leaving only the third to see that his old parents do not starve. But in achieving three sons, the family will probably produce three daughters as well.

The hardest-to-answer argument is: if I want nine children and can feed them, who shall say I may not have them? A big family becomes an important civil right, maybe worth overturning governments to achieve.

Have we a right to shake a sanctimonious finger at India when the same danger threatens vast areas of our globe in China, Africa, and South America? India's problem is only more immediate. Will the others do better? Can any contraceptive, any threat, any coaxing, any bribe, curb man's deep urge to increase his kind? Could it be that Malthus, unheeded now for so many decades, is the true prophet of our age?

Clinic workers say that most women who have had three children come eagerly to the clinic when husbands allow it. Or they come secretly. But our Brahman friend (the one who so resembles Julius Caesar) thinks this is overoptimistic, and doubts that it will be true in the villages. Little plastic insertions, he feels, will never be acceptable to village women, because the people have a deep, honest feeling about having children.

Instead he points to Japan, which had a birth rate of 34

per thousand (India's is 40) but then legalized abortions, making them available at low cost in first-class clinics. This has pulled Japan's birth rate down to 16 per thousand; its 100-million population is increasing by only a million a year.

India is his country, so we do not argue. But we wonder if Hindus would accept the destruction of life. Might not such first-class village clinics be picketed by naked, whiskered, trident-waving sadhus?

Something must be done, and quickly, but what? The government's goal is to decrease India's birth rate from that 40 per year per thousand to 18, in time to let her population peak off at 600 million, the maximum (even with improved agriculture) that she can feed. Does India have this much time? For the most recent (and most heart-breaking) news is that the number of loop withdrawals now exceeds the number of insertions.

Sometimes the programs of the ministries seem to fight each other. Take the wonderful campaign against malaria. Prior to the campaign, India had ten million chronic cases, able to do little work, and a million a year died of it. Now with sprays and wonder drugs, malaria has come down to 100,000 quickly cured cases each year, and no deaths. Who will deny that this is enormously to the credit of the Ministry of Health? Who can deny that this triumph has given the Minister of Agriculture a million new mouths to feed each year?

Yet the achievement was not without critics. Fanatical Hindus hold all life to be sacred. Since in your next life you may be reborn a mosquito, the crime of murdering billions of insects cannot be justified on the ground that it saved a paltry million human lives. Letters to this effect reached the press, but most Indians accept the anti-malaria campaign.

Would the fanatics have accepted it from the British?

Maybe they got out just in time. Had they stayed, they might have been blamed, either for letting millions of Indians perish from famine and disease—factors which have held down the population in past millennia—or for the heartless butchery of mosquitoes.

Now India is on her own, to cope with such fanaticism. Let us pray that she wins, for the free world has here a vital stake.

Wistfully abandoning the New Market we go back to the Grand, where the hall porter gets us a car and a somewhat-English-speaking driver, who at least knows the names of the principal sights. He points out Calcutta's great parks, sport stadiums, and stately public buildings. We pass a memorial in marble to Queen Victoria, a vast but beefily British translation of the Taj Mahal, set in a park that occupies several city blocks. How would this pious little Anglican Queen have liked it, could she have learned that here in Asia, four tall Moslem minarets would guard her memory?

We pass a shantytown into which are herded refugees from East Pakistan—roofs of matting or of rusty corrugated iron, supported on rickety poles—walls of anything. Calcutta lacked the funds to house them in a model city designed by Le Corbusier.

We pass a big park, its grass kept down by a flock of sheep and some sacred cows. We pass a handkerchief-sized park, populated only by one cow and three homeless men, preparing to lie down for the night.

How big is Calcutta? No one is sure. An Indian, talking of this, his native city, told us that if there were any way of counting the inhabitants, it probably would be the world's biggest. But how can people be counted when so many sleep in the streets?

We were to see more of Calcutta driving to the airport,

one morning before dawn. For on both sides of the street, for blocks and blocks, sidewalks were littered with disheveled lumps of people sleeping, wrapped in dust-colored, shroud-like robes. Now and then one had a dash of color—the hopeful new orange or pink sari of a sleeping woman.

We saw no family groups, so the street sleepers must be either the unwanted old, or aunts and uncles who have lost track of their families, or, still more likely, people whose relatives have died. For the Indian family is a tight-knit group which, if need be, starves together.

The story of Calcutta's street sleepers is old. Kipling, describing them, called Calcutta "The City of the Living Dead." Still they sleep thus under the Congress Party's raj. But we know what brought them here, to this particular shore of the Hooghly once occupied only by Job Charnock's three villages. It was hope for jobs created by machines—first, cotton looms brought in by the British, then still other machines brought in by TATA and Birla, machines that were creating far better jobs than any they could hope for in the villages they left.

But how strange the mind of man! Now in Calcutta's streets, lean, white-clad, brown-faced figures parade against "automation," denouncing those very foreign machines that drew them here. And the socialist government they chose protects them from "exploitation" by forbidding the importation of still more machines.

Near our hotel is a poster in somewhat fractured English, calling a mass meeting in protest against "automation by foreign oil companies." Since India produces almost no oil, what can be the crime of these alien exploiters who bring it in for sale? Have they perhaps imported an electric tabulating typewriter that now threatens the jobs of thin little brown men scribbling in ledgers?

Our homeward-bound taxi turns a corner and ahead of us we see, coming down the street, a dense ocean of white-clad, brown-faced men, walking rapidly, purposefully now—headed toward us.

Is it a demonstration of ricksha coolies against automation, which will pause to pull our taxi to bits? Or maybe a Boxer-type uprising against all exploiting foreigners? Should we get out and run?

Our driver explains that this moving ocean of men has come from a nearby cricket match. Their determined purpose is to get in the bus queues before all seats are gone.

In this land—so lovely, so tragic, so patient, so turbulent, so vast—all generalizations are untrue, all certainties dissolve.

BANGKOK

I N Thailand (by many still called Siam) we find ourselves in a busy, happy, clean city— Hondas popping in and out through traffic jams of shiny new cars from all over the world, and neon signs advertising them: Citroën, Volkswagen, Renault, Porsche, Volvo, Mercedes, Datsun, and Toyota.

We have crossed a racial frontier. Our plane has set us down in the most westerly frontier of that Mongoloid world through which we shall travel, and to our Western eyes the people all seem Chinese—yellow faces, straight black hair, slant eyes. They are clean, well dressed, and bustling. But at first we hardly see them, since we are distracted by the roar of pneumatic drills and hammers where apartment houses, office buildings, and air-conditioned hotels are under construction. Little of the building, we are told, is being done by the government; it is part of a free-market economy. Unlike poor India, this country staggers under no compulsion to be self-sufficient, to pour tax money into locomotive works, automobile factories, and atomic-energy plants. Here, foreign firms are not feared as neo-colonialist exploiters. Businessmen who want to move in are welcome, either to manufacture or to sell products made abroad. Thailanders have no suspicions of them and do not harass them with restrictions or force them to compete with state-owned enterprises; therefore, foreign companies have come. Thailanders are delighted to have the jobs and the improved standard of living. Americans are not conspicuous in this investment picture; mostly the money is West German, Hong Kong Chinese, Austrian, French, Japanese, and Swiss.

Although I have a quarrel with those Americans who argue that Asians have no interest in democracy but prefer a strong, authoritarian government, they are right about Thailand. It has what might be called a military dictatorship, and the prime minister is a big, jolly field marshal who believes in keeping order and then letting things alone. Americans here say his economic outlook is conservative— not so far right as Barry Goldwater and probably closer to Nixon or Eisenhower in philosophy.

This plump, tough soldier has been our close ally, and it was he who arrived in Washington in the spring of 1968 to get from Lyndon Johnson whatever assurances a president can give that the United States will never walk out on its friends in free Asia.

How free is Thailand? Our International Press Institute bars Thailand's newspapers from membership on the grounds that they are under heavy censorship. I do not quarrel with this, but Bangkok, even so, has two well-written, properous-looking English-language newspapers that give good coverage of the outside world. Had I not been told of the censorship, I would never have known it existed.

Nevertheless, censorship exists, to a degree. I learned that neither the book *Anna and the King of Siam* nor its movie version, *The King and I,* is permitted in the country. The king of the book and the musical is the current king's great-grandfather, portrayed as operating an extensive harem and owning hundreds of slaves—all of which, however factual, would detract from the "image" of the monarchy, founded firmly as it now is on a prim monogamy and as intensely respectable as the court of Elizabeth II.

Beyond those strictures protecting the dignity of the throne, there probably is still more censorship. I would guess that if either Communist faction, right (Russian) or left (Chinese), sent in a task force with money to subsidize a paper, it would run into rough sledding. But the government is certainly not a tyranny of which its people live in dread. There are none of those sudden pauses in conversation or whisperings behind hands so routine in Hitler's *Reich* or Stalin's Russia. I have never met a happier people, but old-timers say their Buddhist faith is responsible. One of Lord Buddha's commandments is to be happy and smile. Most Thailanders do, and all Bangkok has an air of friendliness about it.

If Thailanders are not obsequious, remember that the country was never conquered by a colonizing power. A century back, the reigning king employed as his prime minister an enterprising Greek, who argued that it might be a mark of status if the country became a dependency of France. When His Majesty had grasped the full implications of this he had the Greek beheaded in a public ceremony. In the following decades all of Thailand's neighbors became colonies either of England or of France, but not this proud little land.

A disadvantage of this for tourists is that few Thais speak a language a visiting Westerner understands. English and some French are spoken at the desks of the leading hotels, by head waiters, and by some clerks in all the better shops. Beyond this, a foreigner must fall back on gestures.

Thailanders revere their king. A pleasant young man who

takes his job seriously, King Bhumibol was born in a Boston hospital, and he wears horn-rimmed glasses, reproduced even on his shining, pure-silver coins. In his lighter moments he loves to take part in jazz combos. Often in the privacy of the palace he plays with visiting musicians, and he is delighted to welcome Bob Hope whenever he comes to entertain U.S. troops stationed up-country.

The young king and his beautiful young queen receive much attention in the press for sponsoring charities and for their affiliation with anything concerning Buddhism. Both are devout members of this gentle creed, the established religion of their realm.

Our hotel in Bangkok is one of an airline-affiliated chain that caters to the round-the-world jet tourist trade—usually the elderly, well-to-do people who have dreamed of seeing Asia but now are a little afraid of it. They are not really prepared to smell, taste, or feel Asia. They would prefer to see it through the windows of the bus chartered by their tour company. True, they will climb a few flights of steep steps to peer at the Golden or the Emerald Buddha. But that night they want the certainties of Beautyrest mattresses and American toilet paper. Above all they distrust the local food. For these unventuresome souls, our hotel's coffee-shop menu provides the answer: steak or baked chicken. You would think you were back home, which is where these round-the-world tourists often wish they were.

Our hotel is vast, and the only new hotel in Bangkok that has gone to the trouble to put into its architecture a dash of the native pagoda tradition. On our first evening we noticed what seemed to be a birdhouse on a high post not far from the pool, an elaborate one with a gilded, peaked roof and upswept gables like a tiny temple. We remarked that the hotel servants often went over there, presumably to feed the birds, but also to decorate it with garlands of flowers picked from the hotel's garden.

It then developed that no birds ever came, for this was a spirit house for the souls of departed Siamese ancestors. The servants brought the spirits food, leaving it on the portico around the tiny house. This food, we learned, was packed each evening into the begging bag of an orange-robed monk, who then trudged back to his nearby monastery. We asked why our hotel was wasting its stockholders' money building spirit houses. Because, we were told, no self-respecting Siamese would work in an establishment of this size which did not have the decency to provide a spirit house.

We were to learn more. I had an item of business with the hotel's assistant manager, a plump American. At the desk they said he was at a meeting, in the executive offices on the floor above. If I went up there, maybe he would step out. As I climbed the stairs, I came closer to what sounded like a Gregorian chant. I opened a door and found the executive office, furnished in the latest Danish modern. In front of its slick desk, two Buddhist monks with shaved heads and saffron robes, palms together, were chanting as they kneeled. Behind them knelt the Assistant Manager, in his neat, gray, American suit, also with his palms pressed together. Behind him knelt the Thai clerical staff of the hotel, palms together and chanting. The deep-pile carpet was ideal for kneeling.

The Assistant Manager rose and came to the door. This, he explained, was a purification ceremony, necessary, before he could occupy the office, to drive out the evil spirits that had caused the recent death of his predecessor, dead of a coronary. The evil spirits, he whispered, were being driven out by the prayers of the monks. The Assistant Manager pointed up to a long cotton string, one end of which was Scotch-taped to the desk. The string then rose to the ceiling,

where it was held by more Scotch tape, and then crossed
the room to an open window, where the other end trailed
down from the sill. The string, whispered the Assistant
Manager, acted as a lightning rod. The evil spirits, under
pressure of the monks' prayers, would follow the string out
the window. In another half hour they should be gone.
Then it would be all right with the Thai employees of this
foreign-owned hotel if the Assistant Manager sat down at
the Danish-modern desk of his predecessor, and then he
could take care of my little request.

That afternoon we tried one of those hotel-arranged tours
of the town with a somewhat-English-speaking driver. Everywhere, even in the smart district, we saw little shrines—a
sitting Buddha, inscrutably smiling, squatting in a handkerchief-sized park, fenced off so that he would not be profaned.
Around the fences little office girls stopped to pray, kneeling
with palms held together, before hurrying back to work.

Bangkok's streets glow with the blazing saffron robes of
Buddhist monks, heads shaved and each with his begging
bag. Why, we asked our driver, are there so many monks,
and all so young? Because, in this Buddhist kingdom, it is
the custom for every boy, beginning at about age fourteen,
to spend at least three months as a monk in a Buddhist
monastery, a sort of religious equivalent of compulsory
military service. A monastery is more than a place for
meditation and prayer. The boys receive instruction on a
high-school level, and some monasteries offer college-level
courses. In the villages, primary schools are in charge of the
monks.

A boy does not become a monk for life unless he desires
to, and he may leave the monastery at any time. Sometimes
a young monk finds that he is needed at home because of
some family trouble. He goes to the head bonze, explains
his problem, takes off his yellow robe, dons the street clothes

stored for him, does what he can to help his family, and then returns to finish his service as a monk.

Our driver took us to a famous monastery where the king has gathered from throughout his realm all roadside statues of Buddha in disrepair. Mended and regilded at His Majesty's private expense, they were stockpiled in a parking lot for gods and would soon be put back in service. In one court-yard of the monastery young monks strolled about. It could have been a school recess, except that there was no playing or shouting. To preserve the placid expression of Buddha in contemplation is not easy for teen-agers. Occasionally we saw one giggling at our Western clothes. As we passed one strolling group our driver almost roughly pulled Kathrine aside. Then he apologized and explained. Had she brushed against a monk, the boy would have had to spend many days isolated and in prayers for purification for having touched a woman.

Our driver explained that the life of peaceful meditation on Buddha's love is a good one. He himself was married, but his wife was dead and his children grown. He had no real need to earn money, and might well return to the monastery to end his days as a monk. One who is not a Buddhist, he said, can never know how satisfying such a life is.

Indo-China was aptly named because in both race and culture it has been a battleground between India, just across the bay, and China, up north, for more than a thousand years.

India's dark races and Hindu religion were there first and came to a flowering in the giant temples of Angkor Wat, in the neighboring state of Cambodia, which were rescued from the jungle by European scholars while France was in control of that country.

As one digs deeper into Asia, Europe in terms of history

shrivels. English travelers of the eighteenth century returned wide-eyed, telling how much greater India's cities were than little London, how much richer and more powerful her rajahs and Moguls than England's Hanoverians.

The Hindu civilization of this peninsula was first disrupted in about the year 1200 when Genghis Khan invaded China and so frightened its peoples that one southern Chinese tribe started running south, and stopped running only when it reached Siam.

This is more than legend, for the Siamese language is clearly related to dialects spoken today in Yünnan, the most southerly province of China. Although the brown-skinned natives were crowded back into the hills, there has been some mixture—among these yellow, slant-eyed faces one face is occasionally darker, with a higher Indian nose.

In the past century a second wave of Chinese has come by sea. China's answer to her population problem was to pour it into every seaport of the Pacific—from San Francisco to Calcutta to Singapore, and all down the Malayan Archipelago and into Bangkok, where they blended well with their blood brothers who had arrived 500 years before.

The second wave of Chinese migrants now makes up more than half the population of Bangkok. As in all the other cities of South Asia they are its merchant class. They work hard. Trading is their lifeblood, and they are also fine craftsmen. In this city (as in the other South Asian cities) they live apart by choice in Chinatown, where they have built their own temples and Chinese-language schools.

Hard-working and useful as the Chinese are, the Siamese have been uneasy about them since the rise of Communist power on the Chinese mainland. In case of a threatened Chinese Communist invasion, what would these Bangkok Chinese do? Therefore in recent years there has been heavy pressure on the Chinese to take out Siamese citizenship (which few had bothered to do) and to send their children to Siamese public schools.

The Red Chinese, we learn, are clashing even with neutralist Burma where Chinese children, coming to Burmese schools wearing red Mao pins, were told by the teachers that foreign political emblems were improper whereupon Peking loudly and angrily protested to the world. We were presently to find that in Cholon, the Chinatown of Saigon, Maoists are trying to take over the Chinese-language schools.

Siam has been increasingly nervous about the Bangkok Chinese since the start of Communist guerrilla activities in the villages in the north. Although the Siamese now have no common frontier with Red China, guerrillas drift over from the neighboring Communist-held areas of Laos. It is not always clear whether Mao or Ho is back of this, but the pattern is familiar: armed guerrillas enter the village, kill the headman if he offers resistance, and take over. We have been helping the Siamese train their rural police. Even if the nuisance is still minor it can grow.

Mao's supporters argue that he has improved on the tactics of Lenin, who based his power on organizing the city proletariat, according to Marx's formula. Instead Mao reached for the peasants, taking over the villages by guerrilla tactics (we see this in Vietnam) and slowly strangling the cities.

In dealing with the Chinatowns of Southeast Asia, Mao shifts his tactics. He ignores the proletariat of such huge cities, since usually they are of native blood stock and are suspicious of all Chinese. So the Red Chinese operate in these Chinatowns from the top down, trying to make business connections with the leading Chinese bankers and merchants, slowly infiltrating Communist teachers into the Chinese-language schools. Thus Mao moves to control not the proletariat, not the peasants, but the Chinese bourgeoisie.

The situation of such huge Chinese colonies in all the

port cities of South Asia is tragic. The people are not Communists, or they would go back to the mainland, which few have done. Marxism goes against the whole grain of their mercantile way of life. But dare they be openly anti-Communist? For in case of a Red Chinese take-over, vengeance would be terrible. They would be traitors as well as enemies.

The reverse of this recently happened in Indonesia, whose cities also have huge Chinatowns. When Sukarno was playing with the mainland Communists, Chinatowns had little choice but to go along, and some may have done it with enthusiasm, since, after all, were not these mainland Communists their blood brothers? And were not the Chinese now top dogs in Indonesia?

But when Sukarno, by an anti-Communist *coup d'état,* was sheared of his power, vengeance against the local Communists was terrible. Two million may have been killed, and surely the most savage blows were struck in the local Chinatowns.

Poor people! I like them, particularly in this Bangkok Chinatown. They have kept here a way of life that goes back almost to the days of the pigtail and bound feet. Walking down Bangkok Chinatown's narrow streets, you see them busy in every craft: stringing pearls, hammering out ring settings or chains of gold, making and gilding furniture in the old Chinese style. One street is devoted entirely to the manufacture of Buddhas—all of them depicting him as sitting cross-legged, and all of them of brass and of any size, from double the size of life down to one that would rest in the palm of your hand. You see thousands lined up for sale, covered with cellophane against the dust of the street.

This faith still lives.

Again that lesson: if you would know a land, get out on its farms if you can; if not, go into its shops. In Asia, from Constantinople to Tokyo, buying clings to an ancient pattern. Siam offers some of the world's best star sapphires.

We wanted (for a modest gift) such a stone to be hung from a small gold chain. A man at our hotel desk directs us to a nearby jeweler. Will he get a small cut? Probably, since this is Asia, but the jeweler must be dependable, otherwise complaints might cost him his job. The jeweler has sapphires of the size and price we require. When this is clear the Chinese boy who runs the shop produces bottles of cold Coca-Cola. In Asia this means we have reached a point of no return. The Chinese has decided we are serious customers. Were we still looking and pricing, we should probably refuse the drinks.

We bring up the matter of hair-thin gold chains. The Chinese boy explains (we should have known) that his is strictly a jewel shop, but, outside, the firm's Volkswagen and driver are waiting, and he will ride with us to a gold store, run by a cousin in the heart of Bangkok's Chinatown. Will this Chinese boy get a cut on the chain? Certainly, for the price to us must include Volkswagen and driver, plus his services as interpreter. Without him we would be lost in Chinatown.

In Bangkok most shop signs are bilingual—the top line in Siamese characters, the bottom in Chinese. Tourist places add a line of our Roman letters. But as we enter Chinatown, Siamese and Roman letters drop away, leaving only Chinese —usually gold characters against a background of red.

We pass Chinese pharmacies with window displays of bottles of Chinese herbs—everything from ginseng root (an unfailing aphrodisiac, imported from Korea) to powdered dragon's teeth (which have even greater powers). We pass Chinese butcher shops with rows of ducks, varnished red and dangling from cords through their beaks. We pass Chinese grocers' shops with bins of delicious-looking vegetables for which there are (says our guide) no English names. The people wear the dress of Old China—flopping black trousers for the women, with an occasional old man wearing a long mandarin gown. We pass huge movie theaters featuring films made in Hong Kong or on Taiwan.

Then we turn into a wide street with many large and solid-looking Chinese banks, but on almost every street corner is a new type of shop. Each is open to the street and has a long counter, against which crowds of buyers wait— you would think it was the candy counter of an American dime store on Saturday afternoon. Clerks stand on the other side of the counter—and behind them is what seems to be a shimmering golden waterfall.

This is the gold store. Chinese people, our Chinese boy tells us, like and trust gold. All this merchandise, including the chains dangling against the wall, is divided into three grades: 24 karat (pure gold) for those who want high value, 18 karat for those who cannot pay so high a price, and 14 karat for the poor and for Europeans, most of whom, our Chinese boy tells us, know little about gold, or maybe don't care.

In size the chains range from the hair-thin ones to ones whose links were bent from rods of gold thicker than a pencil—far too heavy, Kathrine remarks, for any woman to wear. The Chinese boy smiles and says these are called "smuggler's jewelry," bought usually in 24-karat quality by people who want gold, live in lands where bars may not be imported, and hope to persuade customs people that the necklaces were bought only as jewelry and not for the high value of their metal.

The chains are in a dozen different designs, but the Chinese boy says that all are put on a scale; then one pays by weight according to the day's price of gold, posted behind the counter. There is a further ten-per-cent markup for profit and workmanship.

Should we want gold even cheaper, the boy says, we should buy it as the Chinese do—by the tael—and he points to a tray of these in the showcase. The tael, he explains, is a

Chinese measure of weight, a little more than an English ounce. Each tael is about the size of a little-finger joint, and is shaped like a bathtub. The boy points out that each is stamped with Chinese characters for the name of the Chinese bank or jeweler which issued it, guaranteeing its weight and purity. The price of a tael depends on the market for the day, and I may read it posted there on the wall (1 tael = US $44.73) just as it was on the market page of the morning paper. The shop's markup above this is only half of one per cent; after all, the people must live.

Then I remember a story out of New York, to the effect that, for the first time in recent history, none of this year's new-mined gold went into the vaults of governments to back their paper money; all was being bought privately by what the story termed "speculators or private hoarders." These people must be willing to pay a slightly higher price than the official $35.00 an ounce, or they would not be getting all the new gold. How much of this is coming into Chinese gold stores, here or on the rim of Asia?

Asia's gold hunger is as old as written history. It was the cause of Julius Caesar's sumptuary laws. Rich Romans wanted silks and spices, brought from the Orient by caravan. In exchange Asia wanted none of the barbaric West's crude artifacts and would accept only its gold, drained from the coffers of Rome; hence Caesar's law against importing Asia's silks and spices.

We ask the Chinese boy if we may wander deeper into Bangkok's Chinatown; he says the driver will wait. In one block, craftsmen hammer and sell only brass. In the next, they weave and sell only straw. Further on in each shop a blacksmith squats near his forge: he will sell you a newly hammered knife or duplicate any broken part in a Honda.

The workers all seem too busy to stop to eat; little bowls of food—rice, chicken, soup—are brought them by small boys from nearby food shops. Here is a shop that sells precious stones—from rubies and pearls down to agates—sorted in little wooden bowls. The shopkeeper squats as he eats a bowl of chicken broth, in which float a few mushrooms, some bean sprouts, and a pale pink cockscomb for extra flavor. As we pause he looks up, lays down his chopsticks, and rises, in case we are serious customers.

Farther down the street a money-changer offers baskets of old dollar-size silver coins of many nations. Once these were the common currency of Asia, their value depending not on the country of origin but on weight of silver.

In the trays are Spanish pieces of eight reals, Mexican pesos, big silver piasters struck by the French for Indo-China, and British trade dollars struck in Singapore. Usually the coins bear the stamped-in chop marks of local Chinese bankers, a further guarantee that they are not counterfeit. But in some counterfeits, no swindle was involved. Mexican silver pesos were so well known that Chinese bankers often would copy them down to the last detail of familiar design, and in silver of the required purity and weight; nobody was cheated.

With world-wide inflation and Gresham's law (bad money drives out good) all these dollar-size silver coins now are worth far more than face value. For that reason they have been driven out of circulation and into the sacks of Asia's money-changers. Where will it end? I know only that in this highly solvent kingdom of Thailand, modern silver coins bearing His Majesty's profile are handled by every cab driver, that our hotel will still cash our traveler's checks although silver has vanished from our American coinage, and that the hotel's pretty little Thai chambermaids (in anticipation of our tips) giggle and wish us a "Melly Chlistmas." So the paper dollar still buys a Thai giggle.

The Vietnam war moves closer: even down to the poolside where often I sit under an umbrella, working up my notes.

Around this pool there usually are three or four polite young pilots, down for their pitifully few days of R&R from the base we have up-country, from which they fly their missions over North Vietnam. Occasionally, because I am an American and they are homesick, they talk to me. More often they talk to the two daughters of a local American businessman. One of the pilots has fallen in love with the elder sister; her sister tells us that he couldn't be nicer. He must go back to base Thursday and won't get his next leave for another three months. But, she says, there are always three or four down here on R&R, and romances often bloom. She thinks it is because they are so lonely, particularly for American girls.

This afternoon the one who is in love arrived disturbed—maybe "hurt" would be a better word—from having read in today's paper dispatches from an American reporter in Hanoi. The dispatches told of damage from our bombs to civilian houses within the city limits.

"Is this fellow an American? Then why would he want to write things like this? Because everything in that area is *beano*."

And what was *beano?*

"That's a word we use at our base. The directives we get on our bombing targets always read: "There shall BE NO bombing, of this, that, or some other place, so we call these *beano* areas. Like the airfields their MIGs take off from—they are all *beano*. And anything within a big circle around Hanoi is *beano*, unless we can get permission from away up top—clear back to Washington, it sometimes is—to go in and take out a specific military target—like, say, a radar installation directing the Russian SAMs that are trying to shoot us down. We have to say just what and where the target is, and why it matters. Even then, usually we don't get permission.

"The people in Hanoi," said the pilot, "must have really

given that reporter a snow job, because in Hanoi they know all about the *beano* areas; you would think they had a Pentagon chart showing the limits down to a yard. Because from the air we can see the North Vietnamese, stock-piling ammunition on its way down to the South—right on the edge of a *beano* area, where they know we aren't allowed to touch it: in a *beano* area it is just as safe as if it was stacked around the Lincoln Memorial. Then, on some day when overcast keeps us grounded, they whisk it down South by truck or pack trains, and the next time we come over, those stock piles on the edge of that *beano* area are gone."

Did I think Hanoi had given that American writer a snow job, or did he have some reason for playing with them? I said probably a snow job.

Another thing about those SAMs, the pilot said, was that all our crews had noticed how little regard the North Vietnamese gun crews have for the lives of their own people. Because sometimes one of our planes would be assigned a course which took them fairly close to Hanoi. Of course the SAMs opened up, you expected that. But often, if they missed you, the trajectory curve would bring the SAM back down in the heart of Hanoi, killing who knew how many of their own civilians. Apparently their gun crews couldn't care less. But was I sure the man writing this stuff out of Hanoi was an American? Because it was bad enough dodging Russian SAMs, without having an American trying to shoot you down in his paper. And had those two American girls been down to the pool this morning?

I said not yet.

The pilot said he had mentioned them in a letter to his bunk mate up at their base camp, and the bunk mate had answered, asking whether, if he wrote the younger sister, she would answer him. The bunk mate had no idea when he would get R&R to Bangkok—maybe never. But it was nice to be able to write letters to an American girl—even one you had never met—and get answers. You got awfully bored up at that base camp, he said. Nothing to do on the ground but slap mosquitoes, and the only excitement those Russian SAMs when you flew missions. And wondering what had happened to crews that had not come back; if they had lived to be taken prisoner, how were they being treated? Many had been good friends. He had sent his bunk mate a snapshot that had included the younger sister. And he hoped she would say yes and then really answer the letters.

We are now on the Trail of the Dragon, for these Thais are blood brothers of the Chinese, each a branch of what anthropologists call the great Mongoloid race which dominates the Asia ahead of us. That race is yellow of skin with slant eyes and black, straight hair. This physical type speaks countless dialects, includes our American Indians, and in Asia lives under many flags—from Japan, Korea, and Mongolia down through Bhutan and Tibet which border India, into Indo-China and Indonesia and even including the Filipinos.

The original homeland of this Mongoloid race was northern China, so scholars tell us. But, starting here in Thailand as we traveled through Asia, we noticed many customs common to most of these Mongoloids—from Thailand up to North Korea—which must go back thousands of years and which set them sharply apart from Caucasoids whom we last saw back in India.

One of the common customs is their method of carrying babies. In India it is in the mother's arms, as in Europe. In this Mongoloid world it is often on the mother's back, a custom taken to the New World by the American Indians.

Another common practice is the use of chopsticks, a custom not old enough to have been carried across the Bering Strait, but a practice followed in villages from Indonesia in the south on up to Tokyo.

Still another custom in common is the wearing of the round, conical straw hat by peasants from Thailand to Korea. The hats are cheap and enormously practical but unknown in India, where peasant men wear turbans or a bit of twisted cloth.

How are burdens carried? Among India's Caucasoids it was on the head, as Abraham's wives (Jews are Caucasoids) carried water from the well, and as Indian women do today. Here in this Mongoloid world of Thailand the natives use the carrying-pole. The burden, divided in two parts, is tied to opposite ends of a bamboo pole, the center of which rests on one shoulder. The flexibility of the pole makes the bearer walk in what appears to us to be a gay little dance. In India or Europe we never saw the carrying-pole method put to use. In East Asia it continued with regional variations.

There are also the customs pertaining to food. You would think that if people are poor enough, they would eat anything they could digest. It is not true. We Caucasoids have a violent prejudice against eating dog which Mongoloids regard as irrational. In China, and throughout most of the Mongoloid world, dogs were (and in many areas still are) raised as choice articles of diet. The Mongoloid ancestors of our American Indians brought dogs with them across the Bering Strait, and their custom of eating them deeply shocked the later European arrivals.

But Mongoloids have their own food prejudices. One is a taboo against drinking milk, which they hold to be as filthy as any other bodily fluid, and fit only for calves. Today the milk taboo prevails largely in the villages. In downtown Bangkok we saw milk bars. Milk seems to be nearly as popular as Coca-Cola, but both are acquired tastes.

Another difference between Mongoloid and Caucasoid has to do with language sounds. We Caucasoids, whether we speak Swedish or Arabic, make a clear distinction between L and R sounds. The Mongoloids of Asia have countless

spoken languages, but apparently make no distinction between L and R, having instead one sound which is halfway
between. Here in Thailand they have trouble with R—they
make it "Melly Chlistmas." Japanese have trouble with L in
English words taken into their language. They say "meron"
for "melon," and "hotel lobby" becomes "oteru-robi." This
offers proof, I think, that although scholars can find no trace
of resemblance between Japanese and Thai either in grammar
or vocabulary, still, millennia back, all these Mongoloids
spoke a common tongue in their original North China homeland.

The Chinese written language, maybe the world's oldest,
unites some but not all of these Mongoloid peoples. Thai
writing, for instance, derives from an Indian script, and this
is also true of Tibetan characters. But the ancient Chinese
ideographs were used in Vietnam until the French stamped
them out, and although the Japanese have greatly modified
them, most Japanese can make a stab at reading Chinese.

There is even some unity in architecture and art. We first
saw the up-tilted gable ends on pagodas here in Thailand,
and continued to see them on palaces and fortresses in Japan
and Korea. So with the dragon as a motif in art. Probably it
was a Mongoloid symbol of sovereignty, for we saw entwined
dragons on the big, dollar-size silver coins struck in the last
century by the emperors of Annam (today Vietnam), of
Japan, and of China. So in entering this vast and fascinating
Mongoloid world—from Thailand to Korea—you could say
we were starting out on the Trail of the Dragon.

We are packing for Saigon. The focus of my interest there
is political. Yielding to our American pressure, South Vietnam's ruling military junta finally called for elections to a
Constituent Assembly which would draft a constitution. The
election was boycotted both by the VC and the militant
Buddhists. The French, who should know the country, pre-

dicted that not 15 per cent of those registered would vote. They were wrong: the turnout was more than 80 per cent and, sitting in Saigon, the chosen Constituent Assembly is putting final touches on a constitution under which the voters will choose a new president and congress.

My self-assignment is to find out if democracy as we know, it is possible out here in Asia. Do the Vietnamese want it? If not, then why are we here? If we are fighting for freedoms that Asians do not value, we could be making more enemies than friends in this end of the world, and that "dominos" theory would work the other way.

John and Elaine Steinbeck have just arrived in Bangkok from Saigon. We have been reading Steinbeck's Vietnam articles in papers arriving from Europe. His combat reporting equals what he did in World War II. Again he is writing with our troops, not about them, pulling through his typewriter the feel of paddy mud and the smell of jungle sweat— no mean feat for a man in his sixties.

Because, in this intensely unpopular little war, he does not disdain our combat troops or the reasons which bring them to Asia, he has sacrificed on the altar of his country some of the popularity gained from his Nobel prize. Soviet intellectuals who once praised him now snarl at him, as do the Mao-ist Left and many liberals in the United States.

Perhaps he could point me toward my political story in this land so strange to us. For dinner we went to a Bangkok restaurant that specializes in *moules marinière,* the mussels a pink species with translucent shells native to the Gulf of Siam, the sauce containing a tablespoon of absinthe added to each pint of cream and clam juice.

Steinbeck's advice was to get away from Saigon, even though the focus of my stories would be politics, not combat. In Vietnam, politics was an integral part of fighting, you could not separate them, and I would find my political story out in the field where his combat material had come from.

In Saigon I would find a gaggle of reporters from all countries, many of whom seldom left the city, and who made an art of trying to trip up the briefing officer at the daily press conference: the real story—combat or political—was out in the villages.

Before and after winning the Nobel prize, John Steinbeck has been a quiet, painstaking craftsman. Arriving in Saigon, and out to cover his first story, he found a battery of television cameras focused on him for a feature, "A Nobel Prize Winner Covers the War." Just how does this work out? As you are getting your material, TV cameras are delivering the cream of it to the evening news show before you have even got it through your typewriter, let alone out to your newspapers. Not even a Nobel prize winner can earn a living this way, so changes had to be made.

As for me, whatever my focus of interest, I planned to follow Steinbeck's advice and get out into the rice paddies. And so it turned out.

VIETNAM

COMING into Saigon we were not too nervous to notice how beautiful this country is: the great river lying in lazy loops among the rice paddies, every inch of ground beautifully cultivated except for a little brush along the creek bottoms.

When the plane's wheels touch the runway, I seem to be jerked back in time and space to any American overseas air base in World War II—our olive-drab planes with the big Air Force star in sandbag revetments, guarded by smartly gloved and helmeted American MPs heavy with side arms, scuttling about in jeeps. But here, in Vietnam, above the military hardware tower the stately outlines of the posh, round-the-world civilian jets of many nations—just as you see them at Kennedy or Le Bourget. The airport is French-modern, but beat-up before its time by military traffic. Inside the terminal, war again: long lines of patient GIs waiting. Are they arriving replacements or troops waiting to go home now that their time is up? It was

Marshal Foch who first said that war is months of weary
waiting, punctuated by seconds of intense excitement. Here
are the same joyless, resigned faces of waiting soldiers that I
saw in World Wars I and II. And, as American soldiers have
patiently waited under Washington, Lee, Grant, Pershing or
Eisenhower, they wait now in this far corner of Asia.

Once through customs and immigration, we find there are
no taxis. In this war of terrorism the airport is a high-priority
target. Cab drivers do not rate security clearance so we must
scramble, with all our luggage and no porters, into a little
airport bus, every seat taken and hot as an oven from the
tropic sun on its tin roof.

Then into Saigon, and the surprise is, how lovely a city! It
could be Casablanca, Algiers, or any French colonial town in
the tropics. Wide, tree-lined boulevards, not really as battered
by war as we had expected. But our huge military vehicles
are chewing up these pavements, nuzzling aside pedicabs and
the battered little Renaults, which somehow have survived
from French days.

Even from its lobby we knew the Majestic was exactly our
dish—an exquisitely un-Hiltony, old hotel with high-ceilinged
rooms. And in its lobby, who but Charles J. V. Murphy, out
here for the Luce organization, whom we had known since
he and I briefly worked together on *Fortune* in the old
Chrysler Building in the late 1930s. We were all three delighted. As for rooms, Charlie told us that he was checking
out of his. Of course the Majestic had a waiting list, but did
I know Joe Alsop? Because Joe was a great gastronome, always stayed here, and praised the cooking to the point that
they could hardly wait between his visits; I might, Charlie
suggested, drop Joe's name.

I did know Joe, and for people at the desk this was
enough; *un ami de M'sieur Alsop* was *un ami du Majestic*,
and we could have M'sieur Murphy's room an hour after

checkout time, which was three o'clock. So we were in and, escorted by Charlie, we inspected the room. The Majestic (built maybe at the century's turn) and its French-trained staff are rugged enough to have survived all the wars of liberation and *coups d'état* that have afflicted this sad little country in the past two decades. It is rather like old Shepheard's in Cairo before it was burned by the Arabs.

The Majestic is clean but, in its fine old French tradition, not offensively so; we noted, dangling high on one bedroom wall, the crushed and bloody remains of a cockroach that Charlie Murphy must have bagged with a well-aimed Church shoe. When, later, we moved into Charlie's room, the shattered cockroach still dangled, perhaps because it was too high for a Vietnamese to reach without aid of a broom. When, a week later, we moved out it still dangled. And if we compromise this Vietnam war so that Ho Chi Minh can move into the Majestic (Ho knows good hotels), I think Charlie's cockroach may still be there.

Ho will appreciate the fact that at the Majestic, breakfast (*café au lait*—very good *croissants*) arrives in your room on a tray. Its staff is all French-speaking except for the younger elevator boys, who are eagerly learning English, a practice Ho may discourage. The dining room is on the top floor, with big windows overlooking the river and the city. Its European menu is better than most oriental imitations of Western cooking—seldom exactly on target, but usually a near-miss. Yet we barely sampled it, for we found that the Majestic had two other menus—one Chinese and the other Vietnamese, both delicious. From both we could load our chopsticks with fresh-caught local fish and vegetables from nearby truck gardens.

And now the war moves closer. From the bathroom, it sounds as though someone were knocking on the corridor door. When you open it, the corridor is empty. Again the knock, and then you locate the sound: distant artillery is shaking the French doors leading to the little balcony.

The artillery is ours, firing just across the river into an area of jungle called the Triangle, where the VC had been dug in for several years. Our infantry has spent 19 days cleaning it out. Seven hundred twenty VC were killed and 725 suspects are being held for questioning. As we feared, most of the VC had got away. They were a considerable force, to judge by captured supplies—7,622 uniforms, 3,700 tons of rice, 555 weapons (some of them needing a crew to operate), 1,000 grenades—all of it stored in 509 buildings and 1,111 bunkers, and all of this cozily close to Saigon.

But out of this Triangle our troops have moved 10,000 civilians to safety; anybody left in this patch of jungle can only be VC. We still fire into it at night because that is when the VC move around. The technical name for this constant bombardment is "H&I"—harassment and interdiction, and its purpose is to keep the VC from digging in again. Hence the Majestic's windows rattle.

The fine, cutting edge of the VC seems to be boys eighteen and under—many only fourteen—from the villages they control. The VC say that they "recruit" them; we say "kidnap." In either case, how can such a child have a political opinion that anyone would take seriously? But of course they have daring. Tossing a grenade into a crowded market is a wonderful boy's joke in any land. When a handful of them launch an attack on our embassy or on a crowded movie theater or on an airfield, our guards must shoot and shoot fast at these crazy children or die themselves.

When the little half-naked bodies are lifted into trucks, television records the scene and offers it around the world at dinnertime. The U.S. image is not helped. This is television's first war. The Korean war ended in 1953 before TV had really got off the ground, and the effect of its terrific impact—war brought back right into the living room—has yet to be digested.

On the whole a quiet night except for those rattling windows. The morning papers report that yesterday was quiet, too: the VC had brought off only four grenade attacks here in Saigon, killing four and wounding seventeen, of whom two were Americans. This box score for the day was under a small head on an inside page. After all, this is a city of two million, and moving about town and getting settled in, we had seen or heard none of it. It seemed a quiet day, and for Saigon it was.

But some tension is also normal. Nightly before signing off the Armed Forces Radio gently warns Americans not to congregate in groups on the street, and warns them to beware of any pedicab apparently left abandoned near the sidewalk with a package left on the seat: it could be a bomb.

We have a lunch date with Cabot and Emily Lodge. The ambassador's residence is in a smart section, and as our taxi turned into his street it was stopped by a lowered wooden boom. This one did not rise until a marine guard had stepped out to look us over.

Like most French villas of its period, this one was surrounded by a wall sheltering its garden from the street; but the wall around the ambassador's residence was surmounted by coils of barbed wire, and the entrance gate sheathed in steel. In the living room a dark, slender, well-tailored young man rose. Since we had recently come from India I instantly catalogued him as a Brahman.

"We've just come from your country and enjoyed it immensely."

The Brahman pondered this. "What part were you in?"

"The North, mostly. From Delhi up toward the Himalayas."

The Brahman slowly shook his head. "I come from *south-*

ern Alabama." At this point Cabot and Emily entered and we learned the Brahman was a highly competent young Negro in the career service of our embassy, asked to join us so that he could find out just what I wanted to see in Vietnam and point me toward it.

Over the shrimp and pilaff I explained that I had come not so much to look at the war as at the recently elected Constituent Assembly, to find out what these men, fresh up from the voters, were like, and what the people wanted.

It seemed that this could be easily arranged and, returning with the young man after lunch to the embassy, the routine of getting clearances began. Our embassy—a ramshackle office building in downtown Saigon, heavily swathed in barbed wire outside—is surely the hardship post of all time. Desks are packed in so tightly that there is hardly space to squeeze from room to room, but a lot of work seems to be getting done.

Late the next day we go to what is officially known as a briefing. (If you are hostile to this almost friendless little war, you would call it a brainwashing.) The briefing is held in the suburban home of Barry Zorthian, one of the head press officers on our embassy staff. Considerably lower down in the pecking order than Cabot Lodge, Zorthian's villa is surrounded by piteously fewer fortifications, for the VC give him, as a target, an appreciably lower priority. Yet I wonder if they are right for, as John Steinbeck had predicted, we found Zorthian one of the most useful men we have in Vietnam. He has a complete grasp of the situation, a candor that is a little breath-taking, and, in dealing with us correspondents, the ability, if not to suffer fools gladly, at least to handle them gently.

The "backgrounder" was for about a dozen newly arrived correspondents. When it was over, drinks were passed and we gossiped. I remembered that on Air Marshal Ky's recent trip to Australia he had been sharply heckled by a journalist who turned out to be a member of the Central Committee of Australia's Communist Party. Ky had invited him to get in his plane and be his guest in Vietnam, to judge the country for himself.

It had been one of the Air Marshal's better moments. Where, I asked, was the Australian Communist now?

"Right over there," Zorthian answered, "talking to your wife."

He was a gentle little man with curly hair and china-blue eyes, voicing his complaints in flawless Australian cockney. One complaint was that Marshal Ky, striving to entertain him, had scheduled a tiger hunt for the next day. "And what," this gentle intellectual asked Kathrine, his palms outspread in a gesture of deepest despair, "would *I* do on a tiger hunt? They expect me to ride an elephant."

We learned that the Vietnamese had been at a loss as to how to entertain him. So the Americans had taken over, inviting him into "The Group" and asking him to background briefings like this. We could do it because we had nothing to hide, and often such frankness worked. Several "peace delegations" that had come over from the States, bristling with hostility, received the same courtesies from our group. Most, when they saw the actualities of this war, had at least been softened.

With us at Barry Zorthian's was Charles Collingwood, a CBS veteran. I was briefly a CBS pioneer when, in the opening months of World War II, I was holding down Helsinki while Ed Murrow was in London, Bill Shirer in Berlin, and Eric Sevareid in Paris. While Collingwood came aboard CBS a little later, he overlapped with most of my former colleagues, and we talked of the old days and of his hope to film the beautiful little State Museum in Saigon's Public Garden.

At the close of the evening at Zorthian's, I said that while I had just arrived and therefore had no right to any firm opinion, I felt this war was a twin to the Korean war, with one enormous difference: South Korea had had Syngman Rhee, a civilian of character, brains, and courage elected before the war began, a man whom the people trusted and could unite behind; whereas here there seemed to have been a sorry procession of more or less likable dictators, but none of them with any roots among the people.

Barry Zorthian listened intently. There are times when a courteous host who is also a skilled diplomat says nothing. This seemed to be one of them.

All evening I have been walking the streets of Saigon with our soldiers in for a few days' precious R&R from the rice paddies and jungles, now crowding Saigon's sidewalks in their civilian clothes. They throng the restaurants, usually with some buddy from their own outfit, occasionally with a pretty Vietnamese girl. It is all very orderly. Not many MPs are needed. You run into the boys in the bookshops as well as the honky-tonk places. We hear that the girlie bars scrupulously pay "taxes" to the VC, to prevent anyone's lobbing a grenade through the door into the crowded bar. So, rumor has it, do many of the deluxe hotels pay these "taxes" that the VC levy. But how many actually pay off?

As for our hotel, the Majestic, I think I know the answer. It is down on the waterfront where, in the old days, the round-the-world cruise ships could weigh anchor. Facing this river there is a large area that in happier days was the site of the hotel's sidewalk café. There one could sip a drink and watch the sampans and freighters going up and down the river. This wide area is now empty. All tables and chairs removed, and the vacant space fenced off with barbed wire . . . which can only mean that the Majestic refuses to pay taxes to the VC. For if it were paying off, it would be able to run this open-air, highly profitable, sidewalk café full blast until curfew at 11 o'clock, with no danger of business interruption from a tossed grenade. We are rather proud that the Majestic does not pay off the VC, even if this means that we must have our after-dinner drinks inside.

There are some very good places to eat in Saigon. Three blocks downstream from the Majestic there is an old barge, reached by a gangplank from the shore, that has been converted into a Chinese restaurant. It was recommended to us, when we first got here, as the best place for Chinese food in Saigon. Customers eat out on the barge's deck in the evening, by the light of gay Chinese paper lanterns. Then someone else said no, don't go there; the place had once been good, but the food wasn't what it used to be.

"Because of the war?" we asked.

Well, you could say that. The VC had staged an attack on it, killing thirty-four people but doing it in a most interesting way, using two grenades. The first one, planted aboard the barge, apparently had been an ordinary hand grenade, for it killed only a few people. But the second, it was later figured out, had been a big Claymore. It was suspended about shoulder height from a tree close to the gangplank, timed to go off just as the guests, alarmed by the first bomb, were crowding the gangplank to get ashore; it killed most of the thirty-four. This had naturally hurt business aboard the barge, and as attendance fell off the morale of the Chinese cooks had suffered. My friend said that he could now recommend at least three Chinese restaurants in Saigon where the food was even better. And they proved to be excellent.

A reporter in war-torn Asia has unusual problems in protecting his source of information; something this source may say, however true, may six months later land him in jail or before a firing squad.

My source is an old friend, a Vietnamese Buddhist I had come to trust long before our plane put down on its Saigon runway. I arrived here intending to depend on him for the hard facts about the situation. I wanted to know, off the record, about the appeal of the VC to the common people of Vietnam.

I told him we both knew of the propaganda line of his government and of mine: that the VC were only terrorists. But surely these governments must be sweeping quite a bit under the rug. I wanted from him the straight answers, and would not embarrass him by using his name.

He looked at me as if he thought I must be either crazy or Senator Fulbright. Then he said that the only honest answer was that both his government and mine were telling the truth; that the hold of the VC in this country was through terror and only terror; that there was plenty wrong with the present government—anyone would admit this—but these faults could and would be corrected, and nobody in his right mind wanted the VC as a substitute.

He said if I doubted this, I had only to look around. Saigon in very recent years had swollen to a city of two million—refugees coming first from North Vietnam and later from insecure parts of South Vietnam. These people are not rich landlords or merchants. Most are ordinary peasants or working people who arrived with their cooking pots on their backs, to get away from terror—from areas either completely controlled by the VC or areas where the VC came in at night. The refugee situation existed, he said, not just in Saigon, but in all cities and villages where the government is strong enough to give security. If I got out into the countryside, I had only to use my eyes—to see people pouring into those areas held by the government. The VC of course made vague promises of "a better life." But if anyone took them seriously, why was there not some flow of people in their direction?

Terror, my friend said, was a terrible weapon. A few organized, determined people can frighten a whole area.

Terror affected even the newspapers in Saigon. Many of

them feared to speak out strongly against the VC, for one grenade can make a terrible mess of a newspaper composing room.

Still another factor, he said, was the South Vietnamese's fear of the future. The years just after the fall of Diem, 1964–65, had been terrible ones, with the VC closing in on Saigon. Now the war was going splendidly. Honest elections had been held, and the government controlled three quarters of the country's area by day, and at least half of it both day and night.

But talks of peace from Washington frighten the anti-Communist Vietnamese. Surely Washington must know that Ho Chi Minh could accept nothing short of an American withdrawal and a coalition government, which would mean a complete Communist take-over in a very short time. What would then become of Vietnamese with strong anti-Communist records?

So I shall not use the name of my Vietnamese friend because, should we decide to jerk our army out, I do not want his blood clogging the keys of my Hermes portable. Nor do I want anything I write even to send him to jail, since already he has been in several and his story is typical of hundreds of Vietnamese intellectuals who in the past twenty years have suffered through their love of freedom.

I shall say only that he was born of a Buddhist family near Hanoi, graduated from its University, and was an anti-French nationalist. However, just at the end of World War II, Hanoi was occupied by the joint forces of Chiang Kai-shek and Ho Chi Minh. But because my friend's brand of nationalism did not quite conform to Ho's, he was thrown in jail with other Vietnamese nationalists, intellectuals and heads of villages. Executions, he remembers, were always at midnight, when people were killed "with no more ceremony than you would kill a pig" and in the same way: they would loop a wire around the neck, and twist it until it cut through the flesh. He escaped this because a Chinese friend, who had influence with Chiang Kai-shek, got him out of jail in February 1946.

Presently the French returned and, with Emperor Bao Dai, were nominally in control. But when they were beaten at Dien Bien Phu, my friend was one of that million anti-Communists North Vietnamese who moved to South Vietnam. But here, as Diem became increasingly dictatorial, my friend joined other intellectuals in opposition and, because of an article he wrote, in September 1961 Diem's secret police arrested him and gave him a year in jail.

Meanwhile opposition to Diem was rising, and in the Buddhist crisis of May 1963 my friend supported the monks. So did everyone in Vietnam who opposed Diem (including even the VC), for it was the only form of opposition that was allowed.

On June 11, 1963, when Quang Doc burned himself to death in Saigon, my friend, with thousands of others, marched in the funeral procession. A week later six of Diem's secret police dragged him into an automobile. He tried to shout his name so bystanders would hear it; he was very well known in Saigon. For fifteen days Diem's interrogators tortured him in the police station. First they stretched him out naked on a bench and stuffed a tube through his nose, connected with a tank of soapy water above. When his belly swelled, the torturers sat on him to force the water out. They asked him to tell of his and the Buddhists' plan to overthrow Diem. "I have no plan," he told them, and it was true. Then they repeated the water treatment.

At first his wife did not know what had happened. Presently some witnesses who had heard him call out his name when he was dragged into the car got in touch with her. She went to the police, who at first claimed to know nothing. But the tortures stopped, and he was formally charged with having taken part in the abortive 1960 coup against Diem.

Diem fell on November 1, 1963. My friend was let out of jail the following day. Although he suffered more in Diem's jails, his life, he says, was in less danger than it had been in the Communist jail in Hanoi.

And today? Things, he says, are in much better shape. The government now has firm control of about five million people in the hamlets and villages, plus another four million in the larger cities, and this is two thirds of the country. But in the rest of the nation the government cannot give firm protection. The VC still come in at night to cut throats, collect their taxes, and take the fourteen- and fifteen-year-old boys for their army. But the Americans are now breaking up the VC strongholds.

My Vietnamese friend cites a serious problem. Although the Vietnamese people are the most intelligent in Southeast Asia, they are unaccustomed to ruling themselves. First the French kept them down, and then Diem. All over Asia you hear the complaint that corruption is endemic, and my friend agrees this is true in Vietnam. It exists because of the shortage of good men. Find a good leader and *he* will find, in turn, corruption in his entourage. "I am almost more afraid of our own shortcomings than I am of the VC." My friend guesses that because of this corruption, much of what the United States sends in aid is stolen or ultimately distributed through corrupt channels. In Saigon rich contractors ride around in Mercedes cars, for there is no check on their incomes. And their spoiled sons smoke opium, go to bars every night for prostitutes, and also ride around in expensive cars.

I say corruption is not unknown in America, and my friend nods; he has heard that one high American officer over here was charged with selling drugs through a source connected with the VC.

We broke off so that he could take me, in his rattling, ancient, little French car, to dinner at a Vietnamese restaurant on the outskirts of Saigon. The restaurant was in a huge hall, the *décor* in red and gold—a little garish for our taste, but not for theirs. It was fairly full of Vietnamese families. I was the only foreigner there, but no one gave me a second glance.

It is crowded, my Vietnamese friend explained, because we are approaching Tet, the Vietnamese (and Chinese) New Year. We are now emerging from the Year of the Horse into that of the Goat, and then comes the Year of the Monkey; a sequence of twelve animal names follows year after year.

The highlight of our meal was a renowned Vietnamese dish of shrimps, flattened by pounding, then wrapped tightly around a six-inch section of sugar cane, and broiled over charcoal. You then bite the broiled shrimp from the cane the way you gnaw a drumstick on a picnic.

When the bill came, my friend handed the waiter three 100-piaster notes (less than $3) and got back a little change. I remarked that all our troops over here, and the money they spend, must surely be a problem. He said a problem existed because Americans have so much money while Vietnamese have so little. For his modest house in Saigon he pays in rent 3,000 piasters (about $27.00) a month. But the other day his landlady came to tell him that an American was offering 30,000 piasters for such a house. You can hardly blame the landlady, he said.

I asked about land reform. The VC talk much of this, he says, but in this country the issue is not of great importance. True, some sections are crowded, but in other parts vast areas could be farmed but never have been.

But I should see for myself: go out to the villages, for there is the real Vietnam. The trouble is, there has been no communication between the villages and the towns. Under the emperors and later under the French, villages were let alone; they were asked only for taxes, which were not heavy. Now, the village people must learn to think of themselves as

a nation. These honest, hard-working Vietnamese make up
80 per cent of the country.

My task over here is to bring back what facts I can on
democracy in Vietnam in relation to its recent elections. The
official story is that this is the first truly free election the
country has ever had, and there is some truth in it.

There was an election under Diem which, his friends insist, was as free as this and with as many votes cast. Since
coming here, however, I have talked to members of the
present Assembly who were also elected in that Diem ballot-
ing, and either were not allowed to take their seats or presently were jailed by Diem. So there can be considerable
argument as to how free the Diem election and Assembly
really were.

In this latest election purists can charge that nobody with
a Communist record was allowed to run. Those who defend
this procedure point out that a war is on over here, and that
the enemies of democracy have no right to use the democratic
process to destroy democracy.

But is this fair? Had the VC candidates been allowed on
the ballot, indications are that they might well have gotten
as high as 20 per cent of the votes. France and Italy survive
as democracies with such Communist percentages in their
assemblies. Is it not better to have this militant minority
screaming at you in a legislature than shooting at you from a
jungle?

The facts are that there were 117 posts in this Constituent
Assembly to be filled, that 640 candidates filed for them, and
that 540 were cleared after screening and eight withdrew.
But 540 candidates for 117 seats in this assembly seems to
allow for a wide latitude of opinion, even though Communists were not on the ballot.

The facts also are that both the Communists and the militant Buddhists boycotted the election. In spite of the boycott, there was a good turnout. The country of about 14 million has 5,298,000 registered voters. Of these, 4,274,812 (or 81 per cent) dared go to the polls, which is a high ratio in any country.

It is true that many of these voters were not too certain what the election was about. Actually, it was to choose 117 men who would draw up a constitution. But many voters thought they were choosing a legislature that would act immediately to correct various shortcomings in the present government.

Out of the 540, which did the voters choose? The largest group was schoolteachers—22 of them. Then 20 soldiers, 18 civil servants, 17 who had already been elected members of provincial councils, 15 professional men (doctors, lawyers, engineers), the rest being assorted occupations—(farmers, laborers, small businessmen), and even three judges.

The high percentage of soldiers is accounted for by the fact that this country is at war, with most able-bodied young men in the army.

The Constituent Assembly meets in what the French built as an opera house about 50 years ago. From one of its balcony seats, and with John Negroponte, our embassy's observer of the Assembly, at my side, I looked down on the 117. Most of them sat where once an audience of French colonials sat, with the elected officers presiding from what used to be the stage.

My first impression is that security is bad here. The VC have already killed one of the elected 117 and almost killed a second, yet the great French doors are open. It would be easy to lob a grenade in here from a taxi on the boulevard just outside.

I experienced a sense of *déjà vu:* I have been here before. There is one old man with a scraggly mandarin beard wearing the traditional dress sometimes seen in the countryside—

a long, high-collared, Chinese-style gown such as those worn under the Old Empress in Peking around 1911. They are still worn by some village elders, and this old delegate surely was one. But as for the rest, how young they are, and how earnest! And how much like the Kansas legislature, when I sat in it, representing Lyon County, back in 1931!

Differences between this Assembly and the Kansas legislature of 1931 somewhat favor the Assembly. The Vietnamese are all in their seats, not gossiping out in the lobby. When they speak, you need no Vietnamese to realize that what they say is to the point and delivered with a punch.

Except for that one old town father, the delegates wear Western dress: black shoes and socks, black trousers, and a gleaming white shirt. Only a scattered few wear coats, and most of the men wear dark ties.

Today they are debating that portion of the proposed constitution that has to do with the senate—how many members and how long they shall serve.

I ask about their political parties and John Negroponte explains that now they have none, and this is to them a matter of deep concern. They are proposing to write into their constitution many safeguards for political parties—their right to organize, rules for their protection, details that to me would seem to have no place in a constitution.

John Negroponte points out that rules about future parties are vital to these young men. Under the French there were no political parties, only underground conspiracies against French imperialism. It was almost as bad under Diem, who in his closing years treated all opposition as treason.

So what they had, instead of political parties, was a number of secret conspiratorial groups, with differing viewpoints. Eventually, these will "surface" in the form of normal political parties. But before they "surface," these young men hope to make sure that their right to disagree openly with government policy will be safeguarded.

In the lobby during lunch break Negroponte introduced me to a number of delegates, including one handsome man of thirty-one, which again gives me that *déjà vu* feeling; it was exactly my age when I sat in the Kansas Legislature. But there are differences. For this man, Danh Thuh, represents, not peaceful Kansas but a constituency in the Delta, that hotbed of Viet Cong activity.

There are further differences. The delegate tells us he spent eleven years as a Buddhist monk, during which he learned his excellent English. Danh Thuh is proud of two other things. Of the twenty soldiers elected to this body, he is the only private. The others, he explains with quiet pride, are all majors or colonels. He is a member of the Home Guard, not to be sneered at as a rabble of militia. It is the backbone of his country's opposition to the VC. In the past year it has killed more of them than did Vietnam's regular army, and it took plenty of casualties in doing it.

Danh Thuh is also proud of the fact that the 28,000 votes his constituents gave him put him ahead of the other five candidates who sought this job.

Danh Thuh and I are hitting it off pretty well in the lobby of this old French opera house when John Negroponte comes up with an idea. Casually he asks Danh Thuh where he plans to spend Tet, which will span four days of next week. Danh Thuh answers that he will go back to his home district, the capital city of which is Rach Gia (pronounced *Rock-ya*) in the heart of the Delta on the Gulf of Siam.

In that case, continues John Negroponte, if Mr. White went to Rach Gia, might not Danh Thuh find a little time to take Mr. White around? Danh Thuh would be delighted. It happens that during Tet he plans to make a trip around his district, if Mr. White did not mind traveling by jeep and by sampan.

It was a date. But what about Kathrine? It would be impossible to get her down there because if this war has a front, the Delta currently is it. And it would be silly to leave her in Saigon. Better that she keep the Pan Am reservation for Hong Kong, where the facilities for worrying are equally good, and the beds much better. The mattresses of the Majestic are beginning to show the inevitable stresses of Total War. A lot of television people stay here.

Today I break the language barrier which separates us American reporters from the Vietnamese people, in an interview with Phan Quang Dan, who spent enough time in America to get a degree in the Harvard School of Government. He is a prominent member of the Constituent Assembly, and was one of a handful who had been elected to the assembly under Diem. Dan was the only delegate who openly opposed the Diem dictatorship and was not allowed to take his seat.

Time passed, Diem fell, Dan was re-elected, and now he is seated in the Assembly, one of two members who have been targets for assassination. Tran Van Van, the other, was gunned down as he was driving to the Assembly. A grenade was planted under Dan's car, but he got off with bruises.

Both men had been critical of the Ky military government, so was it really the VC? Our people here are sure it was: that the VC shrewdly picked men critical of Ky so that the Vietnamese would suspect Ky of having ordered the killings. Many Vietnamese still suspect Ky.

Both Dan and Van had also been *Caravellists*—a small group who in 1960 had petitioned Diem to liberalize his regime, and for their pains were jailed on charges of conspiracy.

Dan begins talking on the subject of land reform. The article that concerns it is meeting opposition in the Assembly which, he says, is predominantly middle class, many of its members French-trained. Even the military government, he says, is more aware of the need for land reform than many of the deputies. The new government, he believes, should not take back the land which the VC have given the peasants in areas they control: let the peasants keep it, let the government do a better job of land distribution than the VC.

Under Diem's land-reform law, never really put into effect, no man could own more than 100 hectares (250 acres) of land. Dan feels that this top limit should be lowered to 10 hectares. The VC, he says, give each peasant five hectares (about 12 acres), on which a rice farmer can make a good living, also raising ducks and fruit trees. He thinks that after the war the government should give each soldier five hectares.

All rice paddies, Dan feels, should go to peasant owners, and why not consider putting each village in charge of land distribution? This was the old Vietnamese way, long before the French came. Every few years the village heads would redistribute the land, to make sure that each family was fairly treated.

Diem, he says, talked of compensation to the landlords. Why not give them, not money, but acreage now vacant in the highlands? There is much of it, suitable for tea and rubber plantations. If landowners were properly approached, with explanations that it was for the good of the country, many would accept a sacrifice.

As for the Assembly, Dan says it all started with the provincial elections—the first fair ones in Vietnam. Its members met in an administrative congress, in November 1965, and asked that the government convene a constituent assembly; the government was so frightened of this idea that it allowed the Congress to meet only for two days. But, meeting again in March 1966, the Congress again pointed out that a national assembly and free elections were important for the stability of the country.

Then followed the Buddhist agitations in Hué, and at last the military-junta government realized something must be done. It convened a National Political Congress for building democracy and called for elections to the Constituent Assembly.

What, I ask, is the real appeal of the VC to the people?

In the villages, Dan answers, the real appeal is land reform. The VC also point to corruption in the government. In Saigon the principal implement is terror. Of course, the VC claim to be fighting an anti-American war. Also the Vietnamese troops were not well trained, and often behaved arrogantly to the peasants—stealing their pigs and taking the best rooms. The VC trains its guerrillas to be much closer to the people. Now and then they may take a chicken, but usually they do some farm work in return or promise to pay.

But now things are much better. The military situation has improved, thanks considerably to American help. And of course things are freer than under Diem. The newspapers are allowed to print and to comment on all the proceedings of the Assembly. There still are incidents here in Saigon—grenades, and things like that. But some incidents, Dan thinks, come from the government side. People are settling old scores, knowing it can be blamed on the war.

He now seemed to be finished, so I thanked him and left. I had not asked if he thought it was the VC who put the grenade under his car. But here, I felt, was a wise, brave man who would make a fine president for any country; even then he was being talked of as a candidate. Presently he was, and he finished third in the list of ten candidates who opposed the Thieu-Ky ticket.

THE
DELTA

TO hear them tell it in Saigon, the Mekong Delta is strictly controlled by the VC outside the towns. It is the rice bowl of Southeast Asia from which the VC supply themselves with food and recruits. At the time of my visit, it was the seat of our most important military operation, for our army was finally moving in on this VC stronghold. Anyone going to the Delta, they told you in Saigon, was sticking his head into the lion's mouth.

The jaws of this particular lion are entered as follows: you arise at 5 A.M. and then drive to that part of Saigon Airport where Air America takes off for the Delta. Air America turns out to be a 60-year-old pilot and an almost-as-ancient Beechcraft that seats six, every bolt quivering for the take-off. The line is to be compared with the Flying Tigers of World War II and, as the world by now has been told, is run by the CIA. I was also told that these Beechcraft sometimes drop pamphlets.

There is this to be said of a 60-year-old pilot: he may not have the eyesight or the reflexes of a boy in his mid-20's, but he knows how to avoid trouble spots or, if they cannot be avoided, how to get out of them. If he did not know these two things, he would not have reached the age of 60.

We move over a checkerboard of canals that connect the Saigon and the Mekong rivers and presently link this Mekong Delta with the sea, toward which we are headed. The square paddies are varying shades of green—pea-green, lichen-green, the yellow-green of an oat field needing lime. Most seem to be flooded from the canals and, when you sight one at a proper angle so that the morning sun bounces off it and glints back up into your eyes, you see that this flooding may be less than half an inch deep.

We pass over a cute little town, the main street of which is a canal bank; it is palm-shaded, and you can make out bikes, pedicabs, and Hondas crawling about.

My seat mate is a young American boy in blue jeans, and over the roar of the Beechcraft's motors he tells me he is a civilian worker with our AID program, under a two-year contract with something called the International Voluntary Services. He is helping Chieu Hoi refugees get settled in a small camp just outside Rach Gia.

I already had heard of Chieu Hoi; it literally means "Open Arms" and describes the welcome given defectors from the VC. Many of the VC, forceably recruited in their early teens, are disillusioned and would leave the VC if given amnesty and a chance to start a new life. So we scatter leaflets to attract them, and are getting defectors by the thousands.

Why should some Americans think this shameful? Reestablishing former enemy soldiers is cheaper in both blood and money than sending out platoons to hunt them down.

I tell the boy I hope I can learn more of his Chieu Hoi program, and he says that he will look me up in Rach Gia. He gives me his name but says everybody calls him Skinny.

We are sliding over a big river that must be the Mekong

on its way from the Himalayas to the sea; at this point it is a lazy river, flowing in wide spirals. From the spirals, canals take water to the rice paddies. The fields can be planted several times a year, depending not on the sun, which in these tropics never changes, but on the level of the Mekong. With the monsoon rains the river rises, flooding the paddies; this means rice, for the plants sprout only when under water. Then, when the summer sun melts the glaciers of the Himalayas, a month or so later snow water comes down, pouring out over the paddies a second flood, and there is more rice.

Many small villages—two rows of houses along a canal. But where is the supposedly VC-infested Delta jungle? There is also an occasional row of palms, their roots in the water of an irrigation ditch. And if this country is so VC-infested, what about a little ground fire? We are hardly at 2,000 feet and should be getting our share.

In Bangkok, U.S. soldiers on R&R who had been making regular runs over Vietnam had plenty to say about VC ground fire—at night winking like fireflies both ahead of and behind them, and sometimes tracers reaching up toward them. Why nothing from here?

We are close enough to those coils of the Mekong to see that they are dotted with sampans. It is silly to let the VC prey on this traffic. If Grant could control the Mississippi from Vicksburg to New Orleans, we should be able to control the coils of this Mekong with twenty-five PT boats. Have we gone soft? I was soon to learn that we have not, that the Mekong is being patrolled.

Far below are what seem to be curious yellow craters. As we head down for Rach Gia airstrip, the craters turn out to be threshing grounds for rice: circles of smooth-packed dirt rimmed by piled rice hulls and straw.

On a turn we see the ocean—that Gulf of Siam on which the town of Rach Gia lies. Out of the gulf, above the mist, rises an island off toward Cambodia which I learned is VC-controlled, except for its little port village. Someday something will be done about that. For the moment, the island is not bothering us, so we do not bother the island.

Beside the Rach Gia airstrip is the Vietnamese driver of a Land-Rover-type vehicle who knows only one word of English—my last name. I climb in and we start off. We pass Lambretta busses carrying eight passengers in the back and two more beside the driver. We pass a slate-gray buffalo.

At close range are some Vietnamese straw houses. Most have roofs of thatched rice straw, although an occasional rich farmer has one of corrugated iron. But always the walls are woven straw, supported by bamboo or cane. In front there is a shaded porch, on which children often play. Usually, a bike leans against the thatch, and always there is a belly-high clay water jar that the children keep filled by carrying bucketfuls from the nearest pond or canal.

The peasant costume is black, with bell-bottom trousers for both sexes. Over the trousers women wear a long gown, slit up the sides. Both men and women wear conical hats, of woven rice straw, about two feet in diameter and held on with a chin strap. When peasants come in to market, the men usually wear European shirt and trousers; the women cling to the old costume, which has both beauty and dignity.

The business district of the Delta town of Rach Gia is concentrated in a large square, around which are the rows of small shops selling ballpoint pens, transistor radios, nylon dresses, name brands of perfumed soap, rubber sandals, cigarettes, tooth paste, and such debris of our factories as has become, in the bazaars of Asia, the coveted hallmarks of Western civilization.

Shops border three sides of the central square. The fourth side is a wide canal in which fishing junks are anchored. Fish are sold from straw baskets by women who squat along the stone esplanade that divides market square from canal.

This little business district might in scale be adequate for a sleepy, midwestern county-seat town of 4,000. The population of Rach Gia is many times that size, and it is the capital city of this Kien Giang province, washed by the Gulf of Siam and bordering on Cambodia.

The driver turns into a lane of prosperous-looking residences, each with a wall sheltering it from the street in the old French manner. He stops in front of an imposing, one-story villa and indicates that this is where I get out. The top of its wall is ornamented by barbed wire, not needed today, I later find out, but a relic of colonial rule when the Viet Minh (who preceded the VC) fought the French. Through a gate lies a little court, and I open one of a pair of doors leading into a huge hall paved with beautiful tiles of the type the French also used in their North African colonies. This hall is 54 feet long × 18 feet wide, with a 15-foot ceiling. The house must have been built for an important French colonial administrator or businessman.

It now serves as a bachelor officers' quarters for Americans. In one corner of this central room leans the tail assembly of a Cessna, painted with the markings of the Vietnamese army and reaching almost to the ceiling. In the center is a massive teak library table. Against the wall stands a small bookcase, packed tightly with well-chosen paperbacks.

From outside comes the noise of a jeep, and presently in comes a handsome man in his late forties with a mop of dark, curling hair and a heavy black mustache. You would take him for French, partly because he speaks it very well, but he turns out to be Francis M. Withey of our Department of State, in whose charge I shall be during my stay in the Delta.

He introduces himself but then brushes his name aside. "Call me Pancho," he orders. "Everybody does." Pancho may be State Department, but he is as far from striped pants as anyone can get. Even up in Saigon this is a shirt-sleeve, tieless war for all ranks.

But down to business: how long would I be here?

As long as was needed to get the feel of the country, an answer that delighted Pancho. They had had some journalists, he said, but none stayed more than twenty-four hours.

I remarked that the people down here seemed to be happy, well fed, and contented. He agreed and said his job was to co-operate with the Vietnamese government in its "Revolutionary Development" program to raise the living standards. But up in Saigon, they often had strange notions of conditions here.

Not long ago, the Mekong River and its tributary canals started rising, whereupon Saigon classified the whole district as a disaster area, calculated that 31,000 people must be flood victims, and shot off a signal asking Pancho, as Their Man in Rach Gia, to estimate how much of what materials would be needed for relief.

Pancho had had to explain that this high water was a seasonal occurrence that had victimized nobody. It meant only that 31,000 people were in water a little deeper than normal. None had left their homes, although sometimes they had moved their sleeping mats from the floor of their straw huts to the table top. They regarded the high water as a boon. It was flushing their floors, a sanitary measure. It was filling their ponds. It would insure a better rice crop and was filling the canals with better fish. Where was the disaster?

There is in Rach Gia, Pancho said, a hotel of sorts, but he thought I would be more comfortable if I stayed in the villa. He occupied the right-front bedroom. The left front was occupied by a Marine Corps major he thought I would like. In the room behind the major was an earnest boy who used to be in the Peace Corps in North Africa, but had recently transferred to AID to work out here.

The room opposite that of the Peace Corps boy was at present occupied by the Baron. Would I mind doubling up with the Baron? I said whatever was easiest for them. Well, Pancho said, the Baron and I should make out all right because the Baron had recently eaten and would be sleeping off his dinner for the next two weeks.

He led me to this rear room and opened the door. I saw a large, high-ceilinged bedroom, starkly furnished with a tall French armoire, a folding chair on which lay a couple of green plastic coat hangers, and an army cot made up with two white sheets. At its head lay a large, lumpy pillow.

I said the Baron must have stepped out. Pancho said that wasn't likely because after a meal the Baron only moved when he had to; he would be someplace around quite close. Then Pancho walked over to the army cot and picked up the pillow. Out slithered a nine-foot python.

"See how smart he is!" said Pancho. "He always gets in the warmest place." The python flowed like molasses, first out onto the sheet, then slowly down off the bed, and over against the wall, where he stopped. His coloring was a mixture of the gray-brown of jungle bark and the dark green of jungle leaves. At his thickest, which was his middle, he was as big around as the calf of my leg. Pancho saw me looking at this lump.

"That's his dinner," said Pancho; "he gets a chicken every three weeks."

"Where'd you get him?"

"A friend," said Pancho. "He had two. . . . Here's the bathroom." Next to the tub was a window and a hand basin. Beside it a chrome-plated towel rack lay on the floor. "The Baron did that," said Pancho, "just before his last meal. When they get hungry, they always start climbing, looking for birds. He must have got up onto the towel rack, because it looked like the branch of a tree—didn't it? You old rascal you!—but it wouldn't hold him. He weighs quite a bit, you know.

"I think I'd better take the Baron in with me. You might leave the door open and the Baron might slide out of the house. The Vietnamese would catch him and, of course, eat him. Pythons are a delicacy around here."

I said if the Vietnamese ate the Baron, wouldn't this help raise their living standards? Pancho said it would, but how could you write a report making this clear to them up in Saigon and back in Washington? "And anyway," turning to the Baron, "we don't want you to get eaten, do we, boy?"

"How do you know he's a boy?"

"Nobody here can prove that he isn't. Come along, boy, you and I are going to bunk together."

Moving his hands slowly he picked up the python, one hand well back of its throat, the other back of the lump made by the chicken. In the front bedroom, Pancho put him gently down against the wall.

We walked back into the big hall, and there was that tail assembly of a Cessna. I asked if the markings were those of the Vietnamese Air Force. Pancho said they were, and would I like to know why he kept it here?

Pancho had known the pilot, a brave Vietnamese kid. Well, one night this kid gets telephoned orders to take off for Can Tho, on some mission that was important to a Vietnamese general. The kid tells them the general should be reminded that he has not been checked out for night flying.

"Well, maybe this general thinks the kid's lazy, or maybe he is a ground general; anyway, the message the kid gets back is that an order is an order. Well, the kid has a wife, and a child four months on the way. But he goes out to that field, warms the Cessna up, and takes off. There is some fog and no moon and, of course, the kid can't read the instruments so, three minutes after take-off, the Cessna rams down so hard that the only thing left sticking up out of the rice paddy is this tail assembly. Two other people in the Cessna also were killed.

"Next morning everybody was sorry, and trying to get the whole thing forgotten fast on account of the general. But because I knew the kid and his little four-months-gone wife, I didn't want it quite forgotten, so, since nobody seemed to want the tail assembly, I had it hauled in, where any of our guys who get to feeling sorry for themselves can always look at it. Also to remind us that there are some Vietnamese who are not just brave, they are very brave. . . . And how about a Coke?"

We had just opened the Cokes when a jeepload of Americans arrived in the compound, some military, some civil; all, I think, come to get a look at the new arrival, for in Rach Gia these are rare. And sitting around the big table I get to work—firing questions at them before I have even got their names straight. Just what is the appeal of the VC around here?

There isn't any, is the consensus; it's all forced accommodation. And what is forced accommodation?

When the VC arrive with guns, the farmers feed and sleep them because they have to. And of course pretend to sympathize with the VC. What else can they do? The VC have the guns. When they control an area, they set up their "government," which includes military service. The regular Vietnamese army does not draft boys under twenty. The VC go down to age fifteen and often lower, and a kid has two choices: he can either join the regular VC army, in which case he is sent away for intensive training, or he can stay in his own neighborhood, attached to a VC guerrilla unit, which lets him eat and sleep at home.

When a boy is taken, his family is nailed down. They may not like the VC but they don't want anything bad to happen to that kid, and can you blame them?

The VC try to levy taxes, but this depends on how firmly they control the area. It can be 25 per cent of what the peasants raise, which is a lot higher than government taxes.

Pancho breaks in here with a point of information: on canals that the VC control, they take 15 per cent of the rice if it is moving in the direction of Rach Gia; but if it is moving away, then only 8 per cent. They preach hatred of towns. Rice moving toward Rach Gia, they argue, is going into the hands of exploiting merchants, or might even go on to Saigon. So they ask a bigger lug.

What do they give in return?

All agree that the rub comes here. They give vague promises of "a better life" someday, which not too many believe. What these people really want is schools, for the Vietnamese were raised in the old Confucianist tradition and want education for their kids. In spite of these years of war the country is 65 per cent literate.

Land reform?

Well, this might be important in some areas but not down here, where there are few large holdings. And anyway, often a man is better off sharecropping for a good landlord than owning his own paddy. Because rice farming takes capital. Someone has to put up the money for fertilizer, see that the needed ditches are dug and the canals dredged so that the crop can get to market.

There is also the matter of security. If there is no militia to guard the area, what good does it do to own land when the VC take from you a bigger lug than a landlord would ask? Why else would farmers be leaving paddies in VC-controlled areas, and crowding into government-controlled areas where at least they can keep what they raise, and their fifteen-year-old kids will not be taken by the VC? Security means a lot more to them than land reform.

Why do reporters believe, in Saigon, that this Delta is a dangerous VC stronghold?

Because the few correspondents who come down usually are brought by MacVee (Military Advisory Command, Vietnam—the collective name for our armed forces in these parts) and are impressed by MacVee's heavy security. They never move out of Rach Gia in a convoy of less than three vehicles, each armed, and in radio communication with the base. Even when they drive out to the airport to pick up someone, they must wear side arms.

Another breaks in here to say that I mustn't get the idea that MacVee is chicken. MacVee is only following regulations. An American in uniform is a top-priority VC target, far more so than an American civilian. But a correspondent, brought down here by MacVee, and seeing all this hardware flapping, naturally goes back to Saigon and makes quite a production out of all the danger he has been in. And, of course, there *are* VC around.

How do they know?

The people tip you off. We American civilians, working out here with them, co-operating with the local government and village heads, are getting ourselves liked. They know we are really helping, and not out laying their women or spending a lot of piasters which runs up their prices. So if you start to leave a village they may say, "Better not take that road today." Or, if you are driving to Ha Tien, near the Cambodian border, they say, better not come back on the same road the same afternoon. Because if the VC see you go by, they will be laying for you on your way back. Maybe plant a remote-controlled mine so that as you pass they can press the plunger without danger to themselves.

Vietnamese love it when you travel with them, the boys explain—either in those little Lambretta busses which hold a driver and ten people, or in the taxi sampans which hold about twenty, and go from village to village on the canals. Both the busses and sampans are always crowded with Vietnamese carrying their chickens or ducks in baskets, along with their produce. When you climb aboard they always giggle at the sight of a *round-eye* * traveling the way they do, instead of in a jeep or armored car. They soon begin peppering you with questions—who are you, and what are you doing in their country? They like it when you are not too proud to squat with them.

But if the bus or sampan is scheduled to move through VC territory, they don't want you around—try to talk you out of getting aboard. If you insist on going, the driver won't let you sit next to him. When you get in at the back, all of them try to squeeze as far away from you as they can, and there is no giggling. They know that any round-eye—in or out of uniform—is always a VC target. Can you blame them for not wanting to get killed by mistake?

Yet in this entire province of Kien Giang in the past eight months only two Americans have been killed. Both were captains, and both were advising the Vietnamese army during operations rounding up the VC—you could say they were asking for it. But during those same eight months, one boy says he has logged 8,000 miles on his gray-painted jeep, running back and forth all over this province—"in civilian clothes, sure, but they can see I am a *Mei,* and if it was VC-controlled, I wouldn't be alive today."

Since he is alive, he gets up and goes into the back room and returns with some cans of cold beer.

Sucking my beer out of its can, I asked, what about this Delta as the rice bowl of Southeast Asia, now controlled by the VC, who are said to be shipping its surplus rice to

---

* Marine Corps slang, highly useful in East Asia. The phrase distinguishes any European or American from the slant-eyed, Mongoloid peoples of Thailand, Vietnam, China, Japan or Korea. They in turn have words equally descriptive of us. The Chinese call us "Big Noses" (Mongoloid noses are flat). The Japanese use this, but also call us "White Eyes" (Mongoloid eyes are always black). An American in Vietnam is a "Mei," and up in China he becomes a "Mego."

their troops up north by canal and trails, so that we have to send American rice to supply Saigon?

Well, they said, start with this rice-bowl thing. It was true that under the French the Delta raised a big surplus. But changes had been made. First, a lot of people had moved in here to get away from the VC. Second, the population bulge; out here in Asia, when people have a little more to eat than they need, they get busy and raise more children to take care of this surplus, and a lot of babies had been raised in this Delta since the French pulled out. Third (least important), also since the French left, canals had tended to silt up, irrigation was not as efficient as it had been, so some of the land was not yielding its potential. Although the Delta people are well fed, there is no big surplus down here.

As for the VC, remember they are smart, and if they need rice up north, how smart would it be to try hauling it from way down here, when they can buy all the rice they want in the Saigon market?

Then I asked about the forthcoming military drive to liberate the Delta from the VC.

Someone said there were two important VC strongholds— the U Minh Forest area, and the area around Three Sisters Mountain. Someone else said he hoped MacVee would take it easy down here, because this terrain was different from up north. If they came in with a lot of heavy stuff, it would get stuck in the mud of rice paddies while the men stood around slapping mosquitoes. The whole over-advertised parade might produce only a couple of dozen VC casualties, and we would end up with a bunch of badly frustrated generals.

Another said that up in Saigon they probably knew all about this terrain. What this spokesman feared was getting too many of our troops down here spending their piastres and the effect it would have in these hamlets. So far, the

Delta had avoided most of the inflation they had up in Saigon.

Another said he had heard talk from Saigon that they hoped to prevent this by making enclaves for our troops, fencing them in. Still another said, don't be stupid; you can't keep American boys penned up in any stockade; he just hoped they would not send down more than necessary.

My new friends seem to have run out of talk, but they told me there was no use going out to find more people to interview; siesta time had begun. It lasts from twelve to three. During that interval everyone in Vietnam—including the VC, who after all are Vietnamese—eats dinner and then lies down to sleep it off.

Someone wonders how the Baron is getting on since he has been moved into Pancho's room. At the base of the door Pancho has rigged an 18-inch plank so that, if you open the door, the Baron cannot slither out. Someone opens it and there the Baron is—or at least two feet of his tail, his other seven feet being back under Pancho's cot. The two feet are still as though they were carved out of gray-green marble.

After siesta I ask the boys about the VC propaganda line to the people in the Delta.

One said, well, that bit about "a better life." But the rice farmers weren't buying it, because government taxes were lower than the VC taxes and about all you got from the VC were your fifteen-year-olds taken to serve in the VC army.

Another said that in the past propaganda had been pure opportunism: "We're bound to win—you can't afford not to join us." But in the past year, this argument has backfired.

A third said when our navy started patrolling the canals with those fiberglass PBRs (Patrol Boat-River), stopping and searching sampans, the VC tried to start a propaganda campaign that these *Mei* were monsters who cut off and ate the breasts of women. But word gets around. One fisherman wrote to his cousin, a rice farmer, that his sampan had been stopped and searched, and the *Mei* not only let him go but gave him a present—a plastic bucket to dip up water, plus a ballpoint. He ended up by writing, "These *Mei* seem to be nice people."

Another said that the most successful VC propaganda campaign has been against defoliation (we go along canals and roads to spray brush that the VC use as cover). We use 2-4-D which every farmer back in the States uses. But the VC have spread the story that it is a deadly poison, and have been distributing herbs which they say are an antidote. This is one thing the farmers really believe, and the VC has a lot of them chewing those herbs.

Still another of the boys said I should remember there was nothing new about the VC toll on sampans. This Delta had a tradition of river pirates who had exacted tolls long before the French came. Also, bad feeling between rice farmers and the towns or the central government was a tradition; there was an old Vietnamese saying: "The Emperor's law stops at the town wall." It would not be correct to say that the VC were only perpetuating centuries-old customs, only now with an ornamental top dressing of Marxism—but there would be a little something in it. River pirates always sprang up and took over when the central government was weak.

I remarked that in Saigon I heard that in the old days you could go from there to the Delta by canal in two days, whereas now because of the VC it took two weeks. What about this?

They said it was true, but the VC had nothing to do with it. It was because nobody had dredged the canals since the French had pulled out. The military couldn't be bothered with little things like canal maintenance, so people on sampans spent most of their time pushing the vessels off mud banks. But it was silly to think that here in the Delta you were in a VC stronghold, cut off from the world. Because down in the main square at Rach Gia you could buy the Saigon morning papers when they came in by bus at two o'clock in the afternoon—almost every day.

Another man noted the Saigon bus was useful to him; before starting on a trip he always checked to see if it had got through. If it had not, this meant that the VC had blown a bridge over some canal, so he delayed any trip in that direction.

It was about dusk and a big, blond, blue-eyed captain who had been listening to us but not saying much got up and stretched.

"Where you going, George?"

"Ovah to the MacVee mess. Ah heauh they're unfreezin' a case of sirloins they jes' got in fo' dinnuh tonight, en Ah'm figgern' on a-gitten one of them abo-d, so's that tomorrow Ah kin go out and win this-hyuh battle fo' the Ha'ts an' Minds of Men."

We were still sitting around the big refectory table when a jeep drove into our compound. The lieutenant who came in asked if we knew the town was on fire.

We said no, we didn't.

He said well, it was, and in case we wanted to watch it burn, we'd better get going.

Outside there were enough jeeps to hold all of us. On the other side of the main canal that divides Rach Gia we could see black smoke billowing into the sky, yellow flame tongues just under it.

Driving over, someone said it was easy to figure what started it—the firecrackers and roman candles these crazy Vietnamese had been shooting off all day in honor of Tet, which would begin at midnight . . . that the civil authorities of Rach Gia were stupid to let them shoot those things off in a town where so many roofs were of straw; they should know something like this would happen.

Then someone else said it happened every year; in half the towns of Vietnam roofs caught fire from the Tet fire-crackers. But if the civil authorities tried to stop it, the people would get themselves a new set of authorities. The people cared more for the celebration of Tet than for a few straw roofs that would take only a few days to weave again.

We found that everyone else was coming to look at the fire, so we had to park our jeeps and walk. Every automobile, Honda, and bike in Rach Gia clogged the road. Even the dozen ricksha coolies who parked in the main square of Rach Gia now had customers, mostly fat old dowagers wanting to make sure they missed none of the goings on. We found the coolies very skillful—pulling their old ladies over and around terrain impassable to cars or to Hondas, to get to the heart of the fire.

It was in an area of nice, clean, comfortable straw houses—each with a raised floor and a big clay water jar in front, houses such as 80 per cent of Vietnam's people live in. By the time we got there most of it was out, and the smoke came from smoldering straw, dampened by the town fire department. This consisted of one steam pump on a truck. Water was coming from a hose line, the other end of which had been dropped into a nearby canal (in the Delta there is always a nearby canal). Firemen operated the nozzle end to spray the thatched roofs of houses near those that had burned.

Because this is the dry season and there had been no rain for several weeks, the people had not had a great deal of time to escape the burning houses. For if an ember falls onto one of those crackly-dry thatched roofs, it and the bamboo rafters go up almost in a puff. But there had been time to chase out all the children and to carry out the old, the beds, tables, chairs, pictures, bric-a-brac, and even dishes,

which were piled in the yard with the family standing
around, more or less to guard them. We saw no signs of
looting; these people were neighbors, busy helping each
other.

We heard that even the governor of the province, a general
appointed by the Ky government in Saigon, had left a big
Tet dinner party to see that everything was going as it
should. The people liked this.

Pancho was all over the place, talking to the fire department, to the mayor, to various aldermen. I was beginning
to learn how important he is in this picture. There are in
all 125 Americans in this province divided into the military
—which is MacVee, headed by a lieutenant colonel—and our
civilian AID program, which sprouts out of our State Department and is headed in this province by Pancho. In rank
Pancho and this lieutenant colonel are equal; neither can
push the other around. Both understand this, and they like
each other.

Tonight Pancho was busy because this fire was going to
require American aid. One way to channel the aid would
be for the Vietnamese military governor to call his uniformed
opposite number—the American head of MacVee—and tell
him what was needed. But this efficient procedure—soldier
dealing with soldier—would by-pass the civilian officials of
Rach Gia, and at a time when all Vietnam is sick of military
rule and looking ahead to the day when a civilian assembly
of their choice will be in power in Saigon. Should we
Americans let civilians be ignored? A fire is not a military
matter. So should not the civilian officials say what they
need, directly to our American civilian AID program?

To uphold the prestige of Rach Gia's civilian officials,
Pancho was busy hunting them down tonight. Most were
at the fire, and had even set up a little office near the fire
engines, where data was being collected. Pancho's final box
score was: 75 straw houses, occupied by 150 families, had

burned; about 800 people were temporarily homeless; there were no dead, actually no one even scorched, so medical supplies were not needed.

New housing? It takes only a few days for a family to weave one of these houses out of local straw and bamboo. The big clay water jars that stand in the front of each take longer to mold and bake, but all would be righted long before the rains. They needed only rice, mosquito netting, and maybe some blankets.

This American civilian aid would reach them through Vietnamese civilian channels. A lot of work and words, you say, to prove a small point in a tiny town? Yet wars have been lost because of such small points.

On our way back we crossed a little square down by the main canal, overlooked on one side by a 24-inch television set in a steel housing, perched on a tapering concrete tower about 20 feet above the cobblestones. How and why?

I was told we Americans had done it; at least we provided this set and others. They picked up the government programs originating in Saigon—about three hours daily, mostly Vietnamese folk songs and opera, with maybe fifteen minutes of news bulletins or action rushes on the war.

Propaganda?

Not really—pretty straight news. And most useful, because when the VC radio was claiming some big victory, this station would come on that evening with the bare facts—casualties and all. The TV set was very popular. During program hours at least five hundred people—usually more—would gather in the square, looking up at it.

This had annoyed the VC; they used to knock out those little concrete towers (paid for by the government of Vietnam) by lobbing a hand grenade at them. But we had fixed this. Blasted towers were replaced by money raised in the villages through a PTA-type organization. This stopped the grenades. When the towers had been paid for by the Saigon government you could almost say the VC had a duty to blow them up. But when the towers were built with piasters collected by the villagers, that was different. Grenading them would anger the villagers, and the VC are very sensitive to local opinion. Now they content themselves with taking spot checks on who watches—what per cent soldiers, what per cent women, what per cent rice farmers, and so forth—or so we heard.

Today I am to go out with Danh Thuh, the delegate elected by this district to the Constituent Assembly. When I left Saigon, I knew only superficial facts about Danh Thuh. He was handsome, likable, taller and a shade browner and less Mongoloid-looking than most Vietnamese, and spoke good English, learned from an American teacher when he was a monk in neighboring Cambodia. He left the monastery in 1962. Under French rule, Cochin China and Cambodia had been adjoining provinces of Indo-China, and not sharply split into separate nations with a frontier guarded by soldiers as they are today. And this Cochin region of South Vietnam today includes a sizable Cambodian minority related in language and blood to the Cambodian Khmers on the other side of the frontier. Danh Thuh belongs to that minority.

Most are devout Buddhists. In this faith, I had already learned, a monk's vows of poverty, chastity, and obedience are not necessarily for life. Danh Thuh in his eleven monastery years clearly had got the equivalent of a good high school and college education, plus something else: the deep sweetness of that faith, its selflessness, its tranquillity, and its high purpose.

Our rendezvous with Danh Thuh this morning is at a Buddhist pagoda on the outskirts of Rach Gia. The large building, they tell me, is about thirty years old. It has the sharply upcurving gables that we had seen on Buddhist wats in Siam. Saffron-robed young monks stroll in the court and, seeing our jeep, go inside to call Danh Thuh, who has been the overnight guest of these old friends. Quickly he comes out. He wears an immaculately pressed black suit, a gleaming white shirt, a black tie, and shining black shoes—dressed as these people expect their assemblymen to look, but in sharp contrast to me, who will ride beside him today wearing a beat-up sun helmet I bought in the local market for fifty cents, no tie, sleeves rolled up, unpressed pants, and a pair of rubber sandals such as ricksha coolies wear. Neither had planned this contrast but there it was: our disparate ideas of what to wear when visiting Delta villages in a sampan. I think both were right. I was only a visiting round-eye, so it did not matter how I looked; he was their assemblyman.

Danh Thuh had his own jeep in which I was invited to ride. He also brought a friend—a young, orange-robed Buddhist monk who climbed into Pancho's jeep. The road was single-track, and once—probably back in French days—had had a top dressing of crushed rock.

We passed Vietnamese straw houses near little ponds dotted with yellow ducks, and after about a mile we pulled up in front of a house. Out came a smiling young Vietnamese of about Danh Thuh's age, also wearing a neat dark suit and carrying a black brief case. Clearly he was Danh Thuh's political right bower. With him was a deliciously pretty Vietnamese girl, probably his wife. She had both a brief case and a stenographer's pad, and it developed that her duty was to refresh Danh Thuh's memory, when he came to each village, as to which villager had recently written him about any legislative matter.

It was the same kind of political team as that which backs up an American congressman when he is out mending political fences, shaking hands with notables and gossiping with county chairmen—with, maybe, the exception of our orange-robed monk.

Jeeps are built to stand up under just such roads as the one we traveled, and after another two miles of it we approached a canal spanned by a narrow bridge. Across the bridge was a little concrete blockhouse, dating back to French times, the purpose of which was to protect that bridge and keep it standing. Inside the blockhouse was a young, uniformed Home Guard soldier cleaning his rifle. The blockhouse was hedged about with coils of barbed wire, and on this the soldier's wife (or maybe she was his girl) was hanging out his laundry.

The soldier spotted Danh Thuh, and his first instinct was to grin and wave. Only then, being Home Guard, did he remember to salute, using the same hand with which he had waved.

Danh got out of his jeep, the soldier left his blockhouse, and they gossiped a minute, pointing away toward the horizon. When we were rolling again, Danh told me that this was a man from his old unit, a unit not to be underestimated. First contact with the VC is usually made by the Home Guard, who are defending their own families and villages. Danh Thuh felt the Home Guard deserved better arms and a little more training.

He said that the soldier, pointing out that the Tet truce was supposed to have begun, had asked what he should do if VC approached his blockhouse. Danh had answered that this should depend on whether they were armed and how they acted; nobody wanted trouble during the Tet truce.

Presently we turned off to visit a straw village, guarded by a little blockhouse perched on a tower. From the tower two soldiers could see the road and over the thatched roofs to the paddies beyond; by day, at least, no one could sneak up.

In the village's central square was a town hall made of masonry. From the hall came the village headman and several elders who had heard the rattle of our jeeps. Ordinarily a round-eye in such a village gets a little attention, if only from curiosity, but here every eye is on Danh, their representative. They are all old friends.

On our way to this place Danh had told me that while in the election he had got 17,000 votes, which had put him ahead of the other five candidates, this had not been one of his villages. But he had run second here and thought they would be friendly to him.

They clearly were. They offered us tea, but Danh said we had just had breakfast. The headman led us across the little plaza to the school. It had long, plank benches, in front of which were equally long desks, with holes bored in them at intervals for inkwells—exactly like the country schools in Kansas hardly a century ago. This school seemed fairly new, for not too many initials had been carved into the desks.

The headman spoke to Danh with a glance at me, whereupon all looked at me, nodded, and smiled. Danh explained that the headman had told him this school had been built in part with American aid. Then followed a long colloquy that was translated for me. It seems that this school was closed because its teacher had been drafted into the army. The government rule was that the village must continue paying his salary as long as he was in service, for military pay is low, but it meant that the village had no money to pay the salary of a replacement teacher. Could not Danh explain this to the government in Saigon? Why should it not pay that former teacher's salary? Then this village would use its money for a new teacher and reopen the school.

Danh told the headman that his business in Saigon was to draft a constitution; then a new government would be elected which surely would correct this situation. The headman said he understood this, but many rice farmers down here did not. They had voted in this election as a protest against the VC, who had tried to frighten them away, and this election had sent Danh to Saigon. Why couldn't he help them?

Danh said perhaps he could. He would go over to the Ministry of Education and try to get this regulation changed, for it must have closed schools in many villages. In any case, when the constitution was finished, and a new government put in to replace this government of soldiers, they certainly would correct this.

Then we went on out to the road, the headman escorting us to our jeeps. Our bumpy road ended a quarter of an hour later on the bank of a canal, where we drove the jeeps into an improvised parking lot and got out. It was a big canal—about 30 feet wide and not quite choked with hyacinths, which moved downstream by a current at about half a mile an hour. Water in this canal network originates in the Upper Mekong Delta and, after flooding all the rice paddies in this vast area, ends up in the Gulf of Siam.

Three sampans snuggled into the bank of the canal, waiting for us. Danh Thuh had arranged it by some political bamboo telegraph of his own. In the old days sampans were poled along by a man standing in the stern, but this skill is now deader than the horse and buggy, killed by a low-cost outboard motor perfected by the Japanese at a price that Vietnamese sampan owners can afford. So we go popping along, making about the same racket in this quiet countryside that a Honda does on the boulevards of Saigon.

In about a quarter of an hour we see two men on the bank, waiting, as it turns out, for us. They try to help me up the bank, treating me with deference, not because I am a round-eye but, I think, because I am so old—at least as old as the venerable monk heading up the local pagoda, usually the oldest man in a Vietnamese village.

On the canal's bank we find we are in the heart of a straw village. Nearby is a blockhouse that once protected a canal bridge, one remaining end of which still sags into the water;

it was blown some time ago by the VC. The headman asks
Danh Thuh about getting it replaced and here Pancho comes
in, for this could be an American participation program.

It is a cute little village, with Cochin China hogs (a breed
that came to America from this country) scratching their
backs against the bamboo supports of the straw houses. But
the headman has some problems. Seven kilometers of road
need repairs; they have crushed rock for only four. Could
Saigon help with some rock or money? And their school
was once big enough, but now with refugee families crowding in here from VC areas, they soon will need another
room. Danh Thuh can make no firm promises, except to
say that as soon as the constitution is written, matters like
these will receive attention.

On we go through drifting hyacinths toward the next
village. In the straw houses bordering the canal people look
up, smile, and wave when they see Danh Thuh, and he waves
back. The people, he says, are newcomers, refugees from the
VC, and their children need schools. As we chug through
the hyacinths, he watches the bank alertly as a good poli-
tician should, answering every wave—even from comfortably
half-naked children—with a smile and a wave of his own.

Over the canal bank we see the spire of a Catholic church.
As we put in, Danh Thuh tells me his district is 60 per cent
Buddhist, but the young Catholic headman of this village
is a fine leader. He is waiting on the bank with his city
treasurer, and Danh goes into a huddle with them. The
village children have gathered, mostly to stare at me. Edging
nearer, one dares to pull the hair on my forearms. They
all giggle. Then several others dare. The arms and legs of
Mongoloid peoples are bare of hair. To them I seem like a
monkey, and they never tire of staring.

The mayor now leads us to a school of two classrooms
where they try to teach 250 pupils, divided into seven grades.
The school needs two more rooms and two more teachers.

The mayor points out the newly built town hall, explaining that the old one is now being used as the school, and then he leads us across the square to the dispensary. Some of the drugs I recognize, but most are herbs, used for centuries in treating local diseases. A nurse is in charge but she needs an assistant, and they should have a hospital.

They, too, have a road problem: no money to buy crushed stone that they could spread and roll themselves. But the most urgent problem is the school; the extra nurse, hospital, and road could wait.

Back on the canal, Danh Thuh resumes taking bows and returning waves. Then we make a right-angle turn into a smaller canal, and I ask Danh Thuh how old these canals are. The biggest, he says, are three or four centuries old; they were here long before the French. The canal we just left was built about 30 years ago under the French. The little one we are presently on—about 10 feet wide—connects two hamlets, is about a meter deep, and was dug 10 years ago.

Its banks are so low that we can see the rice on each side; it could be standing wheat. The rice, a local variety called "floating rice," recalls one of the fumbles in our AID program. We had brought in and induced some of these Delta farmers to plant a newly developed variety, bred to yield less straw and more grain which, in other parts of Asia, had doubled the yield per acre.

The new rice rooted beautifully, but then came the annual flood. The rising water submerged and drowned the new variety, while the same floods stimulated the growth of the long, "wasteful" straw stems of the old "floating rice," holding the heads high above the flood as they had been doing for centuries.

Over the canal bank we see the upcurved gable ends of a pagoda roof; it is Ak Dinh Phuoc, our destination and a village of some size. A glance around its central square shows that it is a Buddhist settlement. Opposite us rises the pagoda.

On the left is a large building—for this size village, a palace—which Danh tells me is the residence of the head bonze, whose title translates into English as "The Venerable." On the right side of the square is a less majestic building, a residence hall for the younger monks.

In the center of the square is what to my Western eye seems to be a temporary bandstand, of the kind from which American politicians speak to the people in small towns on the Fourth of July. The bandstand is reached by a flight of wooden steps—almost ladder-steep, as always in Asia—and on its top level there is a small speaker's stand, with pitchers of fruit juice and glasses. Tet, I know, combines the principal features of Christmas, New Year's, Thanksgiving, and Fourth of July: firecrackers are still popping in this village. So from this grandstand Danh Thuh, their congressman, will speak to his constituents.

But first we are taken to the Vatican of this Buddhist village, to meet The Venerable. The double doors open into a spacious audience room and here he awaits us, robed in orange and seated on a dais. He is a wizened, frail, kindly little man, flanked by slightly less venerable monks. All clearly are old friends of Danh, and they greet each other with warm smiles and with those little bows, palms pressed together, that are the Eastern equivalent of a handshake. Then Danh introduces Pancho and me. He singles out his old teacher, and we gather that Danh, as a young monk, spent some time in this monastery.

This could be an old man's room in any country, filled with the things The Venerable has collected and loved over a lifetime. There are little statues of Buddha—some Cambodian, some Vietnamese, some old, some new—in various attitudes. There are framed photographs of other pagodas and of robed monks who were his friends, including one killed by the VC in 1947, hung now in a place of honor.

We go out into the square where people are gathering.

(This hamlet, they tell me, has 1,300 inhabitants.) The monks produce a little camera and take pictures of Danh and these old friends from the monastery. They try to include Pancho and me, but Pancho pulls me away. Suppose, back in Washington, some new government might decide to let go the rope out here? The photographs of Danh with us Americans could murder him five years from now, and not just politically.

And he's too important—a fine, dedicated boy. Pancho and I want him alive, working to get schools for his people, no matter who is running the show up in Saigon.

We cross the square to visit the school, a self-help project, they explain. The government furnished the materials, but the work was done by the fathers of the schoolchildren. The school has seven grades, 130 children, and two teachers, one of whom is provided by an American Protestant church.

Here my notebook comes out: "Which one?" They do not understand. "Is she Presbyterian? Or Methodist?"

If I mean the teacher, he is a Buddhist. The American Protestant church gave the money freely, with no religious conditions.

Back out in the square, we pass the town hall and Danh Thuh, still trailing a comet's tail of orange-draped, admiring young monks (clearly he is their Monk Who Made Good), tells us that, as a young monk, he helped to build the hall. We are taken to the refectory where the younger monks live, and where a feast is being prepared. The monks invite me to sit down, but are we really expected? Where is Pancho? He seems to have left, for they point outside.

I ask again. They point down the square and around a corner. I turn the corner; nearby is a small Vietnamese restaurant; maybe we round-eyes will eat here. When I ask in the restaurant, they shake their heads but point down a lane. I can overtake Pancho if I hurry, so, breaking into a dogtrot, I start down the lane alongside a small canal.

Presently I come onto a Home Guardsman with rifle on patrol. An American? He beckons me on up the trail, and I puff and pant, trying to maintain my trot. (I should overtake Pancho any minute. But which minute?)

A yellow dog, out for a noonday swim in the canal, looks at me curiously. I hear footsteps behind. It is the guardsman who overtakes me and sprints on ahead, apparently to run down Pancho.

Pancho, I have learned, is a master of the seemingly inexplicable which, given the passage of some time, turns out to be brilliantly sensible. And here he is, coming toward me down the trail at a trot, followed by the Home Guard. Briefly he pauses. Little matter of private business. And wouldn't I join him in a run back to the village? No? Well, then, he'd see me later.

It was half an hour later. The monks were assembled in their dining hall—three tables full of them, and us. They in brilliant orange, we in shirt sleeves. In Saigon, restaurants offer chopsticks of white plastic, imitating ivory. Down here in the country, chopsticks are of honest wood, their sharp corners eroded by many washings. The cooking is a Chinese treatment of local foods—bite-size chunks of fish that surely had been caught in the canal that morning. Then a pork dish from one of their local spotted pigs. A final course is a quart-size bowl of what seems to be a soft cheese, beautifully aged. It can't be cheese, for Mongoloid peoples do not normally eat it. It turns out to be eggs, beaten with herbs for flavor and set aside to ripen. It is a lovely country dinner of things raised within the village, prepared following traditions, and delicious as such meals are in any land.

Through the open door come young voices in what could be a Gregorian chant. We go out. In the center of the square is that bandstand which I had thought decorated in honor of Danh Thuh. I was wrong. The stand is filled with young monks sitting cross-legged and chanting, with palms together, to an audience of villagers. Nearby Danh Thuh talks with The Venerable and the mayor—their own boy who lived, worked, and prayed with them, and now speaks for them up in Saigon.

I ask to see the pagoda. They seem pleased that a *Mei* should care, and half a dozen lead me there. It is dim inside (it is always dim in Buddhist temples). On the dais is a huge Buddha and half a dozen smaller ones. Around the walls are primitive frescoes that depict scenes from Lord Buddha's life.

Outside people are moving toward the sampans. Even The Venerable totters down to see Danh Thuh off, the younger monks at either side, ready to steady the head bonze. It is a great day for this pagoda. Even the chanters have come for the send-off.

We are on our way. How lovely to travel in a sampan! We pass an old man paddling another sampan, the first we have seen without an outboard. He sees Danh Thuh's black suit and white shirt, recognizes him, grins, and takes off his conical straw hat. Soon we pass a straw farmhouse and, in front of it, at the canal's edge, squats a wrinkled, gray-haired old grandmother, scouring a crock. She looks up, recognizes Danh Thuh, and breaks into a snaggle-toothed smile.

We put into the canal bank at the village of Bhuyeb Van Nam, a poor hamlet. This is clear, from the appearance of the ramshackle straw houses. All Vietnamese know how to weave straw houses, and in this village they did a sloppy job. Why? There is an old saying among farmers, "Poor folks, poor ways."

On the canal bank two little Home Guard soldiers are on duty. The headman has a patient, careworn face and gnarled hands. He leads us into what he tells us is Trom Chet pagoda, which seems to do double duty as the town hall. It is a modest building, housing a modest sitting Buddha, hardly larger than life, which, however, was made in Cambodia; this apparently gives it status. To one side of it is a small table for offerings left by the faithful—two packages of Kent cigarettes and three bottles of the local root beer, rendered unto Lord Buddha but really intended for the monks.

We sit on straw mats, in front of the Buddha but at a respectful distance. For a time the talk is general, and Pancho translates snatches of it.

Some local VC are dug in about four clicks (kilometers) from the village, which makes the people nervous. Also, says the headman, there may be some in this poor village who sympathize with them; he is not sure.

There is a pause in the translation. Danh Thuh then takes out a notebook and jots down notes. There has been, says Pancho, a big screw-up in this hamlet. The headman has just told Danh that two months ago he made application to Saigon for help with a school, but has not even got an answer, which Danh does not like. This is the central pagoda for 1,200 families, and the hamlet badly needs a school.

Pancho listens some more and then whispers to me that the trouble goes back to the practice of drafting teachers. Of course the government will assign no teachers to a hamlet unless it has provided a satisfactory school. This hamlet, although poor, could manage to build one. But suppose it hired a teacher who then was drafted? It could not possibly raise enough money to pay both the drafted teacher and a replacement.

Danh Thuh tells the headman there is no excuse for Saigon's not answering his letter; when he goes there after Tet, he will see that the headman gets a reply. He and the village council seem to have forgotten that Danh Thuh is only a delegate to an assembly drafting a constitution. Already he is acting as a congressman—Their Man in Saigon.

A young monk comes with bottles of root beer of the kind offered Lord Buddha on the little altar table. We drink the warm drinks; in so poor a village there is no money for ice.

Pancho and I are vibrating on the same wave length; each

fishes out a 500-piaster note—a considerable sum for this village. But to whom do you hand it? Pancho solves it by laying them with the offerings to Lord Buddha between the Kents and the root-beer bottles. The monks look at those 500-piaster notes and incline their heads toward us in thanks.

Back into the sampans and on to another village where the headman escorts us to the town hall. We sit on chairs and they break out more bottles of root beer. We remark how cold it is, and they explain with quiet pride that this village has ice, brought up the canal by sampan from Rach Gia. A rich village!

The problem here is medical, so we are taken across the square to the dispensary. It is run by a Buddhist monk and contains an orderly array of druggists' bottles and chests of small drawers, filled with the herbs needed to treat tropical ailments. The monk is proud of the building's corrugated tin roof, put on only recently (because during the monsoon, he says, straw roofs often leak on medicines). The floor is of dirt, with cracks at least an inch wide left from the annual flood. But never has the water got high enough to spoil the medicines.

What this village needs is not penicillin (they don't trust it) but a registered midwife. The old women who do these jobs have no training. The monk is skilled in prescribing medicines, but, even if monastic rules permitted him to act as a midwife, no woman would want it. Can Danh Thuh, in Saigon, find out where such midwives are trained, and tell them that one is needed in this village?

We squat on mats, and children—friendly but intensely curious—swarm over me so thickly that I can hardly take notes. I could be a strange marsupial from another continent. Their little hands are everywhere—touching the sides of my cheeks, patting my belly, tugging at the hair on my forearm, squeezing the muscle above it with their little fingers; to them it must seem huge.

On the way back to the sampan, I ask Danh Thuh if there is anything I can do about the children.

He smiles, and shakes his head. "You strange to them. You very big man. Also, many children like Americans."

Our sampans nosed into the bank for a final village call. Danh Thuh said it was a hamlet of 1,700 which, in the election, had given most of their votes to one of his opponents. "I am not sure they like me," he added, "but we stop anyway."

Nobody was waiting for us on the bank, but a small boy recognized Danh Thuh and raced away to notify the headman, who came out of his straw house, looking a little surprised. Danh Thuh explained that he happened to be passing and wanted to know what was on the minds of the people of his district.

The headman nodded. He said they appreciated Danh Thuh's call, and there were some things they should know about, up in Saigon. Their needs were similar to the others'—another schoolteacher, but also more security against the VC who, this headman said, had come into this village trying to collect taxes, and might be back again.

People were beginning to see, the headman said, that money given to the VC for "taxes" was really thrown away—they received nothing in return. We learned that in one district the VC boasted they would set up a school, and even went so far as to paint an old building and hoist their VC flag over it. But the teacher they provided had had only two years of school himself and could barely teach reading and writing; the people were disgusted. With the money the VC took for "taxes" they could have hired a real schoolteacher. But what choice did people have without protection? Lawmakers up in Saigon should understand that.

Danh Thuh said he understood it, because he had been in the Home Guard. The headman said he had heard this during the campaign, and also had heard that Danh Thuh had been a good guard. He went with us to the canal bank, helped Danh Thuh into the sampan, and waved us good-by.

When we were out of earshot, I congratulated Danh Thuh; he had really softened that headman up. Danh Thuh said yes, for the time being. You couldn't be sure it would last, but he was glad he had stopped by.

I told Danh Thuh that I envied him: his beautiful country, his youth, his prospects in politics, and these sweet, happy, hard-working countrymen whom he was helping. He said nothing. I know he liked it but he is a devout Buddhist and it is hard for them to accept praise; it is too close to the sin of self-glorification or vanity.

The sun was low in the sky when the sampans put in to the canal bank and we got out where we had left the jeeps. Pancho and I climbed into the back seat while Danh Thuh rode with the driver. He slowed down every now and then to avoid hitting someone who had sat down in the road.

I asked Pancho what this was about, and he said it meant the area was secure. He explained further that the Vietnamese are cold-blooded; every evening, when the sun gets low and the temperature drops under 80 degrees, they come out and sit or lie down on the black-topped road, which still holds the midday heat. Kids do it and of course old people, and they even bring babies and lay them on pallets. Dogs come, too, and lie down on the warm pavement, and sometimes even the ducks out of their ponds. All the people gossip and giggle and enjoy the warmth of the pavement until after dark—provided the area is secure.

When he asked me what I had got out of our trip, I said a lot of little things, all pointing in the same direction. With all the men and hardware being sent down by Hanoi, the war had to be won by MacVee. But until these people had a government that they had elected and could trust, it would not stay won; the VC would close right back in on the tracks of the tanks, as MacVee moved out.

Pancho said that was the trouble; the whole thing could come unstuck again unless the people cared. Today we had watched these Delta rice farmers looking to their own elected representative to get things done. I said they were reacting to democracy exactly like the people of Kansas, and that when the new assembly got down to work, giving the people in these straw villages what they asked for, might not the war fold up sooner than anyone dared hope?

Pancho said the Vietnamese would jump at the chance of free government.

We had now come to the blockhouse guarding the canal bridge where, in the morning, the guard's laundry had been drying on the barbed wire. The laundry had gone and so had the guard: inside the blockhouse was only his wife (or his girl) and she seemed scared.

Danh Thuh leaned out to ask her why the guard had left his post, and she pointed down the road. About half a mile away we found him with a dozen other guards, milling nervously. They told Danh that they had reports that a fair-sized body of VC was on the move, off to the left and very near. They asked what he thought it meant and what they should do.

Danh Thuh pondered a moment and then said these VC probably were boys taken from homes in the neighborhood, now going back to visit their families for Tet which, under the rules of this truce, they had a right to do. The guards had been right to gather, but they should not shoot unless the VC shot first, which he doubted they would do. At least, if he were on duty here, that is what he would do.

We could see the guards' relief. They had not wanted to take on the VC, with a chance that someone would get hurt—particularly during Tet.

In the courtyard of the big pagoda where we had picked up Danh Thuh, we made speeches of gratitude. Although he knew we meant what we said, Danh, the modest Buddhist, was embarrassed.

Back at the house, our servants had started their four-day Tet holiday: beds were unmade and floors unswept, but we didn't mind. In Pancho's room the Baron had left the shelter of the bed and lay coiled in one corner. This restlessness, Pancho said, meant that the Baron was beginning to get hungry.

Pancho had some paper work to finish, so I went for a stroll around Rach Gia. This day must be the climax of Tet; every street of the village has turned into an Easter parade. Families, reunited from far and wide, stroll in their Sunday best, a Vietnamese modification of the old Chinese dress. Down the cobblestones each family moves as a unit—parents, children of all sizes, and grandchildren, smiling and bowing to other families as they pass.

There are, today, smiles even for foreigners. The focus of one approaching family is its great-grandmother, a plump, spry, splendidly decked-out old lady, surrounded by an immense school of daughters, sons, grandchildren, and freshly scrubbed great-grandchildren—a brood to be proud of in any land. Stepping to the wall to let them pass I bow to her. Grinning broadly with pride she bows back, as do all her sons, sons-in-law, and grandsons.

In Rach Gia's little square I encounter Skinny, the midwestern boy who, on the Beechcraft coming down, told me he was working with a Chieu Hoi project under our AID program; he is on his way to eat and asks me to join him at a waterfront food shop; he thinks every other place in Rach Gia will be closed for Tet. I know the food shop to be a tiny shack down by the waterfront, roofed over but otherwise open to the sea breeze, run by a Chinese with his two teen-age sons as waiters, I call it my "Pointing Restaurant," for no language is needed; all its small menu is right before your eyes, either on the tiny stove or beside it—kettles of soup and of boiled rice, straw baskets of fresh-caught crabs, shrimp, and mussels. You point to what you want and presently it is brought to you at one of the little tables along the quai, where the warm salt water laps the rocks just below.

Sure enough, my "Pointing Restaurant" is open, and as we down chunks of fresh-caught crab (fried in oil) along with bowls of rice, Skinny, in answer to my questions, sketches in his short (he is twenty-three) but happy life and tells me of his job down here in the Delta.

I told him that I wanted to know the truth concerning the Chieu Hoi program and in exchange would withhold his name. He answered that he would go along with the bargain if I would make it clear that the program was really a good one; he believed in it, and its seamy side was far outweighed by the program's virtues.

I note that Skinny skillfully handles his chopsticks in the Vietnamese (not the Chinese) fashion, whereas I am getting pretty well splattered with fried crab. He admits that he is (as I had guessed) a conscientious objector, not because he feels that there is anything particularly wrong with this war, but because his people are Mennonites who don't believe in killing anyone for any reason, however noble. After Skinny got his degree in civil engineering from his state university, he looked around for something as an alternative to military service. His church had such a program, called PAX, but in this, one pays one's own transportation abroad, and the living allowance is not enough to get by on. He did not want to ask his family for money, since he has two brothers still in college.

The answer for him was International Voluntary Services, an old, well-established organization. (The Peace Corps later patterned itself on IVS, Skinny says.) Its head is a Roman Catholic monsignor. On its board are prominent Quakers and Mennonites and, while it does not stress the conscientious-objector angle, many COs such as he have joined up with it.

He had picked Southeast Asia because in college he had met several students from there; he assumed they were from high-class families. And while he had never been under the illusion that he would be able to do much to alleviate human suffering in Asia, at least he wanted to find out for himself how the common people lived. He had been given a choice between Laos and Vietnam, and he had picked Vietnam. (Could it be that Skinny wanted to be with the American boys of his age—sharing their dangers if not the sin of killing?)

Skinny likes the IVS approach. They told him to avoid living in a foreign enclave with other Americans: to rent a house for himself and his interpreter only a little better than the Vietnamese average, to keep it tidy, to set a good example.

He says that before you start to improve things in this country you must know what you are doing. The Vietnamese are set in their ways, and unless you realize that their way may be best, you can do more harm than good. And you must always use your head.

For instance, during the recent high water U.S. soldiers, trying to be helpful, distributed entrenching tools (collapsible shovels) with which the farmers could repair irrigation ditches. But the GIs gave no instructions for opening the entrenching tools, whereupon the farmers, finding them useless, sold them for 70 piasters each to Chinese merchants. The merchants opened them up into shovels and resold them to other farmers for 500 piasters.

For a while Skinny worked on a water-purification program. (Most villagers dip their water from ponds or a canal that may be contaminated.) He dropped in on one district chief to get acquainted and was told of a village that badly needed a well, plus a pump and gasoline, which Skinny assumed must be for a storage reservoir for drinking water.

Checking into the matter, Skinny found a number of similar wells had been built. However, they were unused most of the time, and then only during the dry season as reservoirs to provide irrigation water. For the rest of the year the villagers refused to pay for pumps and fuel to get pure drinking water. Pure water, Skinny says, could be piped into every village house, but the Vietnamese see no reason to pay the cost of pumping, when they have plenty of children to dip water out of ponds or canals and carry it home, as children have done for centuries.

Now and then, Skinny says, you suspect a little graft. Once he was asked to check into a request for an irrigation-drainage project. Going to the hamlet, he found the man who wanted it, but also found that his request had not been made through proper government channels. Perhaps the man wanted Americans to pay for improving land that he himself owned, with no benefit to the others.

Skinny also suspects that maybe some of the rice farmers, settled on land that once belonged to the French and is now owned by the government, could be paying a squeeze to some local official. Such land is supposed to be rent-free, but the farmers fear to complain lest they be thrown off. Situations like this can be corrected, Skinny says, only when the farmers have learned the procedures and when they have a voice in an elective government.

As for the local Chieu Hoi project, it is a quadrangle of houses around three acres of damp land, grown up in marsh grass. To drain this, workmen are digging ditches and putting culverts under roads. Then, by irrigating it in the dry season and draining it during the rains, the peasants can raise vegetables and support themselves. With his college degree in engineering, Skinny is in charge of this project.

I ask about his house and daily routine. For the house he pays a monthly rent of 5,000 piasters (less than $50) plus 2,000 piasters tax. (Most Americans would be charged 20,000 piasters for such a house, but he speaks a little Vietnamese.) He gets up at about eight and comes to the food shop for his breakfast, a special Vietnamese soup—chicken broth, noodles, and scallions—which costs 20 piasters. Then he goes out to his Chieu Hoi project, where he checks the grade on the ditches and then picks up a shovel and digs along with the Chieu Hoi, "until I start getting blisters." This would usually be around noon. He goes home to lunch, prepared by the cook for him, the two other IVS workers who live with him, and their interpreter. Lunch is probably rice, a bowl of clear soup with a little cabbage and meat floating in it, a dish of fried pork (to be dipped in a *nuoc mam* sauce), string beans, and a glass of limeade.

The cook-housekeeper gets 3,000 piasters ($27.00) a month, which Skinny says is very high for Rach Gia, but she is highly competent and trustworthy, careful to boil their drinking water and even the water her own family drinks—most unusual in Vietnam. It comes from a well about 50 meters from the house, fetched by her little boy in two buckets balanced on a pole and poured into the big clay crock in front of the house.

After lunch comes siesta. Then Skinny goes out to see how the digging is getting on and also supervises training programs for the Chieu Hoi, which are not just to keep them occupied but are really needed. Most of the Chieu Hoi were drafted by the VC when they were only twelve or thirteen and, having spent several years in their army or as guerrillas, they have no idea of any trade except fighting. They must be taught farming, carpentry, and how to use the simplest tools. When the land of this project is drained, they will be taught to plant their garden.

Skinny says the boys almost never talk about their VC experience. And, although they are supposed to have been heavily screened to prove they were certified VC-defectors, he suspects that a few have been anti-VC all along—refugee farmers who fled their homes in fear of the VC but are smart enough to claim they fought the government in order to rate the better treatment and free land given defectors. The true refugees get a bare subsistence level.

When they talk to an American, villagers in this area of course claim to be against the VC. And in most cases Skinny thinks this is probably true. But when he asks if they are paying taxes to the VC, he thinks he probably gets "too many no's."

Americans, he says, have a tendency to lump everything into two piles—pro-VC or pro-GVN (government of Vietnam), but his experience is that the majority of the rice farmers have no strong motivation either way, except that they want to be left alone. Yet practically all of them are friendly to the Americans in the AID program and what they are doing. There are days, Skinny says, when everything seems to go wrong, when idealists in his outfit who came out here with the idea of doing good, get discouraged and wonder if anything they do is really helping. He is lucky, says Skinny, for he never had any illusions; his main reason for coming out was to learn how people in Southeast Asia really lived. Which was, I think, the only lie Skinny told me. I would say that this boy who will not kill his fellow man is as eager as any to do good, but too shy to admit it. There is a large chunk of the midwestern farm boy's realism stirred into his hidden idealism.

Next morning my plane back to Saigon leaves at nine. Packing means only zipping my shaving things into a plastic AIR VIETNAM bag. But out in the living room I stop. A huge contraption stands near the door.

Its center seems to be an old-fashioned barber's chair, complete with head and foot rests. Within hand reach of this are control levers. Sprouting in all directions from the chair is what might be the fuselage of a one-man helicopter, if such a thing existed.

Pancho emerges and invites me to agree that it really is a little beauty. He ordered it from the States and it came when we were out in those sampans. It is just the thing he needs to get around the province; a blown-up bridge can stop his scooter, and other villages can be reached only by canal and sampans are slow.

But with this! It cruises at 72 miles per hour, right over canals and forests. In case any VC start shooting at him, it has a 12,000-foot ceiling, far more than he would need. Its 300-mile range will get him anywhere in this province. And safe? It can maintain altitude at 15 miles per hour, needs only 300 feet of runway, and it cost only $2,250, plus another $175 transportation from the States. With this machine, Pancho can really do his job. And now he must jeep over to MacVee for a minute, but will be back in plenty of time for my plane.

I found the marine major in his room, catching up on some paper work. I said I was leaving but that the rest of them absolutely had to gang up on Pancho. This lovely, sweet, useful, crazy guy had ordered that gadget from some mail-order house, probably with an instruction manual on how to make it fly, and had some Buck Rogers picture of himself in orbit over the Delta. Anyone with common sense knew that if he ever managed to get the thing in the air, he would surely kill himself trying to land.

The marine major said I knew only part of Pancho, that he delighted in letting people think maybe he was nuts. The truth was that back in the States there was an organization interested in developing these one-man helicopters. Pancho had been a member of it for years and had checked out on a pilot's license to fly this midget helicopter.

And I learned from the major that the day before, when Pancho had taken off for what I thought was that crazy run around that village, he had been willing to trade his lunch hour for a chance to reconnoiter the outskirts of the village, looking for a good landing strip for his helicopter.

The only truly crazy thing about Pancho was that he had got himself so churned up about the Vietnamese civilians that he would lay out $2,500 of his own money for something he hoped would let him help them more.

Now we heard the rattle of Pancho's jeep. I told the marine major good-by and said the toughest part of a job like mine was running into nice guys and never seeing them again. The major said you could never tell; maybe we would meet some place.

SAIGON

AT the Majestic the slant-eyed, French-speaking little floor waiters and room boys greet me almost as an old friend; the glass in the French doors giving onto the balcony still shakes from distant explosions (theirs? ours?); and a letter is waiting from Kathrine in Hong Kong—so lovely a place, she writes, that she is staying on so that we may see some of it together.

But at the Pan American office I find that Saigon is even harder to leave than it was to get into. It will be several days before I can get away; therefore I accept the invitation of friends to go out to Cholon for dinner. This is Saigon's Chinatown, founded 300 years ago and now grown to half a million. It is a copy of the huge Chinatown in Bangkok—its signs in gold Chinese characters on a red background, replacing the Roman letters that the departed French imposed on the Vietnamese.

Early in 1968, Cholon was to be the scene of the heaviest fighting in the Saigon area. Why here? A repetition, I think, of the tragedy of all the Chinatowns of Asia. Were the Chinese in Vietnam really pro-Communist, they could have gone back to China. But as Communist power moves toward them, dare they resist? In the event of a take-over they would be doubly punished—as Chinese traitors to Chinese Communism. Small wonder they dared not refuse housing and some support to VC infiltrators. But tonight Cholon is still a friendly Chinese town, and in this restaurant are many Vietnamese, for they (like the Japanese) often prefer Chinese cooking.

My friends say that these Cholonese are in deep trouble. They are overwhelmingly "non-political" which means that they hope only to be let alone, an objective shared by most of the human race, but hard to attain out here in Southeast Asia, where in Cholon the Red Chinese have been recruiting pro-Maoist, teenage Chinese assassins. These venomous brats are equipped with tommy guns and mounted on Hondas. First they gunned down the editor of Cholon's leading Chinese-language newspaper (it was not sufficiently respectful of Mao). Then they bagged (also on the street and in broad daylight) the headmaster of one of Cholon's Chinese-language schools (it gave no instruction in "Mao's Thoughts"), darting away from both murders on Hondas which defy pursuing police cars because they can weave in and out of ordinary traffic. More killings are expected, and the Cholon Chinese are increasingly upset and fearful.

The next few days I spend at the Majestic, either typing up notes or talking with reporters, seeking to understand this lovely, tragic land and this explosively controversial little war. However did we get here?

In a sense we Americans followed the French, who arrived about a century ago, who departed only in 1954, and who in that interval built the city of Saigon on the site of a few fishing villages. They first appropriated, as a colony, Cochin China, which is roughly the Delta whence I have just come, and Saigon was its capital. Along the coast to the north of it

two "emperors" ruled—one from Hué governing Annam, one
from Hanoi governing Tonkin. To the west, similar native
princelings presided over Laos and Cambodia. Around 1840,
French missionaries began to penetrate most of the territories.
They survived occasional massacres and built churches,
schools, and hospitals. By the 1880's the French controlled
all Indo-China.

As for education, authorities do not agree on the French
settlers' role. One group blames the French for wiping out
the old mandarin system, which they insist was widespread
and which followed traditions of the Chinese Empire.
Another praises the French for giving Indo-China its first
taste of Western education, building its first university in
Hanoi, and establishing *lycées* in the larger towns and con-
vent schools in the villages. Certainly French schools drew
the upper and middle classes of Indo-China into our Western
civilization, if we can agree that this was an advantage. In
one way, at least, it was a mixed blessing. Young Indo-
Chinese flocked to their university at Hanoi and then to the
Sorbonne in Paris, with the result that there are more Vietnamese doctors today practicing in Paris than in all their
war-torn homeland, where the need is desperate.

French education also brought to Vietnam the Roman
alphabet, a modified version of it being used to give the
phonetic values of the local dialect, all books and newspapers
now being so written. But it displaced the old Chinese
ideograph characters, universally understood by Mongoloid
millions from Tokyo to Singapore, a unifying link as important as that of Latin in medieval Europe. Today in Vietnam these beautiful and enormously useful characters survive
in Cholon. As for the rest of Vietnam, only a few of the very
old remember them, and the French have saddled both Vietnams with a written language useless outside the country.

Authorities agree that the French did not exploit Vietnam;
their schools, hospitals, roads, and peace-keeping soldiers

brought great prosperity and a vastly increased population. To say, as did Franklin Roosevelt in 1944, that the people of Indo-China are "worse off than they were at the beginning" and that "France has milked them for a hundred years" is nonsense. When the French took over in about 1880, the population was 10 million; when they marched out in 1954 it was almost 30 million.

Yet French mistakes were serious, and they were slow to correct them. Whereas in India the civil service was largely staffed by Indians well trained by the British, a hopeful Indo-Chinese graduate of the French university at Hanoi found that government posts in his own country were reserved for the French who, if they deigned to grant him any job at all, gave him a fraction of the pay a Frenchman got for the same work. This the French began to correct only in the late 1920's, but in the Vietnam army they moved still more slowly. Even after World War II its officers were almost entirely French. So under French rule the best of Vietnam's youth avoided the army as a career, since they could hope to end up only as sergeants under French officers. Vietnam's current Vice-President, Air Marshal Ky, was a sergeant when, in the French Air Force, he bombed rebel nationalists in Algiers.

If today the top officer corps of Vietnam's army is mediocre, Vietnamese, agreeing, will angrily insist that it goes back to that colonial situation. After the French left Vietnam, these former sergeants promoted themselves to high rank to replace their former French officers. If they make indifferent colonels and generals, they are even less fit to administer the civil affairs of provinces, to which the military Junta has assigned them as governors; hence the tepid enthusiasm of the Vietnamese for this government the United States has been supporting. . . .

Yet, sitting in my room as I waited for that Hong Kong plane, I could then be most hopeful. After four years of delay (for which we had paid in blood and treasure) the military situation in the villages was at least back to where it was when Diem fell. The Vietnamese press was free and one honest election had at long last been held. Others were scheduled to follow. True, those earnest men from the villages who were drafting the constitution in the old French opera house had been having their troubles.

There was, I knew, a delicate situation between those delegates and the military Junta, which had summoned this Assembly only under strong pressure from America. The Junta wanted, in the constitution, a strong central government with only limited power to the legislature; the Junta furthermore had veto power over anything the Assembly did, as the Assembly well knew. But both wanted to avoid a break. So some things that the Assembly wanted had never got to debate, but had been taken up "through channels" with Ky and his Junta.

One such matter was a proposal to put in the constitution a provision that no military man could run for president. The day this might have come up for debate, there were three uniformed visitors in the gallery overlooking the Assembly: Brigadier General Nguyen Ngoc Loan, head of Ky's secret police, with two equally tough-looking officers, their tunics bulging with what seemed to be side arms, coldly running sharp black eyes over the little assembly. So the proposal did not get to the floor that day . . . nor on any other.

A related proposal also got stopped in its tracks by the Junta. Even we Americans knew the people were tired of military rule; any ticket the Junta put up, we felt sure, would get snowed under. But some of the Vietnamese (they turned out to be right) were not so sure. Because, suppose there were several tickets in the field, representing, maybe, regional groups. Might they not divide the Junta's opposition? The cure proposed was for a run-off election—the two presidential candidates with the highest vote then facing each other in a final election. But when this also failed to get off the ground and into debate, we did not think it greatly mattered. Maybe its proponents were borrowing trouble. Political parties of real meaning would soon be free to emerge and debate the nation's problems; for instance, they would adopt whatever degree of land reform the people felt was wise.

For land reform cuts two ways, and depends on which you want: votes or food. If it is only votes, then by all means land reform, for ten tenants can outvote one landlord in any country. But if you want food, then land must be farmed with thrift and skill, which often means large tracts managed by smart owners working for a profit. If some of the proposed land-reform plans for Vietnam were imposed on our country—cutting sizable farms into small tracts—we would be reduced to starvation in a year. Yet it is not a pretty situation when, as our side takes back control of a region, a landlord hooks a ride in a military truck to repossess rice paddies divided by the VC into five-acre plots.

But let the next legislature decide. It can take care of land reform, and clean out corruption, too. Only then can things start moving for our side.

For as I saw it on that last evening in Saigon, only about half the people of the country were deeply involved in this war—either on our side or with the VC. The other half might not care for the VC, but they also had no desire to be ruled by that clique of Saigon generals, from whom lesser officers sometimes bought administrative jobs, jobs that enabled them, in turn, to put on the squeeze, down to the village level. Even draft deferments could be bought, as the Vietnamese well knew.

Why had we Americans not insisted on free elections years ago? Maybe because Washington had listened to those experts who argue that it is naïve to think that Asians either want or can cope with Democracy. So Washington had avoided this naïveté and we had paid the price for sophistication.

But at last, I was sure, we had learned. I was leaving not only with hope but with something close to love for those gentle, hard-working Vietnamese people and their lovely land.

Now I stare at those final notebook lines, scribbled at my desk under Charlie Murphy's cockroach on that night before take-off . . .

"A wonderful story—wish I could be here longer."

After we left, South Vietnam went to the polls. It has 17 million people of whom 8.5 million are old enough to vote. But 2.5 million of these live in areas then controlled by the VC, which leaves 6 million free to register, of whom 5.8 million did. On election day, 4.8 million went to the polls, but of these only 1.6 million voted for the military Junta's Thieu-Ky ticket. But, because the remaining 65.2 per cent was divided among 10 tickets, Thieu and Ky with only 34.8 per cent had the leading plurality.

Why did Washington proclaim this as a victory for the Junta? If it was, then Barry Goldwater scored a greater victory, when in 1964 he got 38.9 per cent of our popular vote. The election figures give an insight into Vietnamese public opinion that has been badly neglected. Where, for instance, was the VC? True, no candidate suspected of VC sympathies was allowed on the ballot, but a Dove emerged. He was Truong Dinh Dzu, a Saigon lawyer and a former president of Saigon's Rotary Club who, after he had been certified as a candidate, came out for an immediate bombing halt and direct negotiations with the VC.

In the election Dzu ran second. Is Dzu a Communist? This is not likely. His platform did not demand abject surrender, and was not far from the position of Senator Fulbright. He did badly in Saigon but, significantly, his best vote came from areas where the VC is strongest.

What matters is that Dzu's pro-VC vote was only 17.2 per cent of the total, and not quite half the percentage received even by the unpopular Junta ticket. His 17.2 per cent is about what is polled by Communist candidates in French and Italian elections. Should we be shocked to find a similar per cent in Vietnam?

There remained nine other presidential tickets which were both anti-VC and anti-Junta. One criticized the Junta for not fighting the war with vigor; almost all of them attacked it for corruption. Together, these nine tickets attracted 52 per cent of the votes.

In this same election Vietnam was choosing a senate of 60 members, but again from a complicated system of 48 contending slates of which the high six were to be chosen. In the senatorial election, a clear anti-Junta pattern emerges, for the front-runner of the winning six, which called itself the Farmer-Worker-Soldier ticket, although critical of the Junta strongly supported the war. Among the 48 slates were several which could be called "Dove": not one was among the six winners.

Then followed elections for 137 members of the house, from which no clear national pattern emerges, since the issues often were regional—16 seats, for instance, having been assigned to ethnic minorities: Montagnards, Chams, and Khmers, linguistic islands scattered throughout South Vietnam's 14 provinces. But clearly this house can speak for the country.

Following the elections President Thieu had a choice. Even though his ticket had got only 34.8 per cent of the votes, he could have won the confidence of the country by picking a coalition cabinet from among those able, loyal, civilian leaders who had done well in the election. Instead, his first cabinet contained few civilian names. It was the same with his appointees to the governorships of provinces. Both were largely a reshuffling of colonels and generals.

Then came the VC's February 1968 Tet offensive which took the Junta by surprise. Because it was cut off from the people, its intelligence was bad, half its army away on leave, and the VC were able to bring up their new Russian mortars within range of Vietnam's major airfields and cities. The rice farmers knew. But why should they risk their lives to give this information to a government they had tried to vote out of office?

Even so, the VC failed to spark a people's uprising. Their spark hit wet powder. In Saigon, although they briefly held the American Embassy and the radio station, the people failed to answer the VC call. In the panic which followed, the Junta asked the legislature for emergency powers for one year. Both houses voted it down by crushing majorities. Who should be surprised? A move to follow this with a vote of lack of confidence failed by a hair's breadth to get on the floor for a vote.

What Vietnam needs most urgently from us is not more American divisions to prop up the Junta, but more American brains who will insist that this Junta respect the will of its own people. For, if we are not fighting to free the Vietnamese people, why are we there? We insist that we wish to free them, and as a result of the Tet offensive put pressure on the Junta to clean house. Bowing, they shot a token lieutenant for corruption. It was not enough, and pressure continued from our Embassy and Vietnam's legislature.

Even before peace negotiations opened at the Majestic in Paris in the spring of 1968, there were signs of progress in South Vietnam. Its legislature, having established its independence by standing up to the junta, passed by an overwhelming vote an even tougher draft law than the junta recommended, and presumably ended a situation under which draft exemption could be bought.

Presently the Thieu government (probably under American urging) gave a cabinet position to Phan Quang Dan, that graduate of Harvard's School of Government who had so impressed me when, as a member of the Constituent Assembly, I interviewed him in Saigon. The Thieu Government then boasted that the acquisition of Dan entitled it to claim the support of more than half Vietnam's voters, instead of only the 34.8% which the Thieu-Ky ticket had got in the election. But then Dan, later visiting in America, was quoted as saying that if America and North Vietnam could negotiate in Paris, he did not see why Saigon might not open talks with the VC. For this opinion he was fired from his newly acquired Saigon cabinet post.

The Thieu Government's treatment of Truong Dinh Dzu, Saigon's Dove of Rotary who in the election ran second (17.2% of the vote) because he advocated a bombing halt, is equally baffling. Following the election Dzu was put under house arrest, and since then has been de-jailed and re-jailed for expressing kindred opinions. While one may disagree (as I do) with such dove-ish cooings, is jail a proper rebuttal in a land which is fighting for its freedoms?

Mao in his "Thoughts" points out that a guerrilla swims like a fish in the sea of the peasant masses. It is also true that these masses will support such fish only when they have little liking for their government, as is now the case in Vietnam.

In the 1967 election, the masses tried to rid themselves of the military dictatorship, but failed for reasons we have seen. So more American troops are not the answer. Thieu should more drastically re-shuffle his cabinet and administration, bringing in more men who, in that election, proved they had popular confidence. When the peasants know that their own chosen men are running the war and the country, this will make all the difference, and the guerrillas will be flopping around like fish out of water, no matter how many missiles the Russians unload in Hanoi.

But in both Vietnams the people know that American public opinion will decide the struggle. Therefore, as delegates talked in Paris, the positions of our American presidential candidates and our public-opinion polls were being followed as intently in Saigon as in Hanoi. An American president, broken on this Vietnam issue, had abdicated his political future. This meant an interregnum until a newly chosen president could take office in 1969. And then, what would we do? Stand firm in defense of freedom for the South, backing some government its people could respect? Or perhaps cave in by agreeing to some VC coalition that would ultimately mean the end of hope for freedom in South Vietnam?

By the Fall of 1968 the Thieu government had made progress in house-cleaning; replacing stupid and often corrupt officers with competent civilians as province chiefs, and bringing into its cabinet men whose popularity reflected the mood of the 1967 elections. These included "Big Minh," a general popular with Vietnam's Buddhists, who was brought back from exile.

At the end of October, as President Johnson announced the pre-election halt in the bombing of North Vietnam the Thieu government, whatever its remaining imperfections, had a far more valid claim to represent a free people than had Ho's monolithic regime in the North.

HONG KONG

THE city of Hong Kong, built on hills that rise from the blue Pacific to form its magnificent harbor, is as beautiful and as unreal as an illustration for a fairy tale by Maxfield Parrish or Aubrey Beardsley.

Writers sometimes invidiously refer to it as the "candy shop" of the Orient. Taking another approach, it could be said that the most beautiful things of our world have been gathered into five places: Paris, Rome, London, New York, and the island of Hong Kong, which may well outrank them all. For although to this duty-free port come useful or ornamental things from the ends of the earth, only here can you buy the fabulously lovely art of the great Chinese civilization.

Sometimes you feel you are being offered fragments of a great tragedy. Just as, following the Bolshevik revolution, the contents of the czar's summer palace turned up on sale in New York, here in Hong Kong you may buy lovely things of jade, ivory, porcelain, and bronze, shipped in from Red China, which could only have come from the liquidated homes of Chinese who had cherished them for generations. It is probably true that Red China is reserving samples of all the Grade A works of art for its museums on the mainland. It is also true that the Grade B+ items they have put on sale here in Hong Kong, to get gold, would rate a high place in any museum of our Western world.

One of Europe's most costly chinas is Lowestoft, a name used for dishes and platters imported from China by the British in the eighteenth century. Platters that survive sometimes bring a thousand dollars. On Hong Kong's Cat Street merchants sell china, recently arrived from the mainland, which is even older and more beautiful for a fraction of that price.

A cherished American antique is Canton China. Around 1830, in the days of the tall clipper ships engaged in the tea trade, American skippers sailing out of Boston, New York, and Philadelphia brought home to their wives dinner sets of this white and blue ware. They were then handed down as heirlooms, and now often turn up in antique shops.

Since Hong Kong is the seaport for Canton (Kwangtung) province, here surely we would find Canton china. We found that they remembered it, but said that, because of its crude workmanship, it was here called "coolie ware," and years ago had been replaced by better-quality china even on the mainland.

The Communist Chinese import elephant tusks which their craftsmen carve into gracefully curved and tapering ladies and mandarins. They also make ornate furniture of what we call the Chinese Chippendale period, with much (if not quite all) of the old grace in line.

Yet Hong Kong is more than just a Chinese Communist outlet. Here are the famous Mikimoto pearls from Japan, but in Hong Kong the necklaces are better matched and somewhat cheaper than in Tokyo. Here are the best Thai silks and cotton textiles from India, almost as cheap as they were in Bangkok and New Delhi. Hong Kong tailors will unroll bolts of the best British woolens—cashmere and even vicuña—as cheap as you can buy them in England. Here shoemakers buy alligator skins, tanned and cured in France, and of this hide or of other leathers will turn out custom-made shoes for a tenth of their cost in Europe.

Here are Swiss watches, and the electronic gadgetry of West Germany and Japan, often cheaper than in the homelands.

In Hong Kong we again are in one of those airline-affiliated hotels that now dot the globe: a glittering marble lobby with, in this case, an unbelievable shopping arcade.

For my first morning, Kathrine has hired a car and an English-speaking driver named Wang. The oldest part of Hong Kong, Victoria City, architecturally could be any clean, prosperous British town, abounding in names like Ice House Street, Queen's Road, Connaught Road, Wyndham Street, and Albert Road. Its center inevitably is Government House, which adjoins St. John's Cathedral. Nearby is the Cricket Club. The little city is prosperous beyond belief. This surviving vestige of British colonialism shows what free trade can do, if it is left free.

Hong Kong's people are overwhelmingly Chinese. We round-eyes (the Chinese call us "long-noses") form less than 2 per cent of the population. Of course a pink-faced governor is sent out from London, along with a staff of subordinates. But the rest—the girl who sells you stamps at the post office, the clerks and department heads where you renew your visa—are Chinese. Most of the banks, shops, and businesses—great and small—are Chinese-built, -owned, and -operated.

You are lost in this flood of Mongoloids and after a week they become your standard of comparison. It is the occasional European you meet who looks out of place. The trim, graceful little Chinese women with their liquid, black eyes look prettier than over-sized Western women.

Yet on the Hong Kong Chinese, the British stamp goes deep. The men wear black suits, white shirts, dark ties as in London. But Hong Kong has no beatniks: the long-haired Flower People have little appeal to the youth of Hong Kong. When at four o'clock school is out, the streets swarm with charming Chinese children in neat, British school uniforms. And like the British, the Hong Kong Chinese have wonderful public manners. They queue up for busses or to buy tickets on the Kowloon ferry; none would dream of shoving. . . .

But back to Wang, who has now driven our car onto the ferry that will take us over to Kowloon, only a few minutes away, a peninsula that, in its shops and hotels, is only an extention of the island city. On the ferry we learn a little about Wang. He is a native of Hong Kong. But when, after Pearl Harbor, the Japanese took over Hong Kong (they stayed, he says, for three years and eight months), Wang and his family walked for days to rejoin relatives on the mainland, returning only after the Japanese left in 1945.

Ahead of us is a big truck loaded with large clay jars, which Wang says hold century (hundred-day-old) eggs. These jars, he tells us, are probably empty, the eggs having been sold in Hong Kong; the driver is taking the jars back to Red China for more eggs. City people, Wang says, do not know how to make them. Duck eggs are coated with a paste of moistened rice hulls, ashes, and clay, and then buried in jars for the required hundred days. Would we like to see some?

He parks in front of a big department store, owned and operated by the government of Red China. Prices in this Communist department store, Wang tells us, are lower than in their mainland stores, because the Red Chinese government wants the gold it gets by selling in Hong Kong. Inside the store everything is sparkling and modern, including the escalators to the higher floors. The century eggs are in the store's grocery section, still in their hardened coat of rice hulls and ashes—three for one Hong Kong dollar (that is 17 American cents, so the eggs are 6¢ each). Nearby are bottles of ginger, also at a Hong Kong dollar each. The store is well stocked with all the Chinese gourmet items, but why no shark fins?

Wang says they come from the waters around the South Pacific islands, are dried, and then shipped to Chinese grocery stores in Singapore, Bangkok, Cholon, San Francisco, Honolulu, and of course Hong Kong. Once they were prized all over the Chinese mainland but now are almost unknown there, and this store sells only the products of Red China.

On other floors there are bolts of silk and fabulous Swatow embroidery. For generations knowledgeable women the world over have revered Swatow, which is most popular in the crenelated "Wall of China" pattern. Hours of skilled work go into every square inch. When China was in revolutionary ferment such products were bitterly denounced by the Left: it was shameful that Chinese women should ruin their eyes turning out table linen for idle women of the Western world.

Freed from feudalism, the women of Swatow are now back at those embroidery frames, their needles again turning out table linen for export, in the old patterns but with one variant. At the Red Chinese department store we saw Swatow table linen exquisitely embroidered with portraits of Chairman Mao.

In the store we also find a large LP record section, Chinese Communist ski jackets, and clothing of all kinds—Western garb and traditional Chinese. There is a vast and staggeringly beautiful antique section—ivories, lovely Ming porcelain at tempting prices. But none may we buy. The Red Chinese would eagerly take our dollars, but our American customs people would confiscate anything that came from Red China.

Communist China's craftsmen are producing new designs.

In the jade section is an exquisitely carved Chinese partisan
with a rifle, pointed up to the exquisitely carved little
American bomber he is engaged in shooting down, the jade
B-52 suspended by an almost invisible thread. In the ivory
section there is a carving of a fat, scowling landlord, sitting
at an ivory table, while before him grovel five gaunt ivory
peasants. Standing beside the landlord, with an ivory sneer
on his face, is a muscular figure holding a whip: the landlord's "bully." In style the ivories are a tri-dimensional
version of Daumier's ink drawings, with suggestions of
Hogarth. How true is it to any reality in Old China? I was
never there.

On our tour we pass through the New Territories, "new"
because they were acquired in the 1890's. Queen Victoria's
government leased them from the Dowager Empress for a
hundred years, to provide more elbow room for the little
Crown Colony of Hong Kong. The population has swollen
by refugees to a million and a half people, with another two
and a half million living in these New Territories which,
Wang says, raise 20 per cent of Hong Kong's food. The
balance of the food comes from Red China, some brought
in by truck but most coming into Kowloon by the railway.

We pass block after huge block of seven-story housing
units that shelter refugees from Red China who from time
to time, pushed by political upheaval or famine, arrive in
waves. They had built for themselves, up the hillsides, countless acres of makeshift hovels without running water or
sewage and hence a health hazard to Hong Kong. This new
housing, perched on the side of a 3,000-foot hill, replaces
the hovels. Each block of apartments, built on terraces, has
shops on the ground floor and on top an open-air school.
A family gets a room about 12 × 14 feet square, renting
for $3.00 (U.S.) a month, and there is a communal kitchen
on each floor.

This is, however, no manifestation of a welfare state, for

the British taxpayers do not have surplus pounds to house refugees from Red China. The colonial government condemns the land and then sells it to private Chinese investors who agree to follow standard plans in building these units. Even if the British government makes money on them, Wang says, the housing units are a boon to the refugees who, when they have been here for five years, get Hong Kong citizenship. The buildings also accommodate middle-class Chinese families, who pay $14 (U.S.) a month for a bed-sitter with kitchen. The investment must pay off, for the mainland Communists have put up the money for several of them, operating probably through their Bank of China, an imposing modern skyscraper not far from the Cricket Club and the Hilton Hotel in Victoria. Communism and capitalism are cozy neighbors in Hong Kong where the Red Chinese also operate a number of factories.

There is the Hong Kong story that a Communist-owned shipbuilding firm was low bidder on an order for a number of small river craft needed by our navy for use in Vietnam. The deal fell through at the point when both sides realized that, if the story got out, it could be acutely embarrassing to each. The story may not be true, but it could be.

The Red Chinese also own two Hong Kong newspapers, high in decibels of noise if low on circulation, and a number of Hong Kong Chinese have become rich by representing the mainland government in these and other commercial ventures here, some even sending their sons to Peking University as an earnest of their loyalty to Communism, while they are also quietly proud of the fact that they are occasional guests at black-tie dinners in Government House. Friends tell us that during the Communist riots here, when there were rumors that the mainland might take over, these rich Hong Kong Communists were in a panic. Such a take-over would mean that they would have to liquidate their Mercedes automobiles, their concubines, perhaps even their No. 2 wives, and get whittled down to size.

Elections in Hong Kong? Who wants them? Certainly not that handful of Communists here, for the beating their candidates would take would bring massive loss of face. A Chinese who really wants to live under Communism need only get on that green train at Kowloon station, and in hardly an hour is far enough into the mainland to have all he wants of Communism for the rest of his life. Nor do the non- or anti-Communist Chinese want elections, which might force them to make a public anti-Communist record that, in the event of a mainland take-over, might mean their lives.

All the people in Hong Kong know that the mainland, when it is ready for a take-over, could do it even without need to overwhelm the tiny British garrison. Four fifths of Hong Kong's food and as much of its water come from mainland China. Even in luxury hotels the valves of water lines supplying toilets are screwed almost shut so that, when you press the porcelain button, barely a trickle comes into the bowl. During our visit Hong Kong's reservoirs were low, and requests to Chinese Communist functionaries in adjoining Kwangtung Province for more water went unanswered.

Yet, as Macaulay's schoolboy well knows, the mainland Communists need Hong Kong far more than do the British, for from it they get that yearly half billion in gold that they usually need to buy Canadian wheat for their people. So the mainland Communists allow the British Empire here to jog along, little changed in the times of Elizabeth II from what it was in Victoria's day. The British only see to it that the streets are clean and safe by night, and that mail is delivered. From there on out, you are on your own.

Education? Under Britain's colonial system, this is no business of the government, beyond a small subsidy to a church-connected school; therefore the Chinese here provide their own schools. Some were started by the Communists, but the Hong King Chinese, wanting their children to learn more than the teachings of Chairman Mao, have organized schools of their own. And well-to-do Chinese here are developing a University of China, which will preserve the old culture for the overseas non-Communist Chinese. Who knows how many of them there are? I have heard it put as low as 20 million and as high as 40. In this city of 4 million there are only a few thousand Communists, attracted to Communism largely by the privileged position they hope to hold in case (or when) a take-over comes. True, they exercise control of some (not most) of Hong Kong's labor unions, but it is no tighter a grasp than Communist leaders had on some American unions back in the 1930s.

In the summer of 1967, during the Red Guard turmoil on the mainland, came a test of Communist power in Hong Kong when the Communists called their transport unions out on strike, hoping to paralyze the city. It lasted briefly, for the rank and file presently returned to work, were protected by Hong Kong's police (all Chinese) from harassment by Communist thugs who screamed that the police were "running-dogs of the imperialists." The police lines held, but several police were killed and someone started a fund for them. This set off an explosion of Chinese gratitude to their police; dollars poured in, even the tiniest peddler and ricksha coolie eager to contribute.

So Hong Kong's Communist strategists, finding that both the city's masses and their own union rank and file were against them, turned to terrorist bombs (Viet Cong style) placed by hired gangsters at random throughout the city. And a few were not quite so random. One, for instance, was put in a taxi and murdered Hong Kong's most popular radio personality, who had built up a listening audience by making fun of Chairman Mao and his Red Guard. This murder backfired on the Communists and the harassment has been called off (at least temporarily) on orders from the mainland.

We continue our drive through the housing units and overtake a ricksha. We had seen many in India, still more in Saigon, and even more out in Vietnam's villages. Why so few here? we ask Wang. Because taxis are faster and almost as cheap. The best rickshas in Hong Kong—new and very clean—are in front of the Hilton, he explains, and maintained for the use of its guests. These need cost us nothing for we can walk through the Hilton's lobby and get into one, pretending we are Hilton guests. Not far from the Hilton, Wang says, is a public ricksha stand, and the average rate is 64¢ an hour.

We are now out in open country. Peasants are working the fields, one wearing not a circular straw hat but a European-style pith helmet. From his neck yoke dangle two buckets, and he dribbles water on seedlings.

Presently in the near distance we see a walled village above which protrude tile roofs, in the old Chinese style. Wang says it is very old and that all the people in it have the same family name. Outside the walls, the village inhabitants are squatting in the fields, giving loving care to the flowers and vegetables.

Then Wang takes a side road that climbs a hill. Halfway up we enter a parking lot for two dozen cars, and from there we get that coveted glimpse across the sluggish little Sum Chan River into Red China. On the other bank we see rice paddies but no farm houses, and in the far distance a clean-looking, white-painted village. It was at this point along the border that the Red Guard from that village played their little harassing game of kidnaping (and then releasing) Hong Kong border police.

We tarry at the car park just long enough for Kathrine to buy one of those round peasant straw hats Chinese women wear while working in the fields—a modification of the conelike oriental straw hats we have seen ever since arriving in Bangkok. Here the slight difference is a hole in the center of the crown, and a six-inch flounce of shirred black cotton voile that hangs from the round brim. Kathrine is sure that back home it will be fetching.

There is, at the souvenir stands, a low hum of excitement. Princess Alexandra, visiting this Crown Colony incognito, is scheduled to come here this afternoon, and these Chinese subjects of the distant British crown are full of friendly curiosity to see a real British princess. Just as we leave, sure enough our car passes hers—a sleek Rolls-Royce, no doubt provided by His Excellency the Governor—with the Princess in the back seat, eager as we to catch a glimpse of the sluggish border river and the white-painted Communist Chinese village on the horizon.

Returning to Hong Kong by another route, we parallel the railway tracks, and presently a neat-looking dark green British train rattles past us on its way to the border where, Wang says, the passengers get out, cross the river on a wooden bridge, and board a Communist train on the other side which goes to Canton and then on to Peking.

In normal years, he says, as many as half a million Hong Kong Chinese take this train to visit relatives in nearby Canton during the Chinese New Year. But in this Year of the Goat, because of Red Guard troubles, only about 10,000 risked a trip. Because who knew whether the Red Guards would honor their Hong Kong passports, permitting their return? Red Chinese, says Wang, are not allowed out to Hong Kong, except for officials on government business. Nor could Hong Kong give immigrants entrance visas, for the city now is crowded far beyond capacity, as we have seen.

A spur leads off our highway into a cute little Chinese village, and distantly we see its market square. Kathrine asks Wang to stop, and wonders if she might buy there another of those New Territories hats. He assures her that this will

be no "plobrem," which brings up another ancient Mongoloid hallmark—that difficulty with L and R sounds. Wang,
as a subject of Elizabeth II, has mastered the European R
sound but is uncertain as to just when to use it.

On our way into the village we pass a little procession—
mostly of teen-age boys, some banging drums and others
clanging cymbals. Its center is two boys who have a painted
cloth cover over them, forming the front and hind legs of
some animal with a fierce face and a yellow tail, the animal
swaying back and forth as the other boys prance around it.

Wang says this is a "Ryan Dance" (we are bewildered,
but then, of course—"Lion Dance!") and quickly we recognize the noble features of the Ryan, majestic as Metro-
Goldwyn-Mayer's.

In the village square we get out to see the tiny shops.
One has high piles of New Territory hats, and Wang handles
the bargaining; they are cheaper than the first we bought
for here they supply farmers, not tourists. Nearby is a food
shop where shrimp at least seven inches long are frying in a
shallow pan. Again Wang does the buying; three of them for
80 cents Hong Kong, which is about 15 of our cents. We peel
them, eat the tail meat and then suck the shells, particularly
the inside of the head, which Wang says is "very important
for Chinese people."

The Communists denounce Hong Kong as an "evil-
smelling and malignant growth on the body of China" where
the people are "oppressed by brutal colonial masters." I can
document this to the extent that some Chinese resent the
British prohibition, in Hong Kong, against the eating of
dog, even in private homes. In the good old Chinese days,
dog was a delicacy prized by emperors and probably still
adorns the lavish banquets that Peking tenders to visiting
European Communists. Charles Collingwood of CBS reports
that dog was twice included in the menu of banquets served
him in Hanoi.

But not just any dog. For the Chinese breed special strains for the market, just as we prize Black Angus steer for steaks. Yet here in Hong Kong, under the heel of imperialist oppression, dog is far harder to come by than is LSD in New York, and when it is to be had at all, chopsticks loaded with succulent pieces of it must be unburdened behind closed shutters, drawn curtains, and locked doors.

For the rest, British imperialism, here in Hong Kong as in the past throughout the world, allows the natives to follow their own customs in matters of food, religion, and sex "so long," to paraphrase the late Mrs. Patrick Campbell, "as they do not frighten the horses."

Most Hong Kong Chinese do not avail themselves of the Christian marriage rites in St. John's Cathedral. One patriarch of considerable affluence maintained one Chinese family in Hong Kong and another in Singapore, where he had business of equal importance, dividing his time between both cities and families and on trips, carrying the liquid assets of his fortune in a brass-bound ebony box. Finally, full of years and honors, he died in Hong Kong and the Hong Kong branch fell heir, not only to the Hong Kong real estate, but to the ebony box as well. The other branch made no complaint; the Singapore real estate was considerable. As for the ebony box, where it would end up had always been a gamble. And the Chinese are great gamblers.

On our way out of this village, with its rich smells of frying food, preserved ginger, exploded firecrackers, and more or less open plumbing, we return to the highway, packed now with the shiny automobiles of Chinese middle-class families returning from their Sunday afternoon drive out into the New Territories, as New Yorkers drive out on Long Island or up into Connecticut.

To escape this jam, Wang again turned off at a British-style country hotel overlooking a valley. Tea, served on

immaculately white British tablecloths on a terrace overlooking the valley, comes in British-style cups, each with a
handle and a saucer (neither of which Chinese teacups ever
have) with cream on the side, wrapped sugar cubes, and a
pitcher of hot water—British in every detail. We found a
free table with difficulty, for all seemed filled with Chinese
families, their beautiful almond-eyed children playing around
the tables in impeccable British Sunday dress. Kathrine and
I were the only long-noses amongst this thoroughly Angli-
cized Chinese throng. We liked it . . . but not more than
the village so little changed from the China of a thousand
years ago.

We were to find that all Chinese, however Westernized,
have deep emotional ties to the mainland. When, in Peking,
Communists insult foreign diplomats, the Hong Kong
Chinese suffer agonies. "We Chinese are a deeply civilized
people," they will tell you. "This is unworthy of us." When
they hear of Red Guard antics: "They have turned our
youth into a barbarous rabble." And when, as a result of
this, Red China's schools were closed: "They are ruining
our youth—putting us back a generation. It will take us
years to recover." And, with Red China's achievements,
often it is again "we." When Peking announced the explosion of its first atomic bomb, all over this diaspora
Chinese faces glowed with pride. "Isn't it wonderful," they
told each other, "that we have been able to achieve the
bomb! And without Russian help!"

Here in Hong Kong, we learned, is a huge godown, or
ware house, filled with coffins of Chinese who died in San
Francisco, Singapore, Hawaii, and Jakarta, waiting the day
when the mainland people will permit them to be shipped
back for burial in their native villages, although it could
be a village the dead Chinese, in his own lifetime, never saw.

As for the living, all yearn for the day when the Motherland will have a government that will be civilized in the old Chinese tradition, a government of which they can be proud and need no longer fear.

How wonderful in Hong Kong to have a Chinese friend—in our case Sybil Wong—to order a banquet ahead, for only a Chinese has the necessary gastronomic skill. Our friend had picked a Chinese restaurant near the waterfront.

A note, here, on why the Chinese regard us as savages. Their food, they point out, is prepared in a civilized way, by which they mean that it is cooked and cut up into bite-sized pieces, so that it can be eaten with chopsticks—all of this completed in the kitchen. Only then is food brought to the table.

By contrast we Western savages put on the table the body of an entire animal—say a chicken—where it is hacked up by the host with a carving knife and fork (utensils that in a civilized home would be seen only in the kitchen). These chunks of meat are then passed to the guests, who in turn must attack them with still more of those kitchen utensils, to cut the chunks into pieces small enough to chew. Will we never learn the graces of eating?

When we were seated in the waterfront restaurant the two waitresses brought us steaming hot towels to freshen our hands and faces (some American airlines have copied this). Then came a stately procession of eight courses: chicken and walnuts; fried scallops with bamboo shoots and seaweed; shrimp with sweet-sour sauce; and then the climax: Peking duck, a huge beast, specially fattened. In addition to pieces of skin and meat that the waitresses cut for us in bite sizes, each of us had a small stack of paper-thin wheat cakes. The Chinese, with their chopsticks, folded these into a tiny bag that they stuffed with duck, scallions, and cucumbers. Then they dipped the bag into the soya sauce and popped it into their mouths. The procedure was far beyond our skill, so we compromised by taking bites of each in rotation. If the Chinese thought we were funny, they were too polite to say so.

Then followed courses of rice and mushrooms, soya-flavored; duck soup; apple slices in boiling syrup. When we dipped the apple slices into bowls of ice water, the hot syrup hardened into a crisp glaze and could be eaten. The last course was jasmine tea, which ends all Chinese banquets. Sipping this, we told the Chinese it was probably the best meal any of us had ever eaten, and worth all the time it took.

They answered that our banquet was only a shriveled vestige of banquets in the Good Old Days. These were for men only, and lasted a weekend, beginning on Friday night with a feast such as we had just finished. But then the host brought on dancing girls for an hour or so, after which the guests retired to couches and opium pipes, which sent them off into a seven-hour doze. They awakened to begin a second eight-course banquet, followed by more dancing girls and pipes, this sequence continuing until Monday morning when usually they went home, refreshed and ready for a normal business week.

We asked about Peking ducks: how do they get their delicious skin and red glaze? We learned that after the duck is cleaned, a pipette is used to pierce the skin all over its body, and air is blown between skin and meat to separate them. The duck is then hung up and brushed with a mixture of Chinese brandy, soya sauce, and brown sugar. When it has dried, the duck is brushed again; the process is repeated and repeated for about twenty-four hours.

About an hour before dinner time the duck is dropped into slowly boiling peanut oil. When the inside meat is done it is taken out and much hotter oil is poured over the outside to crisp the skin and give the golden-red color. It is then ready to serve.

We asked about the carved ivory group we had seen in the Red Chinese department store over in Kowloon—the fat landlord and the groveling peasants. Our Hong Kong Chinese friends said the display was not really exaggerated—at least not much. In the old days when there was little transportation, a drought in one region would produce starvation. Then tenant farmers sometimes had to sell their girl children to pay their rent and stay on the land. Now the peasants really were better off. But what had been done for them would have been done by any modern Chinese government, had it had the time.

In this pleasant colony of Hong Kong we get occasional whiffs of the Mainland Dragon. Close to our hotel is a Communist Chinese bookshop, one of many in Hong Kong. It could be a typical, neat, Communist bookshop in any land, sells mostly paperbacks and is presided over by a Chinese woman who is polite to curious foreigners. Judging by the English-language titles offered, everything is devoted to Mao—his works, his speeches, his life. Most popular of all are the little red-bound, prayer-book-size volumes of Mao's "Thoughts." (In the riots which were soon to come, these volumes were carried by every young Red Guard rioter.) The bookshop also sells tiny lapel pins bearing Mao's gold profile against a red enamel background.

To stamp collectors the shop offers packets of mainland issues. Some are beautiful: one series is of flowers, another of children's toys. A huge stamp bears the whiskered, catlike face of Mao's last Russian hero, Joseph Stalin. How weird to see him peeping out at us over a line of Chinese ideograph characters!

These Communist bookshops, although spotted in high-rent locations over Hong Kong, we found to be almost

empty, except for an occasional small knot of Chinese teen-
agers—neat but always wearing leather jackets, as did the
younger American Communists back in the 1930s.

For us, Hong Kong ends in a wake, for we read in the
morning paper that Henry Luce is dead. Allen and Beatrice
Grover are in transit at our hotel. When I briefly worked
for *Fortune* magazine in the late thirties, Al was one of
Harry Luce's senior executives. Kathrine's ties were closer.
She worked for Harry when *Time* was a struggling group
on West 45th Street, sharing a part of their space with the
Saturday Review and some writers with the *New Yorker*,
Time then getting its news by scissors and paste pot rather
than from far-flung correspondents. In this period Dewitt
and Lila Wallace were getting the *Reader's Digest* off the
ground from a Greenwich Village loft. Publishing giants
were the *Saturday Evening Post, Collier's,* the *Literary
Digest,* and *Life* (then a comic magazine). Where are they
now? It has been another day, but with Harry's death, even
its sun seems to be sinking.

A phone call assembles us in the Grovers' suite overlooking
Hong Kong harbor, where we order up the martinis that
will be our little wake for Harry, since we are here on the
rim of the China where he was born, and that he never
forgot. We talk of those old days, Kathrine and Al swapping
memories of Harry. Al says since we are going to Taiwan,
we should not miss the chapel that Harry built there in
memory of his parents, who as Presbyterian missionaries
devoted their lives to that China Harry loved so well, and
hoped so greatly would one day rejoin the ranks of civilized
nations.

TAIWAN

FROM the air Taiwan (which the Portuguese called Formosa) is as neat as a park, with planted terraces rising far up the sides of mountains, every inch cultivated as it must be if this banana-shaped island, about 150 miles long, is to feed its 13 million people. Taiwan has roughly the size and population density of the Netherlands. Because the island is well watered and on about the latitude of Key West, Florida, anything will grow at any time of year.

We have come here because Taiwan quivers with political interest. It is Chiang Kai-shek's Republic of China, and its government has experts on mainland China for whom other China watchers—in Hong Kong, in Tokyo, and in Seoul—have deep respect. On this island (Chiang's Elba, if you like) the top people know well the top people in Mao Tse-tung's People's Republic of China.

Chiang, America's World War II ally, in the 1920s commanded China's West Point, Whampoa Academy. Some of his cadets,

generals today, are with him here on Taiwan. Others who
worked, ate, and played with the Taiwan leaders now serve
Mao as generals on the mainland. Lin Piao, who commands
Mao's armies, and is Mao's designated successor, was a cadet
under Chiang at Whampoa.

Lin Piao? Here on Taiwan some remember him well;
remember, back in the academy at Whampoa, his great
talent for dramatics. Whenever a parade or pageant was to
be staged by the cadets, Lin served as chairman of the
Committee; no one else had his sense of showmanship.
When, years later, mainland China's army put on a vast
parade of Red Guards in Peking, marching in review before
Mao, foreign correspondents were deeply impressed, but here
on Taiwan his former classmates chuckled: "That's good old
Lin for you—doing his thing again! Anything that's show
business is Lin's business!"

In Hong Kong we had become aware of how deeply knit
all Chinese families are. A Hong Kong Chinese hearing you
are headed for Taiwan says, "You may run into Uncle Wei—
give him our love." The same man will tell you he gets
occasional family letters from Aunt Tse in Peking, with
snapshots of little nephews and nieces—how they have grown!
—which often they pass on to Uncle Wei, so that little cousins
on Taiwan may not lose touch with little cousins in Peking.
Chinese families have a horror of losing family ties. Governments are transient; the family marches on.

The city of Taipei, capital of Taiwan, certainly is not
luxurious and lovely. Here we are out of British tidiness
and back in Asia, with its haphazard dilapidation. The tone
is set by Taipei's public buildings, erected by the Japanese.
They could be copies of America's dreary public architecture
during the Cleveland administration. But they are sturdy
and still in use for, unlike many "emerging nations," Taiwan
has squandered no money on architectural showpieces.

Chiang's defeated army, arriving here in 1949, has spent all available aid money in developing the island's economy.

But in those shabby Japanese-built offices you get, from the representatives of Chiang's government, first a feel of hearty friendliness (maybe less polished than the suave Hong Kong Chinese) but, more important, a sense of brains and bustle—a strongly American tang. Also there is a slight difference in race. The great Mongoloid peoples have two subdivisions. The southern branch of the Chinese which we so far have met tend to be small, light-boned Malay types. Here on Taiwan we meet northern types—a shade taller, chunkier in build, with high cheekbones not unlike Manchurians, Japanese, and our Navajo Indians (who are also Mongoloid). The differences are slight but perceptible.

In Hong Kong when we praised a Chinese banquet our host would say, "Wait till you get to Taiwan." This they said for two reasons. One is that in Hong Kong you get Cantonese cooking which, however good, still is regional. Because Chiang's armies came from all over China, on Taiwan we would find the best dishes of every province.

We first sampled Taiwan's food at a lunch arranged for us by Jimmie Wei. Everybody knows Jimmie, from Washington to New York through San Francisco to Tokyo, and of course Hong Kong. "Oh, you were in Taipei—well, how's Jimmie?"

He is the top public-relations officer of the Nationalist government: smart, vigorous, amusing, with a knack for getting done anything you want within reason, and getting it done promptly. The American accent of his fluent English is perfect; all Americans are instantly and effortlessly on a first-name basis with him. Without ever having met me, he assembled for the lunch exactly the people he knew I would want to see. All spoke English. Half were seasoned American reporters who know Taiwan well and would have no reason to tell me less than the truth. My questions were answered without pauses or stammering.

Jimmie's lunch consisted of the standard Chinese procession of about a dozen courses, ending with soup. Its climax was Szechwan duck, which, I shall starkly state, is first plastered with moistened tea leaves, then smoked over camphor wood, and is superb. We later learned that it took the assembled talents of four nearby restaurants—each sending over a few courses via cute, slant-eyed small boys—to produce that lunch.

Between and after the courses we learned much. Almost 14 million people live on Taiwan's 14,000 square miles, of which 48 per cent are mountains, 22 per cent is sloping land (here they graze cattle and plant bananas and fruit trees), and the remaining 30 per cent is arable (rice, grain, and vegetables). For the first decade after the Nationalists' arrival this farm land got the most attention. In early 1949 Taiwan's population was 6 million; then 2 million of Chiang's defeated armies and their families arrived from the mainland, bringing the total to 8 million. The island's bulging birth rate has added most of the other six million.

But Taiwan lives in no immediate dread of over-population. The island had a census in 1956 and another 10 years later, which showed that the population had an average yearly increase rate of 3.2 per cent but that it was coming down; in the last census the increase had only been 2.6 per cent. This could be dangerously high were it not that Taiwan is even further ahead in food production. Last year's target was a 4 per cent increase but, because of favorable weather, they got a delightful 8 per cent.

Taiwan has 836,000 farm families, and as a result of land reform the average holding is about a hectare (2.5 acres). Unless on Taiwan I was given a snow job (and I doubt it) this is one of the few countries where land reform has increased production and was in fact the main reason for the increase. Under the system left by the Japanese, 64 per cent of the farmers were tenants, paying 70 per cent of their yield to landlords, which gave them small incentive to produce for the market. One could also add that maybe another motive for land reform was to make room for Chiang's newly arrived mainlanders. But whatever the reason, land reform paid off. Rice production has increased 88 per cent; sweet potatoes, 166 per cent; sugar, 430 per cent; tea and peanuts, 200 per cent; bananas, 700 per cent. Banana production, only a million baskets in 1952, has zoomed to 7.8 million, most of it going for export.

All of this, Taiwan officials boast, was gained not through government subsidies to farmers, but by providing them with incentives. In the old days middlemen got three fourths of the price; so the government encouraged co-operative marketing, which has increased the farmers' share. Beyond this, the government has seldom intervened. An exception is the case of banana production. Bananas grow well on sloping land but were so profitable in the export market that many rice farmers started to convert. The government had to step in, for each hectare must feed fourteen people on this crowded island.

Another factor in Taiwan's enormous production increase was the "brain drain" from the mainland in 1949, by which Taiwan profited at the expense of the Communist mainland. The picture you get from Chiang's enemies is that no one followed him to Taiwan but his soldiers and a few landlords, fleeing the vengeance of their tenants. The truth is that Taiwan also got the cream of China's intellectuals and of its university faculties—scholars in many fields, including some of the world's top experts in agriculture, whose brains now direct the island's farming.

Taiwan's mild climate—about 75° Fahrenheit the year round—makes two yearly crops the standard. But experts have introduced inter-cropping (new crops planted between the

rows of half-grown crops), which makes possible four crops a
year from each hectare. The experts also encourage diversifi-
cation. Formerly Taiwan exported only sugar and rice; today
it exports such luxury items as pineapple. In 1959, Hawaii's
production was six times Taiwan's; now Taiwan is even with
Hawaii, and hopes soon to pass it. It is the same with cultured mushrooms, an experiment started by the professors in
1961. Today Taiwan is the world's largest mushroom ex-
porter.

The land, these professors feel, can become the world's
most important truck garden for luxury items. Already
Taiwan's canned asparagus, pineapples, and mushrooms are
moving into markets in Japan, America, and West Germany.
At present Taiwan's best customers are America and particularly Japan, which buys Taiwan's sugar, bananas, and pineapples, paying for them in industrial products.

Taiwan has a keen interest in helping other free Asian
nations. When we were in Saigon, a delegation of agricultural experts from Taiwan arrived at the Majestic Hotel,
welcomed by banners stretching across Saigon's main boulevard: VIETNAM WELCOMES THE REPUBLIC OF CHINA'S AGRICUL-
TURAL DELEGATION—in English because Vietnamese know
most educated Taiwanese read this language. Now in Taipei
we got Taiwan's report on this visit, which had been financed
by our American AID program.

Taiwan experts had fanned out from the DMZ to the
Delta, going into the villages. They had real respect for their
opposite numbers in Vietnam—fine men, well trained, mostly
educated in France. They visited Vietnam's experimental
stations and were warmly welcomed, but reported that the
real problem of the average farmer is security. "Don't come
so early," the farmers would warn them. "Wait until about
ten-thirty, when the VC will be gone." And when the experts
got back to Taiwan, they said, "If the Americans want to

win that war, they will have to arm those rice farmers so
that they can defend their paddies."

The Taiwanese had found that their new variety of rice—
developed by the Rice Institute in Manila—had not performed well in the Delta. It has a short stem and works well
on Taiwan's slopes, where water levels in the paddies can
be controlled. But in the Delta the Mekong's monsoon
floods cannot be regulated. However, this rice has worked a
miracle in India, where yields per hectare have increased
many times over. Taiwan had sent to India several hundred
tons of it for seed. They also agreed to train several hundred
rice farmers, whom the Indian government planned to send
to Taiwan, but at the last minute the timorous Indians had
backed down. "They became afraid it might offend the Red
Chinese," the Taiwanese told me. Then in unison they
grinned.

As we return to our hotel on the outskirts of Taipei, our
taxi fights its way through dense traffic, much of it battered
American cars, but also bicycles pulling great loads and all
sorts of improvised vehicles pulled by motors or bullocks.
Unlike Hong Kong, nobody seems to be rich here. But great
numbers are comfortably well to do, and (as in Hong Kong)
everyone is decently dressed, obviously well fed, and all of
them working and happy. Or so it looks to the passing
tourist.

Our hotel, the Grand, somehow typifies the island. It was
built by the Generalissimo, of course a passionate Chinese
Nationalist, which explains its architecture. The lobby
squirms with wood carving and blazes with Chinese red
and gold leaf: clearly no Western interior decorator was
allowed to fiddle about with its fundamental *Chinoisité*.
Our rooms (U.S. $15 for a double) have Western-style beds
and plumbing above reproach of the most finicky tourist.
There is a section of the dining room where you can get,
if you insist (we did not), Western-style food.

The Grand also has gables slightly upturned at the end, which we had first noted in the wats and palaces of Thailand (in sharp contrast to the beehive-shaped temples of India) and which we were to see all the way to Japan. In the Civic Museum of Hong Kong we had seen a tiny baked clay house (perhaps a child's toy) that they said was made millennia ago. It also had these upturned gable ends.

Let us go head-on into this matter of a "Return to the Mainland." It is here as much an article of faith as is the Immaculate Conception in Vatican City—seldom mentioned because it is beyond discussion. I did not have the bad manners to bring it up. Back in Hong Kong I had broached the subject with Chinese intellectuals who had close Taiwan connections. They told me that the younger Taiwanese privately doubted that it would ever come off, but tactfully avoided expressing such doubts to their parents who, in the beginning, regarded the island only as a temporary launch pad from which to free the mainland.

Slowly, without open argument, a compromise was reached. Of course all dreamed only of The Return, but might not the best way to hasten this be to make Taiwan bloom like a garden, with high standards of living and education, thus proving to the world (maybe even to the mainland Chinese) what Chinese can do if they are truly free? All could unite on this, and on Taiwan they are proud of what they are achieving. When Chiang's armies arrived in 1949 few could read. On Taiwan today 70 per cent of the older people and 97 per cent of the younger ones are literate.

It is curious that Mao and Chiang passionately agree on many points. Both hold that Taiwan and the mainland are one and inseparable, to be united as soon as possible under one Chinese flag; the only question being which flag.

Both want to recover millions of people who are Chinese by blood and culture but were, in imperialist times, torn away and now are ruled by the Soviet Union or India. Both want these (including those in Tibet) back on the bosom of Mother China. But which mother?

Both want to see Mandarin (the spoken language of the old imperial court) established as a *lingua franca* over all China's myriad spoken dialects; Mandarin is taught in schools both in Peking and Taipei.

In these and related matters Chiang and Mao are as like as chopsticks. Beyond, a chasm gapes. Only once in my talks did I get close to that subject of "Return to the Mainland." I brought up the matter of the 46,000 fighting men which South Korea has sent to South Vietnam. I then asked if there had been any discussion of sending troops from Taiwan. I got a crisp "no." Why not? They were being held for "other contingencies."

Taiwan is one of the few "emerging" nations with enough hard sense not to crave a steel mill, or any other costly symbol of national self-sufficiency. The island has no iron ore, and what little coal it has comes in veins so thin that mechanized mining would not be profitable; so Taiwan imports most of its fuel. With imported crude oil, processed in the southern part of the island, Taiwan manufacturers are going into petrochemicals. In the northern part, a natural gas field has attracted another industrial complex (including Mobiloil and Allied Chemical), which is turning out fertilizer.

In 1960 the government offered tax incentives to industry (also open to foreign investors), and as a result light industry is thriving—textiles, consumer goods, and electronics. When we were there, twelve foreign companies (including Philips of Holland, Mitsui of Japan, and Admiral from America) were operating, while a dozen other plants were under construction.

Their system works, the Chinese told us, because the island so far has not been caught up in the wage-price spiral of our Age of Inflation. Here, food is cheap and wages correspondingly low, while in Japan both are rising, which means higher prices for the goods the Japanese hope to export. So Taiwan-made scooters and motorcycles can start out with a lower price tag. And officials told me that foreigners are surprised by the dexterity of the Chinese girls they hire. In Philco's assembly plant, the girls worked so fast that the company ran out of imported parts and had to cut back production.

Taiwan is also moving into shipbuilding, and the government hopes to expand it to 130,000 tons a year. The country has a labor force (not counting the army) of almost 4 million, of whom only 140,000 are classed as unemployed. Of the workers, 45 per cent are in agriculture; 22 per cent in mining, manufacturing, or utilities; and 22 per cent in business, transport, or communications. The future looks hopeful, particularly if Taiwan can continue to avoid the world wage-price spiral while its competitors move gloriously onward and upward toward boom-bust.

It should finally be pointed out that while the Taiwanese are grateful for American aid, they are proud that they are now almost completely off our backs. U.S. aid has dwindled to a trickle and is now mostly surplus commodities.

On our final night in Taipei we were again engulfed by Jimmie Wei's hospitality. At his behest a group of hearty young colonels in the Chinese Air Force arrived at our hotel, probably chosen because they spoke American English which they had picked up in Arizona where, during World War II, they got their flight training as cadets in Chiang Kai-shek's air force. They came with their wives in somewhat beat-up American cars and, making room for us, drove us to Taipei's newest supper club. It was like dining at a circus. The big vaudeville theater was furnished, not with rows of seats, but with round tables, each seating a dozen to accommodate the average Chinese family group.

Our table was in the front row of the balcony. As we were settled, two things simultaneously happened: the curtain rose on an act of Japanese tumblers and, from the wings, white jacketed waiters converged on the tables, bringing us the first of a nine-course Cantonese-style banquet. We began with hors d'oeuvres—cold smoked pork and pickled mushrooms.

Then followed smoked fish, with a family of Swiss bell-ringers; roast chicken, with an Italian sword swallower; shrimp, with three Portuguese slack-wire walkers; bamboo shoots, with a West German fire eater—and so on throughout the evening. Clearly the crowd loved this show (as did we) and for this high occasion were decked out in European dress. Who were they? Our hosts said most were farmers and their families, since good crops and decent prices have made them prosperous. The acts, they said, came through on a circuit that linked similar supper clubs or vaudeville theaters in Hong Kong, Tokyo, Bangkok, and Singapore.

We hire a car and driver that will take us out for a couple of hours to the Museum of Nationalist China and afterward deliver us to the airport. The car turns out to be a standard Chevrolet but seems huge to us, geared down as we are to the tiny European and Japanese cars now used on Asia's mainland. And for Taiwan the car was surprisingly new, for most of Taipei's cars are carefully preserved and repaired American models, bought from departing U.S. soldiers or government functionaries.

In the twenties and thirties, following Henry Ford's invention of the assembly line, American cars dominated the world and were our principal export item, since they were cheapest and best. Now our wage-price spiral has priced us out of the world automobile market. European and Japanese compacts under-sell similar U.S. cars even in our home market. . . .

Our two hours in the museum should have been two days.

When the cream of China's scholars left the mainland with Chiang's armies in 1949, they took with them the cream of China's art and cultural treasures—at least everything small enough to be crated. Here it is in all its variety—patina-encrusted bronze caldrons, gleaming carved jade, ceramics from all periods, some as chaste in line of pale blue ornamentation as anything turned out by the fifth-century Greeks, others as voluptuously ornate as Europe's eighteenth-century baroque. Here are examples of Chinese printing, dating centuries before Gutenberg, including the porcelain blocks on which the paper was pressed. The museum has historic examples of Chinese calligraphy, an art almost lost in the West but still treasured in China and Japan. Everything is superbly catalogued, with signs both in Chinese and in English. On the day of our visit its five floors swarmed with farmers and their wives and with clumps of bright-eyed, uniformed school children led by teachers, soaking up the culture of Old China which is their heritage.

In the matter of these treasures, Chiang and Mao are again firmly united on one point, which is that they should be removed, with all deliberate speed, back to the mainland museums whence they came. But now the differences: Mao will return them as soon as his armies recapture Taiwan; Chiang, when he lands on the mainland, will have the treasures (carefully recrated) in his baggage train.

Our watch hands pull us away from the museum and push us into the back seat of our shiny Chevrolet and out to the airport. As our bags are being lifted out, an incident: a police captain collars our driver, shouts at him angrily, and, even before I have had a chance to pay him off, sends him away under guard. When I protest, the police captain explains that they want to know how such a man got possession of so new an American car; that there are laws against this, and that the police are fighting corruption to keep their country honest.

Since our plane was being called, we had to go, and never learned the outcome. But others had told us that the government takes militant pride in the honesty and incorruptibility of its officials. This may be a reaction against the stories of American reporters who wrote, as Free China was crumbling, that Chiang's government was almost a synonym for corruption.

Why? Maybe in part because some of what we call corruption was built into the economic tradition of Old China— called "squeeze" by foreigners and accepted as legitimate by Chinese. As the boy in the Bangkok jewel shop surely got (and earned) a percentage of what we paid in the Chinese gold store.

Or the corruption once connected with Chiang could have come from the terrible inflation of the World War II years. Money voted by Congress to help Chiang in the war with the Communists never got to him, so he printed his own money; presently a clerk's monthly salary would hardly buy a meal. Whatever the case, Chiang's government on Taiwan is now militantly trying to live down the reputation it once had.

SOUTH KOREA

W E have come to South Korea because the war we Americans thought had ended in the 1953 armistice shows signs of warming up, perhaps because we have reduced our troops manning the armistice line. Or perhaps because the South Koreans have dared send a fighting force of 46,000 to South Vietnam, along with another 10,000 civilian engineers to rebuild roads and bridges.

To remind us that what we signed in 1953 was only an armistice, the North Koreans (they work closely with the Russians) have stepped up patrol activities along the line that separates the two countries, every now and then killing or wounding half a dozen Americans or ROK troops. North Koreans know how thin we are spread, needing troops to stop the burning in our home cities, needing troops in Europe and Vietnam.

South Korea is one of Asia's most crowded countries: 29 million packed into 38,000 square miles—nearly 800 for every square mile. Most of those square miles are ridges, as our boys who fought over them so well remember, with crops growing only in the valleys. Of this 29 million, 2 million were refugees who, when MacArthur briefly reached the Yalu River, ran south to freedom. Most of them crowded into shacks surrounding this city of Seoul, which had a population of 800,000 when World War II ended in 1945 and is now just short of 4 million. From 1950 to 1953 Seoul changed hands several times, and Americans who lived through that period say the war reduced it to a rubble pile. If much of its building today seems shoddy and ramshackle, what else could it be? Naturally the people are proud of the new multi-storied office buildings that rise here and there from what recently was rubble.

The Koreans are Mongoloids of the far north, which means they are more rugged and often taller than the southern branch of this yellow race. With their high cheekbones, they call to mind the Indian head on our old buffalo nickel. They are tremendously hard-working. The visitor to their country sees them pushing or pulling rickety carts piled high with merchandise over the rough streets, and often their stocky legs bear burdens piled onto big A-frames strapped on their backs, the wheel being a luxury they cannot always afford. Yet they look healthy and are warmly dressed in rough clothes.

Everywhere are reminders of the 1950–53 war. Seoul's traffic jams are made up largely of ancient American jeeps, pounded back into shape and always smartly painted. South Korea has a budding steel industry, its source largely American scrap lavishly scattered over these ridges during the war: it is still collected by thrifty people. Much of the scrap, rolled into galvanized sheets, again goes to war in Vietnam.

Aside from being crowded into this tiny country without enough land to feed themselves, the nation's great problem is that they also lack raw materials for industry. They have a little low-grade ore, but most of their supply must come from Australia. They have some anthracite coal to sell to Japan, but must import bituminous coal, coke, and oil from the United States. An international iron and steel group is putting up a plant here, but almost all of its raw materials must be imported. South Korea is forging ahead in the manufacture of plywood; they buy lumber in Canada, the Philippines, and Indonesia, and sell the finished product throughout the world. Similarly with textiles: American cotton is spun, woven, and sold to Europe. Buying wool from Australia and New Zealand, the Koreans knit it into sweaters so popular that Sweden decided to put a quota on them.

Korea lacks everything, but has one enormous asset in her rugged, hard-working people, who are capable of developing high skills. With low wage scales based on low living costs, she can profitably market these skills in an inflationary world. As Japan gets caught up in the world wage-price spiral, Koreans are delighted: this is their chance.

A millennium ago Korea was a land of high culture. Korean ceramics rivaled those of China. Even today in the antiques world, no ceramics are more highly prized, particularly in Japan, which centuries back kidnaped Korean craftsmen to teach its islanders the art.

Korea was long ruled by the Yi dynasty, founded by a general who drove out the Mongols. Yi rule ended in 1910 when the Japanese invaded the peninsula, butchered the old empress, and held the country until their World War II surrender. The current Yi heir, an M.I.T. graduate married to an American girl, is without ambition to ascend the throne.

The Japanese ruthlessly suppressed Korean nationalism and ruled the land as a *Herrenrace,* thus creating a hatred which smolders today. In what is today North Korea the Japanese built industries, leaving the southern part strictly agricultural. The Japanese language was taught in Korean schools, no Korean could rise above the status of foreman in

any factory, and there was a quota on Koreans in the civil
service. Korean patriots such as Syngman Rhee had to get
their educations abroad and live in exile.

Only after the 1953 armistice did the drive for industrializa-
tion in South Korea begin, but first the war-ravaged country
had to be rebuilt. In 1960 the aging Syngman Rhee was overthrown as a result of student riots, which reflected an im-
patience to get the country moving, and was presently
succeeded by General Chung Hee Park, who was elected
president in 1963. Is this a military dictatorship? Americans
in Seoul say yes and no, but increasingly no. President Park
has begun to replace the generals in his cabinet with civilians.
Elections are free, and a vigorous opposition can express its
views in the nation's newspapers.

But this opposition is not of the Left. There are few
socialists in South Korea, even among the student intellectuals. All parties want to get the country moving and to improve its living standards; the only dispute is which party
can do it best. For a while this crowded little country was
threatened by a population bulge of almost 4 per cent a year.
They tackled the problem, largely with the loop, and have
pulled the birth rate down to about 2.2 per cent.

With fertilizers and factories their production has been
increasing at about 8 per cent a year, and last year (because
of the war in Vietnam) hit 12 per cent. They have been
proud of their handsome fighting men in Vietnam, following
them in newsreels, glad that their soldiers have been so
successful in Vietnam's pacification program wherein they
make friends with the villagers—helping them with the rice
harvest, for example. Furthermore, the VC fear Koreans as
skillful bush fighters who, with their knowledge of karate,
can crack a guerrilla's neck without breaking his skin.

South Korea is taking a lead in bringing closer together
the free nations around the Pacific. During my visit a banner
waved across Seoul's principal boulevard, greeting the visiting

Australian premier: WELCOME THE RIGHT HONORABLE HAROLD
HOLT & MRS. HOLT! All of which will help South Korea's export trade. They hope to increase production so that they
will no longer need American help after 1971. American
grants last year were down to $40 million.

The South Koreans have a passion for education but found
that at first they had got off on the wrong foot, training too
many intellectuals and lawyers who added to the over-supply
of disappointed politicians. Emphasis has now shifted to
technological and vocational training, and education leaders
feel that their young engineers are among Asia's best.

The United States tried to help by bringing 8,000 Korean
students to American universities, but only 1,000 returned to
South Korea and of these, 500 later returned to America,
where pay was higher and living conditions not so primitive.
The brain drain caused by our help actually hurt Korea. To
stop this, President Park planned an Institute of Technology
in Seoul, but found his country could not staff it. Now Korea
is trying to re-attract Korean teachers living abroad, offering
them money for research and good living standards. The
campaign seems to be working.

The South Korea government even plans a tourist industry. By about 1970, it points out, American boys who
helped them keep their freedom in the early 1950s will be in
their middle forties, and some can afford to bring their
families to Korea to see the ridges that Daddy captured when
he was a young soldier. In Seoul tourism promoters are
planning hotels and roads that will be up to American standards.

Americans who deal with Koreans say we are most welcome
here. Nobody wants us to go home, though they are eager
for the day when they will be on their feet and no longer
dependent on us. Americans here have close Korean friends
and are often invited to Korean homes. Unlike the Japanese,
the Koreans are open, friendly, and enjoy a good argument.

The subtle Japanese never argue: a Korean will joyously pound the table in a friendly dispute.

Their attitude toward us is the reverse of an obsequious colonial. An American, entering his office smoking a cigar, reports that the comment of his Korean subordinate was: "What do you think you are—a big shot?"

But increasingly South Koreans are concerned over new threats from the north. Infiltrators, they knew, were being sent through the wire to stir up trouble. One defector told them the North Koreans were getting agents through this wire at the rate of ten a week. It came to a climax when a dozen or so converged on Seoul in a well-planned attempt to assassinate President Park and his cabinet.

Plans were afoot to execute these culprits according to due process of law when the American spy ship *Pueblo* somehow managed to get itself captured, and the suggestion was made that maybe the *Pueblo*'s crew could be traded for those North Korean agents who had failed to butcher the South Korean government. The hint did not go down well. Why should these men not be executed? If we wanted the *Pueblo*, why didn't we go in and get it? Were we going soft?

American political developments in 1968 also surprised and alarmed the South Koreans. They are not a devious people. They think to the point, and then say what they think. Since 1945, America had been the protector of all free nations on the rim of Communist China. Is America about to abandon the Pacific? If so, might not those three Korean divisions, now fighting the North Vietnamese, be far more useful back home, manning the armistice line against the North?

JAPAN

IN any land the airport tells you something of what is to come. Here in Tokyo, how clean and modern in metals and textures of wood the airport is! How smartly uniformed, efficient, and smilingly polite the Japanese officials! A smart, prosperous land at peace. Then briefly we thought—how Europeanized! The throughway into Tokyo is as modern as the complex that connects Kennedy Airport with Manhattan. The road swirls over rooftops from which rise giant neon signs, usually in Roman (not Japanese) lettering, in contrast to Hong Kong, where most such signs were in Chinese characters. Have we left Asia?

So you would think from our hotel: spectacular modern but having no link with Japan, except that it is crowded with prosperous Japanese, the men all in Western dress. Our hotel room could be in any new American motel, so we switch on TV to get our first look at the real Japan. We get a favorite of the late, late shows; but how weird to hear Clark Gable speaking Japanese! We change the channel. A Japanese girl is giving English lessons, teaching the use of our verb "suppose": "I suppose not." "They supposed." "She could not suppose that it would happen."

Next morning from our window we look out over the city. It is shoddy, ugly modern, but there is a reason. During the war old Tokyo—a city of inflammable wood, however charming—burned like a match box, and had to be rebuilt. The Japanese government forbade rebuilding in wood, so the new city went up largely in stucco-covered cinder block—hideous, but practical in any land. To see the old Japan, you must get out of the cities.

On the Ginza there is a department store that compares favorably with any of ours except that its gourmet food section has enticing items nameless to us. But elsewhere one sees Western clothes for men, women, and children. The furniture floor has reproductions of Western antiques—of New England colonial cobbler's benches and dry sinks, of fifteenth-century Spanish cupboards, and of old English milk stools—all being bought by Japanese housewives.

One surprise is the rock department. The Japanese of course love rock gardens, and the store offers choice rocks. One, of pink quartz the size of a cabbage, has been polished to reveal a freak crystalline formation in its center—a big chrysanthemum, the emblem of Japan. It is priced in yen at just a shade over 10,000 American dollars, which we thought considerable to pay for just one garden rock, a view not shared by the Japanese.

We did not need rocks, but were shopping for a pair of those immensely practical and comfortable Japanese sandals, held on by a single thong between the toes. I had worn out one pair in the Delta and needed a replacement. The shoe department handled every type of slipper, but not these. Then they understood—oh—*Japanese* slippers! Those I would find in the *Japanese* department—just take the escalator. On that particular day, in this thoroughly Americanized store, we did not see a single foreigner; its throng of shoppers was all Japanese.

Tokyo is one of the world's great news centers, and its experts (newspapermen and government specialists long stationed here) are generous with their time to a roving reporter. On any given subject largely they agree since, in a city like this, they pool their information. In Hong Kong, an unofficial group of professional China Watchers meets weekly at a little Cantonese restaurant, where resident British and American reporters swap information on mainland China with English-speaking diplomats stationed there. A guest might be a British or French tourist just back from Peking.

Although newsmen in Tokyo largely agree on facts, still each has his separate interpretation. These men agree that in Japan, we Americans for the present lead other foreigners in popularity, in so far as any foreigners can be popular in Japan, which is not very far. This Japanese craze for aping the West is superficial, as one soon finds outside of Tokyo.

The Japanese government realizes that the nation's great strides are possible only because America has shouldered the defense costs of a disarmed Japan. This truth is slowly percolating into the opposition parties and down to the people. Similarly the government realizes that, in Vietnam, we are trying to hold the line against a bit-by-bit take-over by Communism of all Free Asia. This realization is also filtering into opposition parties. It was greatly strengthened by the Red Guard turmoil in China, which shocked the Japanese. They saw that mainland Communism was becoming, not more civilized, but more violent and nationalistic. Even Japanese Communists began edging closer to the Russian branch.

Yet Japanese intellectuals are still hostile to our Vietnam war: fanatical students who attacked an American military hospital caring for wounded flown in from Saigon are perhaps the best example. But such students—probably pro-Mao

—are a tiny minority. Actually if we abandoned Vietnam, we would suffer a serious loss of face in Japan. They are a practical people. They depend on us for their defense, and if they find our Asian allies cannot trust us, Japan will start making other arrangements and will make them fast. But surely, my American friends in Tokyo insisted, I had heard all this before in the other Asian countries I had visited.

There are few attacks on us in the Japanese press. On the whole it tends to be chauvinistic, and also anti-Establishment. During the military rule it was curbed, and now it glories in its freedom to criticize the government.

The Ryukyu Islands will be a tough problem for any Japanese government. The situation is that, although we recognize residual Japanese sovereignty there, 90,000 Japanese are still under American military rule more than 20 years after the war. We point out that we need bases there in order to defend Asia, a benefit in which all Japanese share. Many Japanese go along with this, arguing that if Japan really wants the Ryukyus back, they must allow us unreserved use of the bases.

The Japanese have begun to feel that they are no longer rising from the rubble of defeat, but that they have a role to play in keeping Asia free. They are undertaking aid programs for the less-developed countries, helping them get on their feet. Their businessmen are striving for the overseas markets they must have, and in turn are buying raw materials from the Australians and Taiwanese as well in Singapore and Malaysia and from the mainland Chinese.

While the Japanese are intensely concerned with mainland China, they no longer have any desire to dominate it. They realize that presently this vast nation may outstrip them in power and production. But for the present the two complement each other: Japan needs raw materials from the mainland, which needs modern machinery from Japan. So although they have no diplomatic relations, they cherish trade relations that they hope will grow, and a few Japanese newspapermen are allowed in Peking. They pray for a change in China—for some less paranoid, less aggressive regime they need not fear.

How does an American get on with the Japanese? "Well," one American tells me, "I've lived here for twenty years and I am still a foreigner." This is particularly frustrating to American wives. They study Japanese—even learn it fluently—and are never asked to a Japanese home. In Japan, business between two firms is seldom done in the office, which American businessmen find hard to understand. It is done "out on the town" (on an expense account), making the rounds of girlie bars and night clubs, which American wives fail to understand.

A Japanese, no matter how well you get to know him, never pulls out pictures of his wife and children, nor does he invite you to his home. His family and home are private—never displayed to strangers—even to Japanese. This would be in unthinkably bad taste.

They have an intense pride of race of which they are either unaware, or do not feel it to be a fault for which they should apologize. There was that recent newspaper story of the son of a Negro GI and a Japanese girl. Arrested for rape, the boy explained that he had no choice, for no Japanese girl would look at him. The Japanese were sorry for the boy, but suggested that he move to Brazil, a country that has few feelings about race and would give him a chance, which in Japan he would never have.

It is not so bad with mixed Japanese-Caucasoid marriages here, and during the Occupation there were many. But most couples ended up back in America, where the Japanese partner has a better chance of being accepted than an American in Japan.

Above all they hate *Nisei,* who set up a deep conflict in the heart of every Japanese, and for somewhat the same reason that a Kiwanian is upset by a transvestite: what is this thing,

anyway? It looks Japanese. It speaks Japanese. But it carries
a green American passport. What kind of a traitor have we
here? Other Americans they respect or even admire, often
paying us the ultimate flattery of imitation. Driving past a
row of bookshops adjoining Tokyo University I was delighted
to see some Japanese beatniks in blue jeans, carrying guitars,
and with their long black hair apparently artificially curled
to give it a bushy effect. But the *Nisei* they hate, and delight
in showing it. In an airport queue I was behind a motherly-
looking old Mongoloid woman in American clothes, present-
ing one of our green passports to the official. She was back
here from Hawaii, visiting Japanese relatives. The official
was scolding her in Japanese until she was on the verge of
tears.

I intervened, starting to explain in English that this was
just an old American woman who didn't understand. The
official gave me a quick look, stamped the old lady's passport
with more than the force needed to drive a dagger between
her ribs, and turned to me with a polite Japanese smile.

Japanese universities: why do the students have so much
time for rioting and political snake-dancing? I was told that
entrance exams are very difficult and depend largely on
memory (our achievement tests). But, once in college, courses
are relatively easy. Japanese society seems to be heavily
stratified. Boys seldom start at the bottom. Where they start
after college depends not so much on their final grades as on
family background. A boy is content with the niche in which
he belongs, and there is not much mobility, either up or
down. Yet, in the higher branches of research in electronics
and optics, ability counts, and the Japanese are ahead of us.
Japanese cameras and computers rank among the world's
best. Industrialists rush into production whatever they have
perfected, from cameras to the design of those supertankers
that have rendered the Suez Canal obsolete.

One reason the Japanese seem content with their places

in the social order is, I am told, that they do not think of
themselves as individuals but as parts of Japanese society,
which is an entity in itself. This accounts for their discipline.
Take their birth rate. Once it was enormous, and its outlet
before the war was to have been the Chinese Mainland and
the Greater East Asia Co-Prosperity Sphere. In 1945 when
Japan accepted the consequences of defeat, the birth rate had
to come down and miraculously it did, largely through
legalized abortion.

This disciplined people, foreigners here agree, learns fast.
Before the war the stamp "Made in Japan" symbolized sleazy
merchandise: that cut-rate light bulb that would hardly burn
for an hour. I had need to buy a Nikon camera, with associated costly lenses, for my newspaper, and took this problem
up with a friend who heads the Hong Kong Associated Press
bureau.

"Buy it here."

"Won't the price be cheaper in Tokyo?"

"The price will be the same. But the Japanese are now
applying more rigid inspection standards to their export
cameras than they do to cameras sold in the home market.
They are out to destroy that pre-war image of shoddy Japanese merchandise. So you stand a better chance of getting a
perfect Nikon here in Hong Kong than in Tokyo."

They are also out to beat the British, not only in shipbuilding but in Scotch whisky, and why not? Any barley that
can grow in Scotland will flourish on chilly, damp Hokkaido
Island. A Japanese delegation went to Scotland to study
methods of distilling, aging, and blending. The result presently was Suntory which, in its more expensive grades, equals
Chivas Regal at its best.

One measure of a country's produce is what you see on
display in the shopping arcades of the deluxe hotels. In Delhi,
Bangkok, and Hong Kong we found superb handicrafts. In
Tokyo's arcades there are, of course, cultured pearls, then

shelf after loaded shelf of cameras, tape recorders, stereo-record players, radios, midget TV sets, every chrome-plated electronic gadget ever devised by man—but very little handi-craft. Japan once made superb ceramics, following ancient, intricate designs. Buyers will tell you this art is almost dead. It requires great patience and a skill passed down from father to sons, who now find they can earn more money driving taxis.

We hear that the Japanese are deeply worried. Since 1945 we have not only protected them, but also shared with them our domestic market, maybe as a substitute for what they once sold on the Chinese mainland. But now comes our wage-price spiral in this Age of Inflation, which seems to be a re-take of the late 1920s. In 1929 (as in 1967) the stock market dipped and sales slackened; the following year American business and labor unions began to feel the squeeze of foreign competition in our domestic market, because of our still inflated price structure. We blamed in part "coolie labor," the products of which were threatening "the American stand-ard of living," and our 1930 answer was the Hawley-Smoot Tariff Act against foreign imports. Of course foreigners re-taliated. The result was a shriveling of all world trade until we went off gold in 1933.

Our current answer to our domestic price inflation threat-ens to be a tariff as drastic as Hawley-Smoot, which may hit heavily at products from Japan. The Japanese have been going along with us—even pledging their gold in the inter-national pool that hopes to save the dollar—but where are we leading them? Are we moving into isolation—bowing out of our commitment to defend Free Asia, retiring behind tariff walls that will cut the trade which is their lifeblood? If so, what do we expect them to do?

You answer them: I cannot.

More on the Japanese people . . . However luxuriously modern and expensive our hotel, it cannot be called a tourist trap, for its customers are 20-to-1 Japanese. It has become a Tokyo status symbol. Even a wedding reception for a member of the Imperial Family was held here, and lesser wedding receptions abound. We spot the parties in the lobby: the groom always in striped pants and a cutaway (an English custom which is dying in the West) but the bride and her bridesmaids invariably in traditional Japanese hairdo and kimono—the designs so lovely that we wonder why they ever bother with Western fashions.

I was later told that, although the wedding reception may be held in this Western-style hotel, the honeymoon really begins in one of those traditional Japanese inns, which serve strictly Japanese food eaten with chopsticks, with Japanese mats rolled out on the floor instead of beds, and with floor matting so delicate that you must remove your shoes in the hallway to avoid scuffing it. Here the bride and groom go completely native for their start in married life, to found a strictly Japanese family. All foreigners have heard of these charming inns, said to be far cheaper than Tokyo's Western-style hotels; few venture to go because the staff seldom speaks anything but Japanese.

The luxury roof-restaurant of our hotel, overlooking Tokyo, is packed with Japanese, all in Western garb, using knives and forks to eat *filet mignon* or shashlik *flambé* and *crêpes suzette*. On a lower floor there is a little coffee-shop-type place that is strictly Japanese.

For our taste, Japanese food is delicate and yet, after Taiwan and Hong Kong, somewhat tasteless, a judgment in which many Japanese concur, for they crowd into our hotel's Chinese restaurant. Many Japanese learned to love this cooking during the war when they occupied China.

A final anthropological note: the Mongoloids of these northerly islands are a shade taller and paler than their southerly counterparts, particularly, it seems to me, among the better-fed upper classes. Some Japanese have skins as pink as any Swede's.

A still more final note on their psychology: they have respected us and imitated us not out of love, but because we have succeeded. There is no reason to think that their America Watchers are any less skilled than their China Watchers, and this year their bright, black eyes are on us as never before since the eve of Pearl Harbor. In 1945 we disarmed them, explaining that we would defend them. Do we still mean this? If not, what should they do? Here I have only one prediction: whatever the Japanese do, it will be done coldly and maybe swiftly, but without panic.

COMMUNIST CHINA

I N tracking down that somewhat dangerous yet basically lovable old beast the Chinese Dragon, I talked with professional China Watchers from New Delhi through Tokyo. Many were veteran Dragonologists serving our government or the British. Others were English- or French-speaking newspapermen now stationed on the rim of Asia, some of whom in happier days had been Old China Hands, serving in Peking.

Over-all, none were wiser than the China specialists of the Associated Press. Taiwan's experts had the deepest knowledge of the people involved in the mainland tragicomedy. Hong Kong's and Tokyo's experts have perhaps the shrewdest long-term insight.

I am most grateful for the time they spent with me. It is their facts and their interpretive wisdom that have gone into the chapter which follows, where I have only pieced together a mosaic: the tale then tells itself.

W.L.W.

When in 1949 Communist armies overran mainland China, a bamboo curtain of censorship fell. What went on behind it no one knew and the wisest tried not to guess; the world was allowed to see only the propaganda image of a monolithic China painted on that bamboo. Experts knew it was a façade; and in Hong Kong, Taiwan, and Japan (where they are stationed), they tried to piece together the truth by talking with returning tourists, by studying the dispatches of the handful of foreign journalists which Peking would admit, by monitoring radio stations, and by pondering the daily flood of clichés in China's rigidly controlled press.

Then suddenly in Peking in May of 1966 came a rash of wall posters which, like a flash of lightning, scattered the darkness, revealing that a great power struggle was in progress. Only now have the experts learned enough to trace the history of this struggle.

In February 1956 the world (including China) was startled when Khrushchev, in his speech to the 20th Congress of the Soviet Communist Party in Moscow, denounced Stalin as a dictator. China then fell in line. The Trinity in Moscow had been Marx-Lenin-Stalin, and in Peking was Marx-Lenin-Mao. Following the Russian example, the Chinese also trimmed their Trinity by dropping Mao. The operation was performed in a speech by Teng Hsiao-ping, general secretary of China's Communist Party, denouncing dictatorship and praising "collective leadership." Teng closed the incision with a few words of perfunctory praise for the honorable party chairman. Recently Teng has emerged as an old enemy of Mao, although no China Watcher guessed this at the time.

But Mao, while out of the Trinity, was still chairman of the Communist Party and president of China. Therefore, early in 1958 he announced plans for that convulsive, sprawling, and disastrous lunge which he called the "Great Leap Forward."

Did China need steel? Her workers and peasants could

make it in back-yard smelters. All traces of Capitalism and even Socialism must go—under the people's communes, farmers and workers would live in collective barracks with collective kitchens, while state nurseries cared for children. Farmers must give up their private plots, which would revert to state farms.

While Russia lagged back in Socialism, China, Mao bragged, would leap now into that pure Communism that Russia's leaders promised their people only as a distant dream. The Russians scoffed, at first privately and then publicly.

China then seemed a monolith behind Mao, but was it really? China Watchers now re-read a speech made to the Central Committee in just this period, which soberly warned that "empty words and hollow exaggerations should be avoided," and that no plans ever should be announced "unless realization is assured." The speaker who issued this chill warning? Liu Shao-chi—today Mao's bitterest opponent.

By mid-1958 it was clear that Mao's Great Leap was ending in a disastrous sprawl. If you exclude crops of sweet potatoes and grain, the private plots of China's farmers raise 80 per cent of the nation's food. These farmers were now killing and eating their privately raised pigs, thus inviting a second disaster, for pigs produce most of the fertilizer used on the big state-owned farms; a fertilizer shortage meant a coming shortage of grain. Worst of all, the state nurseries and communal barracks were resented to the point of mutiny, with the result that most of the country had to be put under martial law, with the explanation that the troops were "helping" with planting and harvest.

What to do? There could be no public repudiation of Mao, who is a god to the Chinese people. But at a meeting of the Party Central Committee on December 17, 1958, it was quietly decided not to renominate him for president. A split had come, although no hint of it got out to the China Watchers.

In April 1959 came the planned changing of the guard. The picture presented to the world's China Watchers probably was that presented to Mao himself, and it may have fooled him. His step down from the presidency was in no sense a demotion, for he was still party chairman. He would now be free to plan China's long-range future, leaving the routine chore of running the country to the new president, his closest friend (and sometimes coldest critic), Liu Shao-chi.

There was also conflict in the army. Its professional leaders were certainly neither anti-Communist, anti-Mao, nor pro-Russian. But they wanted modern hardware that only the Russians could provide; its supply was threatened by Mao's increasingly shrill squabble with Moscow over political leadership in Africa and Asia. The army's spokesman in the Central Committee was Defense Minister Peng Teh-huai, who objected to Mao's use of his troops on the farms; Peng wanted to pull them out and start training with new weapons. Guerrilla tactics, he insisted, were not enough. Indoctrination in Marxism-Leninism was no substitute for pilot training.

To Mao this was just short of treason, for it is his romantic but unshakable belief that masses of lightly armed men (China has them beyond counting), under inspired leadership, can sweep modern weapons aside. In Korea had not his masses of lightly armed Chinese Volunteers pushed the Americans back from the Yalu, capturing most of their vaunted modern weapons? And in spite of still more American weapons, had not these inspired masses then held the Americans at the 38th Parallel, substituting a truce for an American victory?

However much the folly of the Great Leap had damaged Mao in the opinion of China's top leaders, he still had the power (in August 1959) to fire this mutinous defense minister and put in his place Lin Piao who, China Watchers now realize, had commanded that Fourth Field Army which had sent most of its men to Korea as "Chinese Volunteers."

With Mao now occupied in Marxist-Leninist meditations, President Liu quietly began the task of putting China back together under what was called the "Readjustment Policy." The back-yard smelters were forgotten. China's peasants and workers in the hated communal barracks were allowed to re-group into families. Quietly the village markets were re-opened; private handicraft industries resumed.

Some hint of all this surely reached Mao on Olympus. Were these measures not a retreat from pure Communism? But Liu and his realists who were now running China insisted they were temporarily needed—even the "retrograde" measure of restoring private plots to farmers in 1961, necessary because 300,000 were dying of famine in Kansu Province alone. Liu pointed out to the assembled Communists at the fortieth-anniversary meeting of their party on June 30 that China could not be directed "by impulse and whim."

But Mao from Olympus could still thunder (and with increasing violence) at Moscow for betraying Communism not only in Russia but around the world, where Maoist parties were venomously battling Russians for control.

Perhaps Moscow's deepest worry was those maps used in China's schools, colored to show large areas of Russia as peopled with races which are Chinese by blood and culture— Uzbekistan, Kazakhstan, Outer Mongolia, and large parts of Siberia—regions which, Chinese scholars pointed out, had in the nineteenth century been wrested from the weak Manchu Dynasty by the imperialist czars, and by right should now return to a Communist China. In addition, Mao was serving notice on Moscow that he wanted The Bomb.

By the summer of 1961, Khrushchev had had it. His intelligence agents within China insisted Mao was tottering,

and in August, Khrushchev let loose with the right hook
that he hoped might topple Mao. Without warning, Russian
technicians all over China downed tools and went home. The
vast dam over the Yangtze, planned to feed countless more
millions, was left unfinished (it still is). Most of China's industry, operating and planned, came to a full stop, a disaster
so extensive that it could be only briefly concealed from the
world's China Watchers.

Early in 1962, Mao on Olympus got a report from Liu on
the country, to the effect that among peasants and low-level
administrators, confidence in the Communist Party and its
promised future had almost gone. If Liu interpreted this as a
backwash of Mao's Great Leap, Mao's view was different. He
announced a new "Socialist Ideological Re-education Movement," further enforced by a purge of 600,000 disgruntled
(and angered) officials at the village level.

China's whole fabric was trembling, although few China
Watchers were aware of it, and at the December 4, 1963,
meeting of the Politburo, Mao called for "strengthening
party unity." Then President Liu rose. If party unity was
weak, this was due to "inadequate understanding of the importance of collective leadership" because some high-ranking
officials (whom could he mean?) "were harboring dangerous
arrogance and egotism; they believe that prestige is above
everything, and that they are above everyone."

That Russian phrase "collective leadership" needled Mao,
and early in 1964 came his response. His "Socialist Re-education Movement" was lagging, so it was now defiantly renamed
the "Re-education Movement of Mao's Thoughts," thus pro-
claiming that China had only one Stalin-type leader.

But Mao had other worries, and there is a school of China
Watchers which believes that he might have stayed contentedly up on Olympus, spewing forth doctrine and grind-
ing out ukases politely ignored by the realists who under Liu
were running China, had it not been for his wife, Chiang

Ching. Before her marriage she was a movie actress, and she delights in using her exalted position to meddle with China's state-run theater. As 1964 closed, a play entitled *Defies the Emperor* was starting its run in Peking. Laid in the remote past, its central figure was a man who had the courage to defy a pompous Ming Dynasty tyrant. Was it a dig at Mao? Probably, for intellectuals of all nations and centuries have an unquenchable compulsion to needle the Establishment. When Mao first started thundering, Liu and his realists had shrugged it off: let the Old Man purge Peking opera; who cares? But it went beyond that; the guilty author, Mao charged, was only an instrument of Peking's Mayor Peng Chen. Now Peng was in addition a member of the Politburo and a trusted henchman of Liu. Was the Old Man daring to start a high-level purge?

A mystery now begins, which has not yet been cleared up by China Watchers. When in October of 1965 Mao appeared before a meeting of the Central Committee, all seemed normal. Then abruptly he disappeared. Speculation started in November. Had he been gagged by the party? Six months later he surfaced in Shanghai. Where had he been?

Only recently has it come out that he had first left Peking for Hangchow. But under what circumstances? Japan's shrewdest China Watcher believes he fled there for his life. But evidence gathered in Taipei is that Mao, gagged in Peking, got permission from Liu and the ruling faction to go south for his health to Hangchow, a pleasant provincial city not far from Shanghai where, they felt, he would be out of the way. But to make sure they sent along General Lo Jui-ching, chairman of China's joint chiefs of staff. Was Mao under house arrest with General Lo as jailer? Surely it was not presented so rudely to the Old Gentleman: General Lo was here only to ensure his safety.

But then came India's war with Pakistan, with General Lo urgently needed to negotiate China's help to the Paks.

Returning to Hangchow to resume his task as protector-jailer, Lo was himself put under arrest by the only man in China with legal power to do this: Defense Minister Lin Piao, who owed his own appointment to Mao.

Together Mao and Lin Piao (Taiwan's China Watchers have learned) proceeded to Shanghai, where Lin Piao had no doubt as to the loyalty of the garrison commander and where they now began scheming to regain power.

Against them was President Liu Shao-chi in Peking, supported by a majority of the all-powerful Central Committee, and backed by the bureaucracy throughout China, most of whom owed their appointments to him. Liu from Peking also controlled the party's newspapers and radio stations throughout China.

With Mao and Lin Piao was Mao's enormous prestige with China's masses, and his title as chairman of the Communist Party. Did not this last give him power to appoint enough new members to the Central Committee to give him control? Mao thought so, and proceeded to do it.

With them was the further fact that, as defense minister, Lin Piao was in theoretical command of China's armies.

With them was the crucial fact that the commander of the Peking garrison was General Yang Cheng-wu, a trusted friend of Lin Piao. So Peking would be theirs when they were ready to move north, which was not quite yet. For some tool had to be devised that would wrest from President Liu control of the bureaucracy throughout China. It had to be good, and by April, Mao in Shanghai announced it: the Great Proletarian Cultural Revolution to check the three Antis—Anti-Mao, Anti-Communism, Anti-Socialism.

Through this revolution, Mao felt, backed with his godlike prestige, he could purge throughout China Liu's decadent bureaucracy. After Mao's death, his enemies had whispered, there would come a struggle for succession. Well, let it come now, while he could control it. Then, resuming

that Great Leap Forward which had been betrayed by Liu
and the opportunists, he could put China back on the road
to pure Communism and Utopia, and then he could die in
peace.

Suppose he did nothing? In Moscow, Khrushchev had
pulled down Stalin's statues and mocked his name. Would
Mao's name be any more tenderly treated by Liu Shao-chi,
who already was prattling about "collective leadership"?
Only if Mao moved now, could he make sure that history
would remember him as the great leader who had brought
first China and then the world to pure Communism, picking
up the torch Moscow had let fall.

Where, clamored China Watchers in the world press, was
Mao? Maybe dead? In partial answer, President Liu's propaganda apparatus in Peking in May released a picture of the
chairman shaking hands with Mehmet Shehu, bitterly anti-
Russian premier of Albania, but without saying where or
when the picture had been taken.

In Peking, President Liu controlled all China's propaganda
organs except the *Liberation Army Daily*, which came under
Lin Piao as minister of defense. Ordinarily this paper only
echoed the propaganda line of the others. But in May it
boomed out, at first alone, plugging Mao's Cultural Revolution, and followed with more attacks on Peng Chen, mayor
of Peking and a Liu henchman. Supporting it were a rash
of screaming posters appearing from nowhere, pasted up
by a strange organization of children—the "Red Guards"—
named after a group which, during the civil wars, had briefly
flourished as a youth auxiliary to the Red Army. These
guards were passionately for Mao (so in theory, was everyone), but who and why were they?

China Watchers now realize that the posters, attacking
Peking's mayor, could never have got pasted up without the
connivance of General Yang, Peking's garrison commander
and close friend of Lin Piao, waiting now to welcome him

and Mao to Peking. When, on June 3, these posters forced the resignation of Mayor Peng Chen, China Watchers could see that the Chinese monolith had a deep crack.

It was time, now, for Mao to move. First in mid-July he staged his well-publicized Yangtze River swim. Some confused China Watchers wondered if Mao might not really be dead, and the picture faked. He was not: he needed the picture to prove to China's worshipping masses that he was no senile vegetable (as his Peking enemies were hinting) but strong, alert, and able to lead the coming power fight.

Mao and Lin Piao now went by plane to Peking, where a meeting of the Central Committee had been called, and where President Liu and his henchman Teng Tsiao-ping, the party's general secretary, were sure they had the votes to control Mao. In Shanghai, Mao had filled his plane with Central Committee members of his own, and this should have been enough to outvote Liu's group, although it was a rump session with less than half the members present (the others discreetly sitting it out in the provinces to see who would win).

On August 1, 1966, the session opened, and at first it was rough going, with Mao's opposition outwardly respectful but inwardly bitter, sure that they spoke for China. In Peking other things spoke louder: the fact that Garrison Commander Yang controlled the streets and directed traffic as Mao for the first time in years showed himself to the masses, who screamed with joy.

Speaking for Mao from the walls of Peking were more posters put up by Red Guards attacking President Liu and his establishment, not yet by name but branding them as that "handful of people in power in the party who are following the Capitalist line."

Behind closed doors for twelve days that rump session of the Central Committee battled, but already the scales were tipped. For dare they defy both the Peking garrison and the mob by dethroning a god? Inevitably its final communiqué—grudgingly approved by a one-vote margin—endorsed Mao, and twice mentioned Lin Piao as his "closest comrade" (successor), thus dumping President Liu from this position and jumping Lin Piao, in the Communist hierarchy, from No. 8 to No. 2 overnight. President Liu was also forced before this rump Central Committee to "confess."

But Mao and Lin Piao, who had organized this pageant, knew it was only that: Peking was not China. They might surround President Liu's house with soldiers, might even, in the hysteria of the hour, persuade his teen-age daughter to denounce her parents. But beyond Peking in the vastness of China, governors of provinces and mayors of cities appointed by Liu were watching this Peking show in bewilderment and some anger. Fifteen years before, Liu had headed China's Youth Movement. Those boys had since moved up into most of China's top jobs. And what of that more-than-half of the Central Committee that had failed to obey Mao's summons? "We are a minority," Mao had shouted to the Peking mob, "but we shall win!"

The military situation was not much better. Through General Yang, Mao and Lin Piao controlled Peking, but what of China's other twelve military districts, stretching from Tibet to Hainan Island? Would they obey Lin Piao, or side with their local governors?

Mao and Lin needed a force to replace or coerce the existing bureaucracy throughout China, and this they had already prepared. China Watchers knew that on June 13 an order had closed down the nation's schools, but none realized what it meant. They found out on August 18, 1966, when teen-age Red Guards with arm bands converged on Peking from all over China, brought there by Lin Piao's army which had, in the provinces, passed out the arm bands, put the youths aboard trains, fed them out of army stores, and even thought to furnish them with portable toilets. As they

marched, screaming, past Mao on his reviewing stand in
Peking, these Red Guard hoodlums stripped women of
Western-style shoes or clothing, even though these had been
made in state-owned factories and bought from state-owned
shops.

The Young Communist League was dead—killed by a
single phrase from Mao, who denounced it as a "poisonous
weed." In its place were these Red Guards—20 million, Mao
claimed—China's youth who, after they had been firmed by
this "revolutionary experience" (like that of his own in the
"Long March" during the youth of Chinese Communism),
would fan out over all China to rebuke or replace Liu's
smug "revisionist" bureaucrats.

Why did not Liu's trained administrators, thoroughly
entrenched in their jobs, rise up against Mao? We in the
West forget that Mao is a god. But the bureaucracy did
resist his purge in a typically Chinese way—by bowing
humbly before Mao's storm, pretending to conform. But
when a province had completed its purge of "bourgeois
revisionists," somehow the same old faces (or those of their
next of kin) turned up in the same old jobs.

In some cities Mao's Guards, pouring off trains from
Peking, would invade city hall or provincial headquarters,
demand to inspect records they could not understand, and
scream at local officials—to the intense mortification of everyone. For, in spite of the Revolution, there still remains that
deep Chinese respect for age and authority. In Peking this
had served Mao in good stead. Out in the provinces it was
now serving President Liu's bureaucracy.

Soon these bureaucrats, again in a typically Chinese
fashion, began fighting fire with fire. So Chairman Mao
wanted Red Guards? Each mayor or province head quickly
formed his own, with identical arm bands, and identically
screaming for Mao's Cultural Revolution, whatever that
meant.

It could mean so many things. In Canton, Red Guards from Peking started to pull down a statue of Dr. Sun Yat-sen, China's first president, but were prevented by Canton Red Guards who defended the statue as part of China's cultural heritage. In Tientsin, arriving Red Guards were "dispersed" by local Red Guards. In Changchow, 10,000 Peking Red Guards were greeted at the station by local Red Guards and marched to the office of provincial government, where their leaders were locked up.

In Anhwei Province, local Red Guards beat up the Peking visitors when they started pasting up posters denouncing the head of the local Communist Party as an anti-Mao revisionist monster, following the capitalist road: the local Guards did not agree.

So it was when the Peking Red Guards invaded the factories. Local authorities encouraged the workers to form their own Red Guards, to go to Peking (this would close the factory), appear before Mao and demand in the name of his Cultural Revolution a better life and relief from his Peking Red Guards.

In Shanghai local authorities, to buy the loyalty of their workers, in the name of Mao's Revolution passed out pay bonuses and extra holidays, actions Mao presently denounced as the sin of "economism."

Farmers, often in the name of this Revolution, began looting granaries; sometimes officials in charge passed out seed reserves to them. Often this sabotage was led by those 600,000 functionaries whom Mao had purged or demoted during his Socialist Re-education Movement.

There was even a sabotage movement, directed against collectives, which the farmers called the Three Finishes:

1. Finish the food (eat reserve grain)
2. Finish the capital (distribute the money)
3. Finish the tools (break them)

In 1967, Mao called what seemed to be a truce. Premier

Chou En-lai, who had stayed apart from Mao's Cultural Revolution, now was moved in as a mediator. The turbulent Red Guards were told to go back to their schools and the army (theoretically in control of Lin Piao) was put in charge of Cultural Revolutionary groups, squabbling in various cities, to get production rolling and also (this was vital) to see that the farmers got on with their spring planting.

As for the future? Since good rains have temporarily saved China from famine, the greatest permanent damage has come in the closing of her schools—her universities for more than two years and her lower schools longer—Mao having turned the nation's children loose to harass his political enemies.

Some are now back at their desks, but teachers are demoralized by having been roughed up by Red Guards. All old textbooks are banned. New ones reflecting the Cultural Revolution are being printed, and they seem to ignore China's past before Mao and reject, as well, "bourgeois science." The damage here to China's future scholars and leaders cannot yet be estimated.

As for the power struggle, China Watchers agree that it has only begun. Until Mao's Cultural Revolution, China's Communist leaders congratulated themselves on having avoided any Stalin-type purge, under which Stalin rid himself of all rivals by a butchery of the "Old Bolsheviks" and by promoting ambitious young administrators of the Khrushchev type to replace them.

But if China avoided this bloodshed, it also means that all of her leaders, including Mao, are moving into senility and soon will be gone. Then must follow—on Mao's death, if not before—the inevitable dogfight among younger men to decide which will come out on top of the pile. Most China Watchers agree that Mao, dead or alive, in the long pull cannot win, for he is bucking the tide of history. It is Trotsky the theorist against Stalin the practical organizer.

As for President Liu, in early 1968 Peking announced that he "no longer held power" but daily denounced him. Was he still in name president of China? The Watchers were pointing out that legally he could only be removed by a majority vote in that National People's Congress which chose him. Could Mao count on such a majority? Dare he convene this Congress? On this point Peking's answer was a significant silence until November when it was announced that Liu had been removed from office, not by the Congress but by the Central Committee "enlarged," presumably for this purpose, by Mao. From this it would appear that Mao still feared the Congress and has not dared summon it.

Instead, China was going through, in almost every province, a badly muffled civil war. All factions invoked the name of Mao, so Lin Piao's army (its generals equally confused in their basic loyalties) was sent out to mediate and restore order. In each province it is typically the anti-Mao Maoists versus the pro-Mao Maoists. What order has been restored in China seems to have come through carefully patched-up, face-saving compromises, with the final coalition making at least nominal obeisance to Peking, and of course screaming loyalty to Mao.

Finally, there is Chiang Kai-shek. Perhaps the idea that he or his Kuomintang could ever again figure importantly in the mainland's future is laughable. If only the Red Chinese could laugh! Instead, provincial radio stations are constantly uncovering what they denounce as pro-Chiang plots, with peasants arrested for having hidden away his picture. And when Peking recently denounced Liu as a Kuomintang agent, this may not have been meant entirely as a figure of speech. Out of China's three-quarter billion people, there are surely some millions who, having suffered under collectives and the current power struggle, are disgusted with Communism's promises. Chiang and his Kuomintang would be the only anti-Communist symbols such people could remember. Any return of the Kuomintang from its Taiwan Elba is highly improbable. Three short years ago, any split in the mainland monolith was even more unthinkable.

China Watchers believe that we in the West exaggerate the importance of foreign policy in the mainland power struggle, insisting that the eyes of China's leaders are turned inward on each other. Europeans view Vietnam as an East-West struggle: the Americans versus Communism. China Watchers are sure that Russo-Chinese rivalry is deeply involved. Mao, they say, likes the Vietnam war because it is bleeding Americans, costing Mao little, and helping him keep us alive as a hate-object to his people. If he entered the war, Mao's supply lines would be long, and the war costly in terms of loyal troops he needs to bolster his position at home.

Mao feels he has a tight hold over Ho Chi Minh in the matter of food. Even under the French, Tonkin Province (now North Vietnam) was a rice-deficit area. China Watchers estimate that Mao, now making up this deficit, could be supplying 90 per cent of Ho's import needs, while the Russians supply Ho with anti-aircraft guns to defend the North, and with excellent mortars which the VC use against us in the South.

While Ho is fulsomely grateful to each for their help, there can be no doubt that he fears China. Before the French entered Indo-China, both Vietnamese kingdoms had had for centuries an Ireland-England relationship with the great empire to the north: allied with it in culture, usually paying tribute to the Celestial Throne, but always fearing the Chinese as invaders, which often they had been. Russia, by contrast, is far away.

The Russians might well be happy to help negotiate, in Paris, a peace that would pull North Vietnam into the Soviet orbit. Ho knows that such a settlement might put him in real danger from the Chinese. Even as President Johnson announced his 1968 bombing pause, Radio Peking urged Hanoi to fight on, chiding the North Vietnamese for leaning toward "revisionism" (they mean the Russians) and for neglecting to study the "Thoughts" of Chairman Mao. It could be that all who hope for a negotiated peace in Vietnam should look, not to the Hotel Majestic in Paris, but to Peking.

But why should Mao want such a peace?

INDEX

Ak Dinh Phuoc, 176–80
Alexandra, Princess, 221
Alsop, Joe, 128
Aryans, 40
Australoids, 39–40

Bangkok, 103–23, 153
Bao Dai, 8ff., 15
Beloff, Max, 79
Benares, 79–82
Bernischke, Hans, 30–31
Bhabha, H. J., 59
Bhakra Dam, 75–76
Bhumibol, King of Bangkok,
    105–6
Bhuyeb Van Nam, 180–82
Bihar, 60–61
birth control, 92–97
Borodin, Michael, 6
Buddhists and Buddhism, 17ff.,
    138, 146, 170ff.; in Thailand,
    108–9
Burma, 111

Calcutta, 89–92, 97–99
Cambodia, 109
Catholics and Catholicism, 12, 17.
    See also specific persons
Caucasoids, 40. See also specific
    countries
Chandigarh, 65–68
Charnock, Job, 89
Chatterjee, R. K., 83
Chennault, Claire, 8

Chiang Ching, 272–73
Chiang Kai-shek, 6, 29, 35, 137,
    138, 231–43 passim, 281–82
Chieu Hoi, 152, 187–90
China and Chinese people, 6ff.,
    267–83; and Hong Kong, 211–
    12ff.; and India border dispute,
    50–51; International Press Insti-
    tute on, 30–36; Japan and, 258–
    59; in Saigon, 197–98; Taiwan,
    231–43; Thailand and, 110–12ff.,
    119
Cholon, 197–98
Chou En-lai, 280
Churchill, Winston, 69
Cochin China, 198–99
Collingwood, Charles, 133, 222
cows, sacred, 58–59, 73, 81–82, 85
Cravioto, Juaquin, 86
Cripps, Stafford, 7

Dan, Phan Quang, 145–47, 206
Danh Thuh, 144, 170–86
Delhi, 25–39, 46–52, 85
Diem. See Ngo Dinh Diem, Jean
    Baptiste
Dienbienphu, 11, 138
"Dom," 45–49
Durgapur, 82–84
Dzu, Truong Dinh, 203–4, 206

Enslinger, Douglas, 64
Escoffier, 5

Fabian Socialism, 68–69
Formosa. *See* Taiwan
France and the French, 3–5ff.,
   121–22, 198–200
Fujikura, Teruo, 32–34, 35

Gandhi, Mohandas K., 54, 93
Ganges River, 79–81
Gaulle, Charles de, and Gaullists,
   4, 7–8
Geneva Agreement, 11, 12
Great Britain and the British: and
   Ho Chi Minh, 7; and Hong
   Kong, 213ff.; and India, 26ff.,
   52–54, 59–60, 68–69, 96–97
Grover, Allen and Beatrice, 228

Hanoi, 117–18
Harriman, Averell, 18, 20
Hilsman, Roger, 18, 20
Hindus, 27, 28, 54, 67, 86–87, 96;
   in Indo-China, 110
Ho Chi Minh, 5ff., 22, 127, 137,
   282
Hong Kong, 31–32, 211–28, 261;
   Ho Chi Minh in, 6–7
Howrah, 88–89
Hué, 18
Hyderabad, Nizam of, 37, 39
Hyderabad Palace, 37, 38, 39, 46

India, 25–99; and Taiwan, 237
Indo-China, 5, 109–10, 198–99. *See
   also* Vietnam
Indonesia, 112
International Press Institute, 25,
   29–36
International Voluntary Service,
   187–88

Jacobson, Sydney, 68
Jains, 46, 48–49, 87

Japan and the Japanese, 7–8, 10,
   32–34, 255–64; and diet, 88; and
   fertilizers, 63; and Korea, 249–
   50, 251–52; population control,
   95–96
Johnson, Lyndon, 19

Kennedy, John F., 11, 14, 19, 20
Khrushchev, Nikita, 14, 268, 271–
   72
Korea, 14–15, 63, 247–52, 270
Kowloon, 214–16
Ky, Air Marshal, 22, 132–33, 200,
   201, 203

La Dany, L., 31–32
Laski, Harold, 69
Lattre, General de, 11
Le Corbusier, 66–67, 68
Lin Piao, 232, 271, 274ff.
Lippe, Jacques, 94
Liu Shao-chi, 269ff.
Lo Jui-ching, 273–74
Lodge, Emily, 131, 132
Lodge, Henry Cabot, 19ff., 131,
   132
Luce, Henry, 228
Ludhiana, 54–59

McCone, John, 19, 20
McNamara, Robert, 19, 20
Mao Tse-tung, 7, 32, 35, 50–51,
   206, 232, 238–39, 242, 268ff.; and
   Hong Kong, 219, 227; and
   Thailand, 111
Mekong Delta, 151–93
Menon, Krishna, 69–70
Mertz, Charles, 87
Momsen, Per, 92
Moslems, 54, 87, 95
Murphy, Charles J. V., 128–29

Nangal, 74–75
NATO, 3–4
Negroponte, John, 142, 143, 144
Nehru, Pandit, 27, 68, 69, 70
New Delhi, 25–39, 46–52, 85
New Territories, 216–21
Ngo Dinh Diem, Jean Baptiste, 10ff., 138–39, 141, 145, 146
Ngo Dinh Nhu, 15, 16, 20, 21
Ngo Dinh Nhu, Mme., 17
Nguyen Ngoc Loan, 201
Nhu. *See* Ngo Dinh Nhu
Nisei, 259–60
Nolting, Frederick, 18, 19

Paris, 3–5ff.
Park, Chung Hee, 250, 251, 252
Peking, 30ff., 268, 273, 275–77, 279
Peng Chen, 275–76
Peng Teh-huai, 270
Phan Quang Dan, 145–47, 206
proteins, 86–88
Pueblo, U.S.S., 252

Quang Doc, 18, 138

Rach Gia, 152, 153–70, 186–93
Rhee, Syngman, 250
Rusk, Dean, 20
Russia (Soviet Union), 3–4, 50–51; and China, 268, 269, 271–72, 282–83; Ho in, 6
Ryukyu Islands, 258

Saigon, 16ff., 123, 127–47, 151ff., 197–207; Japanese in, 8
Seoul, 250–51, 252
Shehu, Mehmet, 275
Siam. *See* Thailand
"Skinny," 152, 186–91
Slocum, Harvey, 75–76
South Korea, 63, 247–52
Soviet Union. *See* Russia

Stalin, Josef, 69, 70
Steinbeck, John, 122–23
Subramanian, C., 62, 64
Sukarno, 112
suttee, 80

Taipei, 29, 231–32
Taiwan, 29–30, 63, 231–43
Taylor, Charles, 30, 35, 36
Taylor, Maxwell, 19
Teng Tsiao-ping, 276
Thailand, 103–23
Thanh Thai, 10
Thieu, 203, 204–5, 206
Tibetans, 50
Tokyo, 256–57, 261–62
Tran Van Van, 145
Tri Quang, 17
Truong Dinh Dzu, 203–4, 206

United States and Americans, 44–46; and India, 71–72, 75–76; and Japanese, 259–60; and Korea, 251, 252; and Vietnam, 8ff., 18–22 (*See also* Vietnam)

Victoria, Queen, 216
Victoria City, 213
Vietnam, 3, 5–22, 116–19, 121–228, 282; Japanese and, 257–58; Mekong Delta, 151–93

Wallace, Dewitt and Lila, 228
"Wang," 213ff., 220ff.
Wei, Jimmie, 233–34, 240
Wichremesinghe, C. E. L., 85
Withey, Francis M. (Pancho), 155–56, 157–59, 164, 168, 177ff., 192
Wong, Sybil, 225

Yang Cheng-wu, 274, 277

Zorthian, Barry, 132, 133, 134

A Note About the Author

William L. White is the son of William Allen White, who built the *Emporia* (Kansas) *Gazette* from provincial obscurity to international fame. The author, born in Emporia, began his career on his father's newspaper as a fourteen-year-old reporter. Later he served on it as circulation manager, managing editor, editorial writer, and associate editor; he is now editor and publisher. White, a Harvard graduate, has also been associated with the *Washington Post, Fortune* Magazine, CBS, NANA, and the *Reader's Digest,* of which he is a Roving Editor.

Political activities for the author have included chairmanship of the Republican County Committee, Lyon County, Kansas, 1933–34, and membership in the Kansas State Legislature, 1931–32. He is on the board of directors of the American Friends of the Middle East, American Committee for Liberation, American Association of Indian Affairs, and the Tolstoy Foundation, and was on the board of overseers of Harvard University, 1950–56. He has been a director of the American Civil Liberties Union, and is currently a director of Freedom House and the Theodore Roosevelt Memorial Association.